IF I WAS . . .

MIDGE URE
IF I WAS . . .

THE AUTOBIOGRAPHY

MIDGE URE

First published in Great Britain in 2004 by
Virgin Books Ltd
Thames Wharf Studios
Rainville Road
London
W6 9HA

A catalogue record for this book is available from the British Library.

ISBN 1 85227 144 2

Typeset by TW Typesetting, Plymouth, Devon.
Printed and bound in Great Britain by CPD Wales

CONTENTS

ACKNOWLEDGEMENTS

I have come to the conclusion that the best time to publish a book like this is when all your friends are dead, or at least you are. None of the content in this book is meant to antagonise, insult or upset. It is just an account of what I remembered and felt at the time. A lot of truths, rants and ravings with a liberal sprinkling of artistic intervention.

Without whose help I could never have remembered: Rusty Egan, Bob Geldof, Chris Morrison, Chris O'Donnell and Chris Allen.

For help above and beyond the line of duty: Robin Eggar; Kate Cons and all at CMO; Berenice Hardman, Dave Claxton and all the crew members past and present; Cerise Reed and Robin Harris; Sue Goulding; Christine Pfannstiel; Michael Lubek; Danny Mitchell, Roberta Baldi, Luca Toccaceli and Piero Sessa from Decam; Julian Alexander and Lucinda Cook at LAW; Claire Clark and all the rest at Clouds House; my peers past and present; Ad Chivers, Josh Phillips, Dave Williamson, Troy Donnockley, Russell Field, Mark and Steve Brezeski; KT Forster, Stuart Slater, Barbara Phelan, Becke Parker, Jamie Moore and Gareth Fletcher at Virgin Books.

Last but certainly not least: my beautiful girls Sheridan, Molly, Kitty, Ruby and Flossie.

PROLOGUE

I'm a musician. That is all I have ever wanted to be, ever since I was a kid in a Glasgow tenement with the ice encrusted on the inside of the windows, listening to Telstar on the radio. For 35 years I've made a living playing my guitar and singing. It's a pleasure that remains undimmed and unspoiled to this day, which is why I'm still plugging and strumming away and not driving a van like my old man.

It's been a topsy-turvy roller-coaster ride. I've had highs: Number One records and a stack of hits in half a dozen different disguises; I've sung 'Vienna' in front of half a million people and jammed with the heroes of my teens. I've had plenty of lows: band splits, relationships collapsed, and I've done plenty of things I'm ashamed of. I've craved fame and fortune and found out that it's not all it's cracked up to be. I've seen friends lose themselves to self-inflicted wounds and a couple of times I've come very close to following them.

I've been rewarded for my successes and for a few of my failures. I've had my share of ups and downs within the music industry, but it has sustained me for thirty years and paid for me to do what I love. But in the end it's not about the rewards or the awards. It's about the music. It's always been about the music. Music enhances the soul; it can give solace and comfort . . . and sometimes it can save a life.

Last year, after I had given one of my 'Out Alone' acoustic shows a man delivered a card backstage. On the front was a picture of a nineteen-year-old black girl. The message was simple: 'You don't know me but this is a girl who received an education via Band Aid. She has just passed her degree, and I thought you might want to see what she looks like.'

I looked at this gorgeous girl smiling out of the picture and there was only one thought in my head: She simply wouldn't have been here. That wiped away the years in a glimpse, brought it all home.

I'm often asked, 'Did Band Aid make a difference?' and there was the answer. That girl is the difference. She is alive. That one person makes it all worthwhile. How do you place a value on someone's life?

People tell me that famine in Africa is indigenous, that it will happen again and again. Yes, it may, but if I have helped to keep somebody alive, if they were going to die and I kept them alive until tomorrow, if I gave them some hope, that is good enough for me.

People say songs don't keep people alive. But I know one that did. People are alive now who would have died. People, like this girl, who might one day make a difference.

That girl is still alive because half a lifetime ago I wrote a song with Bob Geldof. I sent him a jingle he thought sounded like *Z Cars* and he bashed away on his out-of-tune, half-strung guitar while I stared at him in dumb incomprehension. Together we wrote 'Do They Know It's Christmas?', a pop song that caused ripples around the globe and proved that music can change the world.

A song that will be played long after the pair of us are dust.

CHAPTER 1
TENEMENT DAYS

Smells are great revivers of memories. Every time I smell paraffin it makes me think of Christmas in Glasgow. There was no central heating in our flat at all, just a coal fireplace in the living room. We had a paraffin heater for the winter and the smell of the fuel always reminded me it was coming up for Christmas. In winter it was so cold there were icicles on the inside of the windows, and every morning my brother and I would wake up and scrape little drawings on the frosted glass. We slept weighed down by blankets. I got so used to breathing that ice-cold air I can't sleep in a warm room to this day.

My home was a one-bedroom flat on the ground floor of a tenement at 24 Park Street, Cambuslang, four miles from Glasgow city centre. A couple of hundred years before, Cambuslang had been the biggest village in Scotland, but by the 50s it was an extension of Glasgow, home to the Hoover site, a steelworks and hundreds of tenement slums. I was born at home on 10 October 1953.

The tenements are what haunt my memories of growing up in Cambuslang. They have all gone now, and good riddance. There was street after street of four- and five-storey blocks; massive big things they were, all connected, stretching the full length of the street, butted together like a row of terraced houses but much more oppressive. The tenements had originally been thrown up as cheap housing for the poor, a way of hiding the slums, somewhere to put the workers who'd migrated over from Ireland or down from the Highlands and the islands back in the nineteenth century when Glasgow was a booming industrial city. Originally the blocks had been faced in red or copper sandstone, but by the time I came along any colours had disappeared under a thick black layer of soot and pollutants pumped out of the factory furnaces. The buildings were so black that until I was ten I thought stone was black. Because it was the poor who were crowded into the tenements nothing was ever done to maintain them and they crumbled away.

Each tenement block had a communal entrance, which we called the close. In each block there was one flat on either side of the landing before the stairs went on up. Some floors also had a 'single end' – a miserable one-room bedsit. Each floor had an outside toilet, but, as we were on the ground floor, our toilet was *really* outside, in a separate building round the back. When I had to go at night Dad had to take me. The communal areas were all lit by gas lanterns that gave out a gloomy light at the best of times, but most of the lanterns were broken, because if you touched the mantles they just fell apart. A visit to the toilet in the pitch black and freezing cold was pretty petrifying.

Immediately inside the flat was a tiny little space we called the lobby, though it was all of two feet square. Two doors led off it: one led into the living room, and the other into the single bedroom where my older brother Bobby and I slept. The bedroom was very dark even though there were no curtains. The only furniture was a bed and a wardrobe which gave me nightmares. Every kid's room has got a wardrobe in it where all the monsters live and, after Bobby warned me, 'Don't go near the door or you'll get sucked in,' I'd lie there in the dark and imagine the door creaking half open and some vile creature crawling out. In winter it was so cold the bed was covered with blanket after blanket tucked in so tight I was unable to move. Bobby and I lay there strapped in our blanket straitjackets, noses red with cold, equally frozen and frightened, listening to the rats scrabbling away under the floorboards.

Beneath us there was a stream – not a sewer, a proper burn – running right under the floorboards, which meant the bedroom was constantly damp and cold. The rats lived there. When the rain was heavy and the waters rose it disturbed them even more. Some nights I heard them scurrying about, scratching so close to the floorboards I imagined they were eating their way into the room.

Everything happened in the living room. It had a little kitchen area – we called it a 'kitchenette' – it was just a sink with cold-water taps and there was a little gas cooker in the lobby. There was no hot water, just a gas heater, which sat just above the sink. It lit up and heated water came down a spiral tube. I was washed in the sink and I brushed my teeth in the sink. It was the bathroom, and where we washed the dishes. The sink was right next to the only window in the sitting room, so I had to stand there naked for the rest of the street to see. Tony's chip shop was right opposite, which must have been entertaining.

We used to have baths in front of the fire as well; I remember seeing my younger sister Linda getting bathed in front of the fire. There was two and a half years between all us kids. Linda had the same slightly red hair as my aunt – she was very much from my mother's side of the family. She was my dad's favourite, probably because she was the only girl and the youngest. I never heard my dad sing much, but when she was a baby he'd sing the song 'Daddy's Little Girl' to her at night. It was very sweet. Opposite the sink, behind a curtain, was a cavity bed, a hole in the wall with a mattress in it. The bed in the wall was where Mum and Dad slept with Linda.

I was christened James but always called Jim like my dad. He was ten years older than Mum, and they met when he was still in uniform. He didn't actually fight in the war because he drove tank transporters in Italy and North Africa. He admitted a few years back that he had once actually lost a tank, but never told me how he did it. When he came back from the war there was nothing for him, no prospects, no career. He didn't have any qualifications, and that's why it was instilled in me to do well at school, gain qualifications and get an apprenticeship – that way I'd have a job for life.

I have some old black-and-white pictures of my dad and my Uncle George walking down a street in Glasgow in the late 40s. Dad was a good-looking, dapper guy, with a Fred Astaire dress sense, tall and thin with his hair all swept back. He was always very smartly turned out in a shirt and tie, a check sports jacket, cavalry twill trousers and brogues. He had a raincoat that he wore with string gloves. When Mum got dressed up on a Sunday, they looked a very smart couple. When she was younger she was very pretty; she wasn't as frumpy as some of the other mums because she made an effort with what she had – which wasn't a lot. Most of my looks – especially the slightly bulbous nose – come from my mother, although she was shorter at about 5′5″.

Back then women still dressed up to tackle the chores. Mum put on her floral-patterned pinny over slacks and a jumper and wore a head scarf to keep her hair tied back and out of the way. She'd pull on rubber gloves to scrub the steps. Everyone had to take a turn scrubbing the steps. Mum scrubbed the front of the close all the way through the lower part up to the back stairs and our own lintel. Everything had to be immaculate, so the close always smelled of bleach. It was a big thing in the community, and there was a real pride in having done your bit – if Mrs Macintosh hadn't done her turn her ears would be burning. Housework was not something to be done once a week. Every single day rugs had to be beaten and beds made.

At weekends, if she was going to meet somebody for a cup of tea or even wheeling Linda up to the park, Mum put on her best. I always remember her blue-and-white polka-dot A-line dress, while in winter she wore this coat she was very proud of. It was very stylish, with a little fur collar and covered in Anaglypta patterns. It was all about keeping up appearances; she'd look very smart pushing the nice big Silver Cross pram, showing she was as good as anybody else. That's what women did then; she had no career prospects. You grew up, got a job, got married, had kids; the wife looked after the kids, kept the house clean, and the dad went out to work. That's how it was.

We were never allowed out with a jumper with a hole in the sleeve. That wasn't done in our family; we had to be smart, neat, tidy and well spoken. Mum wouldn't let us talk like the other kids, it was one of her foibles. We got a slap if we talked like classic Glasgow thicko kids – 'I didnee dae noth'n'. We had to speak properly. We might have been very much at the bottom of the food chain but she wanted us to do as well as we could. The way we talked was important because she believed that then we wouldn't turn into thugs – which a lot of the neighbourhood kids did.

Dad was a van driver for a bakery. He got up at a hideous time every morning, shaved and then got us all up for school before he left. He came back again at 6.30 at night, except on Saturdays when he worked a half day. He never shaved on Saturday mornings, as that was a different ritual. He waited to do it in the afternoons, listening to the football on the radio. I can still picture his long round cylindrical stick of shaving soap, and its smell will always be associated with Saturday afternoons.

Dad was big into football: Rangers, of course, as we were Protestants. In those days a Catholic player could never play for a Protestant team and vice versa, never mind how good he was. Once we got a record player, Dad bought all the Rangers songs and played them all the time.

There was this huge barrier between Catholic and Protestant, although we were living side by side in the same close. The religious divide was handed down from father to son; you were born into it, and that's why it's still going on in Ireland. The words 'Don't ever marry a Catholic girl' are still etched in my memory, and I've hated the strictures of organised religion for almost as long as I can remember. Sometimes we'd play together but there were times when if it was all Catholics they would say, 'You can't join in, because you're a proddy,' which struck me as ridiculous. My primary school was directly opposite a Catholic school. At playtime there was a constant running battle between the two schools. A boy would run across, whack somebody, then run back into the safety of his mates. Nothing was ever said, it was ingrained: Catholics were different.

In Glasgow you could tell someone's religion from their name. If you were christened Patrick Malley you were a Catholic twice over. Football was a great incentive to be bigoted, but because I didn't like the game I was spared from it. I knew Rangers wouldn't have a Catholic playing for them and I always thought, How stupid is that? I didn't ever say so out loud though.

I didn't have any spiritual beliefs. I went to Sunday School but that was just because it was part of a club all my mates were in. If I didn't go I had nothing to do. I did like the Christmas story as a kid and I'd go to the church because I was into music and I loved hearing a choir bring it all to life. After I hit my teens I only went to church for a wedding, a funeral or because the school made me go. It wasn't until I had spent two years in London that I realised I had a whole bunch of friends and I hadn't thought for a second about what religion they were. That was when I turned my back on what people do in the name of fixed religion. I'd had enough of it.

The Orange Walk every 12 July was nearly as big in Glasgow as it was in Belfast. Mum and my Aunt Jessie always took us, and it was a big day out. We went up to Glasgow Green to watch the pipe bands playing their bigoted songs. It wasn't until I moved away that I realised it wasn't like that everywhere else. In Scotland there were no kind of race issues at all: I didn't know any Asians or any black people. It was very much a white community, a closed shop where nobody was interested in anything going on outside Glasgow.

While I was very aware of the kind of inbuilt bigotry that goes hand in hand with coming out of Glasgow, I wasn't aware of any violence. I did see my mother fighting somebody once. She jumped on the woman's back! It was something to do with us kids but I never knew what and I knew better than to ask in case I got a whack for my troubles.

My mother, Bett, was the disciplinarian. She'd threaten us with 'wait until your father gets home', but my dad never touched any of us. He'd come in and tell us off in as strong a way as he could, probably to pacify his wife. My mother, however, was the tyrant, the one who knocked us into shape, who dished the punishments out, who whacked us across the back of the legs with a plastic bat. And quite rightly so, because we could be difficult. My brother Bobby was particularly good at goading me into an argument, which inevitably turned into a fight. The two of us squabbling in a tiny apartment while

Mum was trying to do the housework made her lose her temper. She'd kick us out of the house and tell us not to come back until Dad was home. We usually went around the corner to see Gran, who spoiled us.

Mum was the money manager. My dad only earned £6 a week. The rent was three pound ten shillings (£3.50). The factor, the man who used to collect the council money, came round on a Friday, and we had to have the rent ready for him. I don't know how Mum did it, but she always managed to feed and clothe us. She did a lot of wheeling and dealing. We were very much an HP (hire purchase) family and Provident cheques were a big thing. We never had a bank account as there was nothing left over to bank. If we needed to buy some bigger item that we couldn't get on HP, Mum would go to the Provident company. They gave her a cheque and she paid it back, plus interest, on a weekly basis. She had everything written down, so she knew that, once the radio was paid off, she could afford to get us new school shoes from one of the catalogues. She made a little bit of money go a long, long way. My dad had nothing to do with it, just worked all the hours that he could get. Every Friday he gave her his wage packet, and she gave him back five bob (25p) for his cigarettes, to last the week. He got his pocket money, and that's how it worked: she made it all happen, kept us all fed and watered and dressed.

Mum worked part-time down at the Hoover factory, and in an off-licence shop in a very heavy area of town, but with three kids and no car it was still hard making ends meet. When I got my first guitar (which I still have today) they paid £2 for it, second-hand. That was a huge chunk of their wages, and they had to save months for it. They always looked out for their kids. From the day we were born Mum and Dad had paid into an endowment policy so on our sixteenth birthday we would get £100 to spend any way we wanted. (Bobby bought a scooter, while I bought a Norton Jubilee 250 twin motorbike. My mother was worried I was going to go and kill myself on it, which I nearly did a few times – but she never said anything.)

Every Wednesday was washday. There was a communal wash house in the back court, and the women fired up this huge copper vat, surrounded by stone and brick, to boil up the water. I'd help with washing the sheets and, because the water was so hot we couldn't put our hands in it, we used big wooden tongs to fish out the washing. It was put into a hand-fed mangle to squeeze the water out and then we'd hang it up in great billowing lines.

The tenements formed a huge square. Round the back where the wash house, the toilets and the middens (where the communal dustbins were kept) were was meant to be a back garden. It looked more like a war-torn mess, a muddy heap full of trashed cars, broken prams and assorted rubbish. There was this overpowering smell of stagnant water. It really stank. Being kids, it didn't worry us, and we just used to play in all the scrap. It was a great adventure playground.

My grandmother Gray lived up on the top floor of one of the blocks and if she saw me out playing she'd shout down, 'Wee Jim, are you hungry?' I was always hungry. She'd make me a jam sandwich, add a chocolate biscuit, wrap it up in a white paper bag and throw it down from the fourth floor with me rushing to catch it before it landed in a puddle. I spent a lot of time with Gran and my two maiden aunts who lived with her. She was my closest relative and if Mum was working I'd go and have lunch in her flat.

When I was older I'd go over to her place to practise my guitar moves in front of the mirror. She always made a meat, potatoes and vegetable lunch for me, and she used to take one potato out before it was completely cooked and was still hard and crunchy in the middle. She'd cut it into four little cubes, put salt on it and that was my treat – 'potato with a bone in it'. I still do that with my kids now. Something Molly, my eldest, still asks for even though my mother won't do it any more is a boiled egg in a cup. Take two eggs and some butter and mash it up into this gooey bitty mess you eat with a spoon. Watching her eat it takes me back years.

My mother's mother, Lizzy, was born in Ireland and her dad, Jimmy, was from Newcastle. Apparently Jimmy was a very stern Victorian man but I never knew him as I was very young when he died. Mum had three sisters and a brother. One sister, Margaret, married a steel worker and went to Canada to find a better life – which she did, owning a ranch-style house in Hamilton, Ontario. Her brother Jimmy (over half the men in my family were called Jim) worked as a steward on ships and in hotels all over the place – like Wales and England. He was divorced with a kid he never saw, which was outlandish in those days. When I was fourteen or so Uncle Jimmy came back to Cambuslang. I'd cycle up to see him, and he was so proud of his little flat, he kept it immaculate. He'd basically come back to die – he looked like an old man to me. He was a great character, maybe because he was a bit of a drinker. My aunts didn't drink; my grandmother didn't drink; my father didn't drink and I'm sure my grandfather didn't because he was so strict. The other two sisters, Jessy and Isa, were spinsters all their lives, so they stayed with my grandmother. But they were always there and, even when we moved to Eastfield, every Saturday morning my aunt would walk down to see us.

My mother didn't get on with my dad's mother. There was a rift, because my mother thought Grandma Ure favoured our cousins over us – they were also called Bobby and Jim. It was the usual family nonsense, but she had this bee in her bonnet and refused to go over except at Christmas. Every Sunday my dad took us, all dressed in our best, to go and visit his mother and father. It took two buses and 45 minutes to get to Carntyne so we must have been a bit of a handful. My grandfather was called Sanny – Alexander – and my gran was Jenny. Their house was the first place I ever ate melon and pasta. She used to make pasta, some sort of tomato macaroni, and we took jars of it back home. Sanny had his own butcher's shop and a house and a car, an Alvis, so in our terms they were rich. Dad used to come home on a Friday night with a bunch of sausages and various bits of meat, which helped keep us alive, and he got bread and cakes from the bakery. The butcher's shop had that horrible dead-cow smell and sawdust everywhere to soak up the blood. I remember his shop being knocked down after he retired – it was closed up and then the whole building was razed to the ground.

My dad had two younger brothers. George worked for the GPO while Alec was a bit of a rogue. He'd turn up at our home at odd times. One night I opened the door to him and he was brandishing a rabbit he'd knocked over. He said, 'Here's dinner,' and threw this thing at me. I was covered in blood and started screaming. Later, when I was eleven or twelve he tried to teach me to drive his mini in a yard with wooden lock-ups all around. I couldn't get to grips with the accelerator and the clutch so I was like a kangaroo jumping all over the place.

I wore very long short trousers that came down to my knees, all year round, and a home-knitted jumper. My aunties knitted all the time but the only colours they used were grey, rust or dark blue. Isa was actually a very accomplished knitter who made amazing Fair Isle jumpers and Arran cardigans which we wore for best. We were so blasé about it because every year we'd get another one.

In winter, because it was so hideously cold walking to and from school, I always wore a balaclava and home-made mittens. When I was very small the smog on some winter nights was so thick I couldn't see more than a few feet in front of my face. If I missed the bus or I'd spent my bus money, which happened quite a lot, I had to walk home. Winter evenings in October or November was when I was most excited with my birthday and then Christmas coming up, I'd look in all the shop windows, wishing and going, 'Oh, I'd love that.' I'd get home so bitterly cold with hacks – chilblains – that when I stood in front of the fire it hurt. My legs, hands, everything, all stung like hell. I stood there in tears, feeling the heat and the intense cold clashing. It burned and hurt for minutes until I thawed out.

Winters were much harsher then. I was given a sledge for Christmas once. We were miles from any hills, so it was straight out into the middle of the road and hoped there weren't any cars coming in the opposite direction. Mind you, there were never that many cars on the streets of Eastfield.

The summers seemed warmer, but they usually do to a kid. I remember sitting in the playground when it was so hot that the tar melted under my feet. I found an old lolly stick, lifted the tarmac up and carved my initials in the tar. We all wore plastic sandals in summer, and one year I was standing on a stank – a metal grid – and my shoes melted to the metal, it was like stringy plastic coming off my shoes.

The tenements were so crowded that any epidemic spread really fast. Lots of kids were sick all the time and polio was rife, which meant many kids wore callipers at school. One year there was a huge outbreak of typhoid – apparently caused by Argentinian corned beef. Illnesses went hand in hand with the environment, and our diets weren't particularly brilliant. It wasn't horrible, that was just the way it was, and everyone else I knew was in the same situation. Everyone was in the same boat, except for a few people who lived in the 'bought houses'. You were rich if you lived in a small house or a bungalow. When I was a kid Glasgow was enough for me. Glasgow and Largs and the Ayrshire coast – that was as far as my world went. England was a foreign country, even Edinburgh was miles away. All I saw on TV was local Glasgow news and Glaswegian newscasters. We had STV and BBC Scotland. My longest-lasting TV memory is of Andy Stewart and the White Heather Club.

One year for our holidays we got really adventurous and went to Whitley Bay, which I knew was in England. I don't remember much about it except that it took a long time to get there and it rained. Not like Largs, where it was always sunny. I have very fond memories of Largs, which was all of 25 miles from the centre of Glasgow at the mouth of the Clyde in Ayrshire. Coming from grey Cambuslang it was a shock seeing these white buildings with brightly coloured doors along the sea front. We used to rent this little flat that was smaller than our home, with an old range in the kitchen which we had to fire up to get any heat in the place. We were there when Marilyn Monroe died in August 1962. I was only eight, but the grown-ups talked about nothing else. (And yes, I can remember where I was when I heard President Kennedy was shot. I was coming out of the Cub Hall on a dark, freezing Friday night.)

The big thing about Largs was that there was nothing to do. We walked up and down the promenade all the time; there was a big boating pond full of disgusting stagnant water and we played in there, sailing boats and running about in swimming trunks, as the sea wasn't particularly clever for young kids who couldn't swim. My dad took us out on fishing trips on these big wooden trawlers where we'd catch mackerel on hand lines. It was so exciting getting the bite, but my dad would have to take it off the hook because we couldn't touch the things. The same year Marilyn died we went fishing but we caught too many mackerel and Dad threw these little tiddlers on the open fire. I thought it was incredibly cruel that this little thing had been separated from its mum and dad and all we did was throw it on the fire.

One year we went to Ayr. My dad couldn't get time off work so he borrowed my uncle's car, drove us down on a Saturday, dropped us off at this caravan and then drove home on Sunday. It rained the whole time we were there and to this day the sound of rain hitting a caravan is one of the most comforting sounds I can hear. There was something really cosy about sitting inside this tiny caravan where we could hardly swing a cat. We played Ludo and snakes and ladders all day to the light of gas mantles, except when the rain wasn't so bad and we went to the cinema.

We had a series of family pets but, like the Spinal Tap drummer, they all died horrible deaths. We weren't very good at keeping them alive and they were all named after drink. At different times we had a Scottie called Mac, and two West Highland terriers, Whisky and Brandy. My dad had had an Alsatian but he had to get rid of it because it started to get a bit aggressive to my brother and myself. One of the dogs was run over, and Dad and I found it lying on the side of the road. He took it down to the Clyde and held it under the water because it was too far gone. Another died when I was at home. I remember shaking him trying to keep him awake and he snapped at me because he was so tired he just wanted to go.

The year I turned ten was full of changes. Dad bought his first car, an old A40 van with only two seats so we kids hurtled around in the back. More important for my mum was that we moved – all of half a mile towards Glasgow – to 9 Buckingham Drive, Eastfield. Because the tenements were due for demolition, the entire community moved together. Our neighbours in the close were our neighbours in this new scheme, four houses together in a block. It was magic for us, all brand new, a proper kitchen where we could actually sit down and have our dinner together, three bedrooms and – the magic thing – an inside toilet and a bath. The garden was 60 feet long, big enough to grow our own potatoes and vegetables. It was still cold though, as they didn't build in any central heating, just an open fire in the sitting room, and there were the same icicles on the inside of every window.

I went to Cambuslang Primary School, though everyone called it Bushy Hill, because that was the name of the road. My mother had gone to the same school, and the same headmistress had taught her. The teachers were mainly spinsters. Miss Munroe looked like she had stepped out of a classic Victorian photograph: her grey hair was pulled back really tight in a bun, and she dressed very conservatively, always in grey. Corporal punishment was still allowed, and some of the teachers seemed to enjoy dealing it out, not that anyone did anything particularly bad. Fairly trivial things – talking in class, late homework or not doing it at all – got us beaten. The teachers used great big thick leather belts with three tongues on the end to beat us. We got whacked in front of all the other kids, so it was not only painful, but incredibly humiliating.

It wasn't a bad school, but school didn't really interest me because I only cared about art and music. The musical facilities were primitive to say the least. There was a piano you weren't allowed to play, a tambourine you weren't allowed to shake and bean bags that didn't make any noise. The art facilities were a paintbrush, some paints and paper.

My brother had got into Rutherglen Academy, which was a grammar school. It was such a big deal getting in that I set my sights on following him there – somehow I believed that if I failed it would shame the family. Eventually I did get in, though I failed the first year because I was one of the youngest in my class. My maths and English were pretty dreadful (though my art was good), but I only got in because it turned out that I had a very high IQ. My mum pushed Bobby and me but there was no pressure on Linda to get into a good school. She didn't feel obliged to either, and as there were no real jobs for women she had no ambitions to do anything. She did that typical Glasgow thing – got pregnant and married very young. Then she moved to Milton Keynes, because her husband's family lived down there.

Academically, Rutherglen was probably far too hard for me. The only things I was any good at they wouldn't teach me enough of. I took the most periods of art I could. Andy Park was my kind of teacher. He was a jazz musician, and he let me paint whatever I wanted to while he wrote out his musical scores. Later, he went on to become the head of Radio Clyde. The school wouldn't contemplate teaching me music unless I was at least Grade 3 on piano. I just had a guitar and knew half a dozen chords.

Had I gone through the whole system and done my O Levels and Highers I would have wanted to go to Glasgow School of Art. As it was I left secondary school at fifteen without an exam to my name. I went to a technical college for six months, and then got a job as an apprentice engineer. While Bobby did an apprenticeship at Rolls-Royce, I worked at the National Engineering Laboratories in East Kilbride. There were five hundred applicants for ten apprenticeships, and I got one of them – maybe because my mother's cousin worked there. I actually got to meet Sir Alec Issigonis when he brought his four-wheel drive Mini to be tested against the hydrostatic car I worked on in the labs.

It was one of the best jobs that I could possibly have landed, right at the upper end of working-class aspirations. It had been drummed into me from an early age by my dad: 'You must get a trade, son, because you'll always be able to work. I didn't and look at me.' At the time it was very true. If I had a trade I had a guaranteed future. To earn a reasonable living – five or six times what my dad was making – all I had to do was work overtime on a Tuesday, Thursday and Saturday morning. Eventually I'd be able to buy a small house and afford to have a family.

Except all I really wanted to do was become a musician.

CHAPTER 2
STUMBLING ON

The musical instrument in my house was the radio. My mother had the Light Programme on all the time she was doing the housework. In the evening we listened to Radio Luxembourg. Some tunes I still remember vividly, even though I was only three when I first heard them. 'Sleep Walk' by Santo and Johnny was a lovely instrumental played on steel guitars, while the Shadows, with their atmospheric and haunting tunes, always captivated me.

My parents weren't old fogies who only listened to Frank Sinatra. Mum was still in her early thirties and she liked the pop music of the day. My dad was really into Andy Williams. One Christmas Bobby was given a Beatles album and I got Andy Williams's *Hawaiian Wedding Song*. As my dad loved Hawaiian guitar I always wondered who that record was really for.

No one in the family was particularly musical. Dad could vamp out a tune on the piano at my gran's house, but generally it was more missed notes than hit ones. I don't know if he had had any formal training, or whether he just had a natural ability to pick a tune out.

Radio Luxembourg was the nearest we got to pirate stations in Scotland. We all bought tiny little cube radios with a single white headphone and I'd sit and listen to that at night in my room trying to tune into Luxembourg – the sound quality was so dreadful. The idea of Radio One – a pop radio station instead of the Light Programme, a pirate station on national radio, something that wasn't going to fade away every nanosecond – was so incredibly exciting. Listening to Tony Blackburn announcing 'Flowers In The Rain' by the Move was this amazing revelation. I could turn on the radio and listen to good-quality pop music whenever I wanted.

Guitars always had this magnetic pull on me, the shape, the sound, everything about them. When I saw Tommy Steele at the movies wearing a white suit and a guitar I thought he was pretty smart looking. I got my first guitar when I was ten. There was this distant relative who had an old 40s dance-band guitar. I was lucky, because most aspiring musicians who told their mum and dad they wanted a guitar ended up with something completely unplayable, because it was the cheapest guitar they could find. I was taught my first three chords by one of the guys in the Scouts, and from there I taught myself. I bought a 'play in a day' book, sat down and figured it out.

I wanted an electric guitar so badly that I entered a competition on the back of a Cornflakes packet to win this beautiful, dark-brown, electric, double-cutaway Burns guitar. At school I was constantly told off because my books and jotters were covered in drawings of guitars and amps. When I got to secondary school, aged eleven, the only place I could play guitar was in the folk club. It was an after-school activity run by a fantastic teacher, Alistair McNaughton, this great tall man with a red beard who'd stand up and sing obscure and dodgy Scottish folk songs – no Robbie Burns for him. My personal favourite wasn't Scottish; I preferred the classic 12-bar blues 'Worried Man Blues'.

The folk club was where I met Jim Potter, who became my best pal. We were inseparable for the next four years, the two Jims, hanging about together all the time, guitars strapped onto backs and riding up and down on our bikes. In our minds Jim and I were the new Lennon and McCartney. We were always in and out of each other's house, working out the latest tune, sussing out every single chord change on The Beatles' *White Album*. We were that close until Jim found girls and I discovered B flat.

Either you played football or you played music, and I was crap at football. I have never been sporty. I left that to Bobby. He was the footballer and the karate champion. I was the Ure with the guitar.

My brother and I chose very different paths. He was a third-dan black-belt karate at a time when not many people had even heard of martial arts, and him and his karate mates used to run around Glasgow – through the snow, the ice, everything – in their white karate suits with no shoes and socks on. That wasn't my idea of fun. One of the great things about having a brother who could do that stuff was that he was on my side. He stood up for me on many an occasion, though I'm not sure it ever came to blows. In our teens the two and a half years between us was a huge gap. Bobby was dressing in parkas and mohair suits and driving scooters. He was a proper Mod tearaway, a bit of a wide boy, in and out of trouble. I was sitting in a café in Burnside when someone came running in and said my brother's car had been smashed up. When I went home that evening he was sitting there looking very sorry for himself – he'd only had the car for one day.

Bobby and I antagonised each other all the time. His job was to wind up his younger brother and little sister, which he did with great aplomb. Sometimes he did surprise me, like when I was sixteen and an aspiring guitar player and we were having a conversation about bands. He said (which was quite unusual coming from him), 'You should be the singer in the band: you're better than that guy you've got.' I told him my voice was way too high but he wasn't having any of it. 'What about that Anderson guy in Yes? He's got a really high voice.' In his older-brother way he was telling me I should be out the front rather than just standing in the back playing the guitar. I still appreciate that.

I've always been able to sing. It was just there. I used to do a paper round in the mornings, and I'd sing 'Johnny Remember Me' (or whatever happened to be the latest hit) as I walked around. Nobody complained, in fact some said it was quite a pleasant way to be woken up. Because the singing was already there all I had to do was learn some chords to accompany myself. I wasn't very good until I was fourteen, which was when I started listening to other guitarists. It was the British Blues boom and after I listened to John Mayall's Blues-breakers with Peter Green and Eric Clapton I realised I was going to have to learn how this lead guitar stuff worked.

My first band – we never had a name and never performed anywhere – came together because the Frazer brothers had a garage we could rehearse in. Their dad owned a little electrical shop just opposite the Barrows. Gordon was the drummer and his brother Ian had an electric guitar and amplifier. The Frazers were rich compared to us: they owned a shop and lived in a bought house – a bungalow. His dad had amplifiers that he had brought home from the shop to repair and then people never came back for them. He gave me my first ever electric guitar. Some days Gordon's dad came home in a foul mood and once he took the guitar away from me. I was devastated until I got it back.

My first proper electric guitar was one I saw in McCormacks, a music shop in Glasgow. It was a 1960 Stratocaster with a small stockhead which someone had hand-painted with a really runny gloss paint so it looked awful. My mother got a Provident cheque for £110 which I promised to pay back at £5 per month – though whether I ever did is a moot point. I took it home and, in front of my horrified parents, proceeded to pull it apart. I took off the machine heads, the neck and the scratchpad until all I had was lumps of wood and bits of electronics. I sanded it all down to the wood, varnished it and put it all back together again. Then I took it straight back to McCormacks and did a straight swap for the guitar I really wanted – a semi-acoustic Gibson 330 which cost £180 and had been way out of my league. That, too, was hand-painted so I went through the whole process again. At this point my parents realised I knew what I was doing.

Guitar practice was never about sitting down doing scales. It was sitting with a mate in his bedroom with a couple of acoustic guitars and a record player, putting the needle on over and over until one of us figured out the chords. I sat and sang along until I learned how it worked.

I have always loved a good pop tune – the Who, the Beatles, Roy Wood: brilliant songwriters with great melodies. The Small Faces were one of my favourites. They were trendy, wrote fantastic tunes and they were small, which at that time meant a lot to me! Once I got my first electric guitar I started growing my hair, wearing ex-army clothes and getting into rock. I couldn't make my mind up whether I wanted to be the next Eric Clapton or the next Stevie Marriott.

I loved Hank Marvin and the Shadows for their sound, but when I first heard John Mayall's Bluesbreakers, early Fleetwood Mac and Chicken Shack, all of a sudden I realised that the guitar could sing. And then there was Hendrix and the way his guitar sustained and distorted. It was totally different to anything I'd heard before. I couldn't figure out how they made those guitars do that – I guess it was talent and I hadn't got there.

My next band was named the Stumble after a tune on John Mayall's *Bluesbreakers* album. We were pretty dreadful. We played everything from blues numbers (or so we thought) to current pop songs. Originally I sang backing vocals and played rhythm guitar. Gordon Appacellie was the lead singer. The original guitarist, Alan Wright, was a fairly good player but when he left the band all of a sudden I was promoted to lead guitarist, so I had to start learning how it worked. The drummer was Alec Baird, who went on to play with the Jags (a late-70s power-pop band); Kenny Ireland was on bass and we had a succession of keyboard players. For a while we had Fraser Spiers on harp; he was a really good blues player, much too good for us.

Some of our gigs were very violent. By the 60s the whole gang thing had kicked in again. Glasgow had dozens of gangs with names like the Calton Tongs, the Gorbals Cumbie (they came from Cumberland Street), the Maryhill Fleet and the Possilpark Uncle. They fought their turf wars with hammers, cut-throat razors and switchblades.

Some of the very fashion-conscious gang members became Mods. There were guys walking about town wearing really smart tailor-made suits, and the jackets had bright red linings on the inside. If they got into a fight they'd turn the jacket inside out so that when they got covered in blood it didn't stain. The really hard men had fish hooks sewn behind their jacket lapels, so if someone grabbed them by the collar to deliver a Glasgow kiss (a head butt) their fingers were impaled on the hooks and they couldn't get away. Others had little pockets sewn inside their jackets to hold cut-throat razors. In a fight they pulled the razors out of their concealed holsters and flicked them open like gunslingers.

I very rarely went into central Glasgow to go to a dance, because by the time I was old enough I was the guy up on stage making the soundtrack to fight to. It happened all the time. Two gangs lined up on opposite sides of the hall and waited for an excuse. The golden rule was that we never stopped, just kept on playing no matter what happened. The thugs crashed in the middle; the bottles and chairs started flying, and once the girls, who were tougher than their boyfriends, got involved there'd be no stopping it.

There was always an undercurrent of violence. If you have a bunch of eighteen-year-old guys out of their brains on Lanliq (a fortified wine – Glasgow's answer to Thunderbird), trouble follows. It still does. Cumnock Town Hall had a dance every Friday night, and every week there was this huge great ruckus. The local farmers just wanted to let their hair down, and their idea of fun was getting drunk, having a massive brawl, beating the shit out of each other and ending up covered in blood.

Bands had to tread a thin line to avoid being sucked into the battles, but sometimes it was unavoidable. If I caught the eye of some girl in the audience and her boyfriend saw it, then I was his target for that evening. At best he'd give me the evil eye and forget about me if there was somebody else to hit, but otherwise I'd disappear as soon as we finished. My brother was the karate man, and he could handle himself without any nonsense, whereas I was useless. All that petrified me.

We often played out in Kirkintilloch, twenty miles east of town, where they spoke in this singsong country brogue very different from the harsh Glasgow accent. They hated us 'city boys' but one guy in particular was notorious. We were playing one night, when this skinhead thug pointed the finger at the band and mouthed, 'You're getting it.' We quaked for the rest of the night. The hall was at the bottom of a valley, and the only road in and out was very steep. We'd hired this guy, 'Ivor the driver', and his beaten-up old van to take all the equipment, and as were loading the gear we could see this gang waiting at the top of the hill.

Ivor, who was more of a coward than we were, tried to drive through, but as the van could barely make it up the hill by the top they had us surrounded and started kicking the sides. Alec, our drummer, was a small, quiet, mild man, but this time he'd had enough. Every time we came to Kirkintilloch these guys got on our case. They were banging on the windows, yelling at us to come out, when suddenly Alec pulled the door open, jumped out and whacked their leader with a hammer. Bang, right in the centre of his forehead. The thug went down like a stone, and the rest of his mates just ran for it, leaving him completely out lying in the middle of the road. I sat there completely agog as Alec got back in the van.

Ten miles down the road the van was stopped by the police. Alec said, 'What the heck, I'm dead, I'll go to prison.' One of the cops asked us to give him the hammer, which Alec used to hammer his bass drum into the stage. Alec pulled it out of his bag and handed it over. The policeman said, 'You might hear from us, you might not,' and off we went. Apparently this thug had been winding the cops up for years, and Alec never heard another word.

We never went back to Kirkintilloch. No thanks. I wanted to keep my boyish good looks and I needed my fingers to continue playing guitar solos.

We played similar gigs in outback towns and villages scattered across Scotland, places where the gene pool was limited. The guys didn't like us playing there because we came from the big city and we dressed smarter, were more fashionable and were more appealing to the local girls. To the girls our band was a glamorous sexy thing irrespective of the crap we were playing, and there were always a few flirty ones down the front determined to catch somebody's – anybody's – eye. At the end of the night, when we were loading the van, there they were . . . and there was time for a snog and a fumble with somebody from Stumble. That was about it, because once the van was loaded we had to shoot off straight away. By the time we'd finished it was usually late, bloody cold and Ivor the driver was desperate to get home to his bed.

The summer before I turned sixteen Kenny Ireland's family went away for a week. We took over his house, kipping down together and playing Edgar Broughton records very loud. I was wandering through the park with a mate where we met this incredibly flirty girl from Hull out walking on her own. She made thi. big show of clocking us, making big eyes. She ended up back in the house with us lads and during the evening she appeared in the front room dressed in nothing but a blanket and proceeded to flash us. This was a slight hint that something else might arise, but it was also frightening for five petrified boys watching this girl running around. We were all a little on edge, as none of us had actually seen a naked girl before. It was a weird night because this very agile fourteen-year-old took everybody on, introducing us each to the wicked ways of the flesh. I had to wait a long time for another chance to have sex.

I didn't have any steady girlfriends at that time, not for a month, not even for a week. Music was the one thing that mattered. The only girls I met were at school dances or record sessions at somebody's house: records were played; the lights were turned off and it was a snogging party. All I got was a cuddle and some ragged, ripped lips from kissing too hard. The girls snogged us boys so bloody hard that everything hurt; my lips were rubbed against my teeth until they were raw. I'd come away with a mouth that looked like a baby had been sucking a dummy for ten hours. I suppose I enjoyed it.

By the time I was eighteen my life was already mapped out. During the week I worked at my apprenticeship and at weekends I played with the Stumble. I was going to train for another year and a half, then the day my apprenticeship finished I'd go out and join a full-time band. Our keyboard player heard that Salvation, who were a well-known band on the Scottish scene, were looking for a keyboard player. We'd supported them a couple of times and as he wanted to audition he asked me to go along.

Salvation was run by the two McGinlay brothers: Jim was the bass player and Kevin the singer. What I didn't know was that they were also looking for a drummer and a guitarist. Jim asked me to play while they auditioned the keyboard player, so I played Neil Young's 'Southern Man', which was one of the standards of the day. Jim offered me the guitarist's position for £25 a week. The keyboard player made a beeline for the cruise ships.

I went home in a turmoil, because it hadn't ever crossed my mind that I'd get offered a gig. I told my parents what had happened. 'Look, I'd love to do this, but I will finish the apprenticeship first. Then, the day it's through, I'll go off and do exactly what I want to do.' The final decision was down to my Mum and Dad. If they had told me to continue my apprenticeship I would have done so. No question. I know that was what my dad wanted, as in his mind it gave me the chance he had never had. They talked it over and then my mother said, 'You've got to do what you think's right, follow your heart.' Throughout my childhood mum and dad let all of us follow our own interests and helped us out when we needed it, but this was their greatest act of faith. It took a lot of courage for them to set me free. It's only since I became a father myself that I've realised how much.

When I quit my apprenticeship it shocked everybody. Nobody had ever left before. One of my bosses said, 'What if the trends all change, and bagpipes become the next big thing?'

'Then I'll have to learn to play bagpipes,' I replied.

The first rehearsal with my first professional band was a shock. I was the youngest and smallest in the group. Jim McGinlay announced in true *Animal House* style, 'There's only room for one Jim in this band . . . and that's me. You are now Mij – which is Jim backwards.'

The name stuck, though it was easier to spell it Midge. That's who I've been ever since.

CHAPTER 3
FROM SALVATION TO SLIK

Salvation were a successful band, albeit in a very local sense, a name I'd see in the Sunday papers every weekend alongside Tear Gas and Nazareth. To me the band was already massive.

I was supposed to earn £25 a week. Of course, it was nothing like that, as we divvied up what was left after expenses, paying for the van, the PA and Joe the roadie – a band always have the one mate who can't play but can lift and carry. Keeping the van running was always a major expense, as we were forever blowing up engines and gearboxes, thanks to Joe's inability to choose between diesel and petrol. But as I was still at home living was cheap. I'd give a tenner to my mum and the rest went into my pocket or to McCormacks to pay off the long-outstanding HP on my Marshall stack.

We'd do two, maybe three, gigs on a weekend but very little during the week. Our agency only worked in Scotland, although eventually they had links with Astra, an agency down in Wolverhampton, and once or twice they did a swap – they sent one of their bands up to do the Scottish circuit for a week, and we'd go down into England. But more often than not it was just the same old places. Scotland was where I cut my teeth, where I learned how to play guitar, and where I became a human jukebox.

Compared to the pub-rock circuit down in England, the live scene in Scotland was non-existent. The Church ran the licensing laws and insisted that a pub couldn't charge an entry fee. There was only one decent pub venue in Glasgow, the Burns Howf. Don't ask me what the name means, but it did have regular bands playing, and we got paid all of a tenner. Bands did it for the prestige, because it was the closest gig Glasgow had to the Hope and Anchor.

On a typical weekend Salvation played the JD Ballroom in Dundee on Friday, the Electric Garden in Glasgow on Saturday night and the Inverness Caledonian Hotel on the Sunday. It took five hours to get to Inverness and five back, all on a dreadful B road.

Glasgow was a musical desert – there were no recording facilities, no record labels. For Scottish bands the pattern was always the same.

Get as big as possible in Scotland then head south to try and see if something could happen in London. It seldom worked. At home they were big fish in a small pond, but down in London there were a million great bands all striving to find a record contract. We saw so many groups go down south full of hope and expectation, and come back a broken band.

Tear Gas were one of the few exceptions. They were a great live band but it wasn't until Alex Harvey came along, announced, 'You will be my backing band,' and turned them into the Sensational Alex Harvey Band that they became successful. Until the Bay City Rollers it was only them and Nazareth who had managed to break out of the circuit. After the Rollers became this huge teenybop band, record companies in London started to pay attention north of the border. All of a sudden they were sending up empty jumbo jets looking for Scottish bands!

The Rollers had been on the circuit for years. When I was in the Stumble we opened up for them a couple of times – though they had a different singer. In the early 70s they had one single, a cover of 'Keep on Dancing' that did quite well, but they couldn't follow it up and came back to Edinburgh. They were big in Scotland for maybe six or seven years before it went crazy. They had been at it a lot longer than I had, so in a way their success was justified, but to anyone playing on the circuit they were a joke. I'd seen them enough times to know they couldn't play as well as we could. After 'Shang a Lang' was a hit we all said, 'It's crap, rubbish. We're a million times better than that.' We were jealous.

The Rollers – or more likely their manager Tam Paton – were smart enough to develop a unique image. Their look happened very organically, not in Glasgow because it was too weird for Glasgow, but thirty miles outside in Ayrshire. Cumnock Town Hall was on the regular circuit, and whenever we played it there were these guys wearing their jeans halfway up their legs with bits of tartan stitched around the bottom and bovver boots – it started as a skinhead fashion. They wore denim jackets and wrapped tartan scarves around their necks like old men. That was where the Rollers nicked the idea. They started dressing like that and the next thing was that half the teenagers in Britain were wearing clashing tartans – Robert the Bruce must have turned in his grave.

In Salvation I was very much the new kid on the block. I was only eighteen, while the others were old men, all in their twenties. Billy McIsaac, the keyboard player, had been in Bubbles, another well-known band in the Glasgow area, though he was working full time as a telephone engineer. Kenny Hyslop, the drummer, had actually recorded an album with a band called Northwind in Germany. At the first meeting Billy expressed his doubts about having me in the band. He was worried that I'd not paid my dues as a full-time professional and thought that I might not be able to cut it. The reality was that all of us were at the bottom of the food chain and none of us was due any pay for a long time.

Musically we worked really well right from the off. Within a couple of years Salvation were pretty well known in Scotland and our fees had gone up from £100 to a heady £125 a night. I'd started to get attention from the girls in the crowd. It wasn't deliberate, but I was young, I had hair halfway down my back and I'd learned some flash moves. In April 1974, at the ripe old age of 28, Kevin the singer decided to pack it all in and go back to being a mechanic. He was the eldest in the band and bored by it.

I took over lead vocals, although everyone sang two or three songs. Jim McGinlay had a great voice and Billy McIsaac did a bit of vocalising as well. Six months later we changed our name from Salvation to Slik.

It's funny how music changes so suddenly. There are long periods with nothing but mediocrity floating along and then, all of a sudden, something explodes. There is this vacuum and suddenly the vacuum is filled not just by a different music but by a whole different style. In the early 70s a new door was flung open. There was an eruption of new talent, new bands – Bowie, Sparks, Cockney Rebel, Queen, Roxy Music – playing new music with a new look.

Bowie was the outrageous side of things, all that red hair and body-hugging catsuits. But off stage the Bowie look was very smart – except when he was in a dress, but even I knew that was for show. We had no idea who supplied Bryan Ferry with suits, or that he was a clothes horse for the fashion designer Antony Price. In 1972 I was an observer from north of Hadrian's Wall – the next time music and image were reinvented together I was right in the centre.

I had always been aware of the importance of fashion in pop. The Beatles caught my imagination because of their haircuts: that long fringe was different from anything else at the time. The next time I really took notice was watching the Small Faces on *Top of the Pops*. There were these little guys with huge guitars, dressed in Mod jackets, flower-power shirts and those fantastic oblong glasses. I watched them open-mouthed, knowing they were who I wanted to be. I was desperate to get that stuff, but financial shortcomings – and my mum – never allowed it.

Music has gone hand in hand with fashion since the Beatles. Before that everyone looked like sawn-off versions of their mums and dads – boys wore suits and girls looked like Ruby Murray. Then the Beatles came along and all of a sudden young people developed their own fashion sense: there were winkle pickers and Chelsea boots. That was the first time I remember seeing an individual style for young people.

In the mid-60s the Mods really made an impact on me with their French bouffant hairdos, the fancy high-cut regency jackets, little rectangular glasses and Italian shoes. Everything was very smart, though whether the look came from the music – the Small Faces and the Who – or the other way round I never knew. I felt this instant connection with the way the Small Faces looked. I don't know where it came from but it gave me this love for their music.

When 1972 came around – with Bowie, Roxy Music and Queen – suddenly the fashion changed again. Everything got outrageous, glitzy and glam with big shoulders, and a lot of emphasis was put on the look. Fortunately the sound was just as important. Roxy Music's 'Virginia Plain' was as groundbreaking as the look they invented. The mix of music and style has been happening ever since – punk, the new romantics, the whole urban dance look with jeans hanging down the backside and pants showing. These days you have got to have the right labels. In 1972 it wasn't about the labels because nobody could afford an Anthony Price suit.

When you're in a band, you can get away with looking outrageous. In fact, you should look good. It should be compulsory. When I first met Kenny Hyslop both of us were wearing cowboy shirts with little pointed pocket flaps and mother-of-pearl lapel buttons. I thought, That's it, he's my soul mate. From that moment the look of the band was our department.

Long hair had to come to an end. Once Kenny and I saw *Dirty Harry* we decided to have these Clint Eastwood haircuts. It was a distinct improvement on the big feather cut I had for a while. I had long straight hair until Max Langdon, one of our managers, who was associated with some hairdresser, announced, 'I know what, we'll layer your hair.' I looked like Suzi Quatro. It was so dreadful I had it all cut off. I had to go short until it was styled and a sawn-off Clint appeared.

Kenny and I devoured the music papers – the *NME*, *Sounds* and *Melody Maker* – to find out what was going on in London. We read about the Bromley Contingent, who had started this cool look: short hair and second-hand clothes. Once we had the haircut, we started to haunt funny old shops in Glasgow that still had 50s clothes. I found some old baseball shirts and it grew from there. (Of course, once we had a hit the management and record company got involved with our image, telling me, 'We need to get some NEW baseball shirts with "Midge" written across the front.' That was the point we lost it. Once it became part of a marketing plan it wasn't real any more.)

The new name came partly from the band and partly from Max. He wasn't the best manager, but a great character who'd come in with these mad, crazy ideas. One day he said, 'Right, I've got it. I've heard the new batch of songs and it's time to think "Slick".' Max wasn't saying it as a name but that sparked off an idea. We thought 'Slick', knocked the 'c' out of it and had a new name. Slik conjured up the right retro-fifties, Roxy Music, David Bowie, glittery camp over-the-top image that was all the fashion down in London. We even knocked up a Brylcreem jar, took all the labels off and replaced them with a Slik sticker.

That set Max off on another rant. 'Right,' he said to me. 'You are still Midge because you can't be anything else. Kenny, you are now Oil Slik. Billy, you are Lord Slik. Jim, you are Jim Slik. Get your hair cut, grow a skinny moustache and try to look like Clark Gable.'

We had the image but our songwriting was never really there. We were always very selective about the songs we played, cover-version snobs who refused to do stuff like 'Son Of My Father' by Chicory Tip. We'd much rather do Bowie's 'Life On Mars'. We chose the best of what happened to be in the Top 40.

We tried to write songs but they were all fairly derivative. I'd bring in something that sounded like 'Ziggy Stardust' and Billy would come up with an obvious Queen rip-off. Jim was actually one of the better songwriters, while Billy wrote some real stinkers. We all did, but his 'Rudolf Valentino' was particularly awful. None of his lyrics rhymed, but we never dared point that out to him. I can still remember some of his words . . . 'Rudolf Valentino / Never has he seen her'. They were all dire, though some original songs did make it onto the first Slik album. We were each allowed to put on one song to pacify us.

I always drove the band's Transit van. One afternoon I spotted Phil Lynott walking around the streets. I'd seen Skid Row do one of their first shows ever at the Picasso, which was *the* club in Glasgow. It was a sleazy place which always smelled of cannabis, but everybody who came to Scotland played there. I saw John Lee Hooker there, and the Edgar Broughton band chanting 'Out Demons Out'. Skid Row's guitarist was Gary Moore; he was only sixteen, with a technique that just blew me away. I knew they really rated this new band, Thin Lizzy (Phil had actually sung with Skid Row for a short time and been taught the bass by Brush Shields before starting Lizzy). A year later 'Whiskey In The Jar' had made Phil a star. He was such a great, unique frontman, an archetypal rock star – except he was black. He did that Hendrix thing; he had the poses of every great guitarist I'd ever seen.

I stopped the van, got out and said, 'Hi, Phil, how are you doing?' We got chatting and I took him home to Eastfield where my mother fed him. Phil was very relaxed considering he'd been taken to a complete stranger's home. He probably thought he was going to have a quiet smoke with a fellow musician and instead he was sat down in front of their parents and eating egg and chips off his lap because we had no table at the house. It was one of the few times I ever saw him eat, because he was embarrassed about his social skills. We sat there for a couple of hours strumming a guitar and playing some of his songs. I was arguing about the chords with him and he'd written the songs. Phil was always very polite. I had to read his lips when he spoke; he was so quiet you wouldn't have heard him behind a matchstick. He was always hunched over because he was so used to talking down to people – especially a little bloke like me.

I drove him back to his gig at Glasgow University and went to pick up the others crowing, 'You'll never guess who I had in the back of the Transit today.' It was huge bragging rights – but only to the band, as nobody else knew who Thin Lizzy were at the time. I never expected to see Phil again but that chance meeting turned out to be the beginning of one of the most important and unlikely friendships of my life.

I got stopped in the street quite a lot. My managers owned the Apollo and, as there were no hire shops when bands came to town and needed to borrow a guitar for the night, they'd say, 'Go down to McCormacks; you'll probably find Midge wheeling and dealing out on the street.' I was something of a McDel Boy because there was no other way to get the gear I needed. I'd go either to the Barrows or Paddy's Market, really dodgy places, looking for gear that I could fix up. Once I saw a bass guitar there for four quid, traded in my leather jacket for it, took it home, stripped it to bits, did it all up, then took it to McCormacks and sold it for ten pounds against something else. Another time I bought a Fender amp and a two-by-twelve cabinet for forty pounds from an ad in the local newspaper. It was some poor wee woman whose son had phoned her and told her 'to sell his amplifier for him'. I traded that in for a stack that was worth £150.

One day this jumpy little guy with a London accent stopped me. 'I just want you to talk to my mate for a minute,' he said. 'It's about music.' I went round the corner and there was a parked car with this very odd-looking character sitting inside. He had a curly fizzy mop-top of red hair and a black mohair jumper with a PVC studded dog collar on it. In 1975 in Glasgow this was a very strange sight. Everybody looked like a reject from the Sweet, and the smart-looking kids wore stack-heeled boots and flared trousers with feather-cut hair.

I sat in this car next to this effeminate-looking bloke who talked in this very whiny, sibilant voice, all about his clothes shop in London and how he used to manage the New York Dolls. He went waffling on and on . . . His name was Malcolm McLaren. I'd never heard of him or Vivienne Westwood or Seditionaries or Sex or whatever the shop they ran was called. The guy who stopped me was Bernie Rhodes, who later went on to manage the Clash.

Bernie had stopped me because I looked different with my James Dean haircut. I was wearing straight jeans when everyone else had flares and stack-heeled boots. It was 25 minutes into the conversation before Malcolm asked if I was a musician. Apparently he was looking for a singer or guitarist for this band he had down in London. It was primarily a fashion thing he was putting together and I definitely looked the part.

As Slik were about to release their second single I declined the offer to join his band. Six months later the Sex Pistols were all over the papers.

When I first met Malcolm I just thought he was a weirdo from down South. Later I realised he was a very clever man. He'd hooked up with Vivienne Westwood and he understood the power of putting fashion trends together with music. His job was to sell clothes and to do that he invented the Sex Pistols. The ripped T-shirts and the outrage have since become a fashion cliché, but at the time you couldn't be a punk unless you had a pair of bondage trousers from Sex or a T-shirt with two cowboys with their willies touching. McLaren did that – he turned punk into a brand.

If you listen to the Pistols' records they are not three-chord thrash songs, over in thirty seconds. They were much more controlled than that. 'Anarchy In The UK' is quite a slow record. McLaren invented the look but he was lucky when he found John Lydon. It would never have worked without him – and it certainly would never have worked with me as the singer, not a chance. Lydon epitomised that snide, distant punk look and was brilliant at it. I can't sneer to save my life. He was the perfect foil for what Vivienne was trying to put across in fashion.

The real reason Bernie and Malcolm were up in Glasgow was because they had some musical equipment to sell. The prices were so low I immediately assumed it had been knocked off, but they assured me it wasn't. They opened a boot full of guitars and amplifiers. I bought a Fender amp for forty pounds. Thanks very much! It would have been two hundred quid in the shops.

Getting a record released had been a long slog. Salvation was a good band. Slik was better. Yet a record deal, any record deal, was still a very elusive thing. After three years it felt like we'd gone as far as we could go. We'd hit a massive wall, and it felt as if there was no way through it, over it or under it.

Slik were managed by Unicorn Leisure, a company run by Frank Lynch and Max Langdon. They had taken on the lease for Green's Playhouse, the big venue in Glasgow, and turned it into the Glasgow Apollo. Unicorn also owned pubs, discos and clubs in and around Glasgow and Edinburgh, and because they had the venues they ended up managing us and Billy Connolly. They were as straight as they could be but they didn't know anything about the music industry. They did their best but it wasn't particularly brilliant.

Frank Lynch had a connection with Bill Martin and Phil Coulter, who wrote all the Bay City Roller hits. One day Bill Martin was in Frank's office in Clouds, a ballroom above the Apollo. We were in there rehearsing Sparks' 'This Town Ain't Big Enough For Both Of Us'. Bill thought it was the record that was playing until he stuck his head out and saw it was a band standing there playing it note for note. He also saw we were a bunch of good-looking lads. That was it: we ended up in the Martin–Coulter pretty-boy collection.

It wasn't the best record deal in the world. Actually it was pretty crap . . . but then again, as it was the only deal we were ever offered, it was a great deal. There was no advance, no cash for us. We got three points on a record, which is not great at all. They also gave us each a publishing deal so that if we did write any songs they owned them too.

The advance seemed amazing at the time, though. I'd never seen a cheque for £1,000 before. I went out and spent it buying one of the very first video machines to come on the market. It only recorded for an hour, so I only ever saw the first half of a movie. As tapes cost £40 each (a week's wages), the second half didn't seem that important. I've always been a sucker for first-generation technology – the first mobile phone I bought cost £2,000, looked like a brick with an aerial and if anybody ever called me on it I was so embarrassed I let it ring until I could find the sanctity of a phonebox to answer it in.

We did have our doubts as to whether we should take the deal or not, but in the end it was incredibly exciting being offered the chance to get inside a recording studio. We knew the song wouldn't be what we liked because Phil Coulter was a 35-year-old man writing songs for fourteen-year-old girls to buy. Don't get me wrong, Phil is a very talented man. I enjoyed working with him, and have done since. Bill Martin was a very different character. Bill was the whiz kid, the ideas man, the businessman, always right in your face. His real name was Wiley McPherson, and I don't know why he ever changed it. It was a great name for a pop businessman.

Bill Martin and Phil Coulter had a formula. They were a hit factory, the Stock, Aitken and Waterman of their day, churning out hit after hit. They had a production deal with Bell Records where they found the acts and paid for all the recordings. Then they'd hand the master across to Bell who were the machine that made it into the hit. Before they got to us they had a whole stable of artists, including the Rollers and Kenny.

The first record we did was called 'The Boogiest Band In Town'. It was released in January 1975 and it died a death. Deservedly. We even shot a promo for it in the Marquee in Wardour Street, the first time I'd ever been to Soho. Slik also made it on to a movie, *Never Too Young To Rock*. Not that we knew anything about it. Someone at the record company knew somebody else who was putting together this movie. It was a *Carry On* film except with pop stars like Mud and Showaddywaddy instead of Kenneth Williams and Sid James. There was no story but every so often they'd stick a periscope up from this van and go, 'Oh look, there's Slik', and cut straight into our pop promo for the next three minutes. It was a cheap way to make a really bad film. The record company saw it as a vehicle to get us exposure.

We'd only sung on the first single, but the deal was we could all contribute to the second. We kept saying to the management: 'We don't want any of this session-player business, we're proper musicians, we'll do it.' When the time came we drove down to London. It took us over eight hours in a three-ton truck full of gear. As we walked into Mayfair studios in South Molton Street we heard what sounded like a Bay City Rollers B-side coming out of the speakers, all these bells and jingling and stuff. We thought it was something left over from the session before, and our recording was about to start. Then Phil Coulter came out of the booth and said, 'Do you like your track, boys? It's done.'

That was our new record – 'Forever And Ever'. The session musicians had been in that morning and knocked it out. The drummer was Clem Cattini, who's played on everything – he's in his sixties now and still doing it – while Phil played the piano. Otherwise it was the same musicians who played on the Rollers and everything else they did. I was really pissed off. I said something to that effect, because Bill Martin took me out to the middle of South Molton Street where he tore strips of me. There he was in the middle of the day, in a very busy shopping street in the centre of London, shouting in my face, 'If you want to be a hit, you've got to sing that bloody song!'

I might have been 22 but I was still a kid, as green as Kermit. I was completely taken aback by his behaviour. So I went back inside and started singing this weird Gregorian chant. It took all day. We recorded on a 16-track tape machine. There were loads of multi-tracks because of all the chanting and multi-layered vocals. Jim and Billy sang on it too, but I'm not sure Kenny did anything. The funniest thing was hearing my voice back on speakers or monitors, as I'd never heard that before. It was a really weird sensation.

I'd always been fascinated by the studio side of things, but before nobody had let me in. It was really interesting to see how Phil worked, using double- and triple-tracking, doing vocals in higher octaves to fill out the sound. In reality the song was like making aural wallpaper. It was a well-crafted pop song, nothing more. It meant nothing to me. However, on New Year's Eve 1975 that song changed my life overnight. Forever.

CHAPTER 4
FOREVER BUT NEVER

It was luck. *Top of the Pops* wanted an angle for their New Year's Day show, so they featured four brand-new bands without a hit between them. Fifteen million people watched Slik play 'Forever And Ever'.

We recorded the show on New Year's Eve but as we couldn't afford to stay down in London we got the sleeper train back to Glasgow. We arrived back first thing New Year's morning and the show went out at lunchtime. It was as if a switch had been flicked. As I walked down the street people went, 'It's you that was on *Top of the Pops*.' Suddenly attitudes towards me changed. Girls thought I was fantastic, that I was wonderful, and wanted to get to know me better. Guys started to get jealous.

In the beginning it was Slik's look that was more important than the record. The other bands were into glam rock, long feather-cut hair, stack-heeled boots and flares, and then there was us with James Dean haircuts wearing baseball shirts. I'd bought a baseball shirt in the Kings Road on the day of the show which I've still got in my wardrobe. Kids just went crazy for those skinny Scots with their retro look performing this bizarre chant-along record. It probably helped that 'Bohemian Rhapsody' had been Number One for months. The public was used to weird vocal hits and were gagging for a new one.

Once the record started getting played on the radio, it picked up its own momentum. It entered the charts in mid-January and climbed steadily until it replaced Abba's 'Mama Mia' at the top on St Valentine's Day. When I got the phone call from Bill Martin I did not feel the elation that I should have. I was so far removed from the song – it was a hit but it wasn't mine, just something that I sang on.

The first time I did *Top of the Pops* I was amazed by how small the studio was. And how few people were actually in the audience, just fifty kids that they shoved in front of whatever stage they were filming. I can hardly remember who else was on that first show. Pan's People were dancing to Mike Oldfield's Christmas instrumental 'In Dulce Jubilo', so my major ambition was trying to catch a glimpse of the girls changing in their dressing room. The only other song that stuck in my memory was the Walker Brothers' 'No Regrets'.

We had knocked up a live version of 'Forever And Ever' straight away. That wasn't a problem. The hardest part was that it had a saxophone featured heavily on it, and as we didn't have a sax player we altered it somewhat.

We shot a video with Mike Mansfield when 'Forever And Ever' was climbing the charts. The night before our manager took us all out for a big Greek meal, and we drank seven bottles of wine in about half an hour. We were so ill the next day. For some reason we were dressed as monks, parading round all day in big, heavy, brown robes, holding candles, hanging onto bell ropes and being hauled twenty feet into the air, but as we were all feeling like shit we had no strength to hold on. No wonder we all looked deathly pale in the video.

The BBC treated everybody the same; there was no kind of special treatment. However, our record company were certainly treating us differently. Suddenly I was a teenybop hero on the covers of *Fab 208*, *Oh Boy* and *Jackie*. Life became one big photo shoot. I did a front cover shoot with Leslie Ash for *Mates* magazine – she looked twelve and behaved 22 while I looked and behaved like a fourteen-year-old. When Valentine's Day came around the *Daily Mirror* photographed us dressed up as gangsters with fake machine guns. It was supposed to be portraying the St Valentine's Day massacre but we looked like a bunch of Glasgow street kids in silly hats.

The worst shoot was up in Glasgow after we got to Number One. Slik was major news up there so people went crazy. The photographer from the *Daily Record*, who obviously had the headline already in his mind, promised us, 'I'll find something really interesting, really good.' We looked a bunch of right twats, dressed up in baseball jackets, standing on top of a horse and cart. The headline was: 'CART TOPPERS'.

Overnight we went from driving our own Transit to not being able to walk out the front door. We didn't have any security guards; we didn't even have a tour manager – our management didn't know how to cope. The record company did, but why should they bother getting involved. They just booked the TV and radio shows and the promo appearances and left us to get on with it.

Now we had bigger fish to fry: the first thing the management tried to do was pull all the dates that had been booked months ahead for £125. There was one we had to do in Ayrshire. It was absolute mayhem. Can you imagine Gareth Gates coming to play the local

Scout hall two weeks after *Pop Idol*? We had to go there and play with no security laid on. It was pandemonium. On stage we couldn't hear a thing because of the screaming girls. Off stage they ripped our clothes to shreds. Our ears rang all the way home as we nursed our scratches.

We realised after that show that this was what it was going to be like once we went out on tour . . . except on a bigger scale. We were booked into the Glasgow Apollo in three months' time and there were going to be 3,000 screaming girls, fainting, crying and waving Slik scarves.

It was the same when we did TV and radio shows. After it was announced that we were coming in to do the breakfast show at Capital Radio the place was surrounded by a sea of screaming teenage girls. We hadn't even had breakfast. Our driver, Bill, was fantastic – he'd done it all before. The only way that we could get through was for the car to mount up onto the pavement. Security guards parted people like a wave as he drove alongside the glass wall. We drove right up to the revolving door where there was just enough space to open the door and run in.

Another time we did a kids' TV programme in Manchester. We were driving out of the studio with kids hurling themselves onto the bonnet of the moving car, hanging onto the windscreen wipers: it was absolute mayhem. When we played the Apollo kids were fainting all over the floor with the police carrying dozens of limp bodies to the waiting ambulances.

The Rollers had fanatical fans and some of them stuck onto Slik. There was this underground fan network, so somebody would send out a signal and they'd all be there. I don't know where they got all their information, but they knew whenever we got back to Glasgow, and when we would turn up for a radio show. Occasionally I tried to talk to a fan, but there was nothing much to say: they were all mad thirteen-year-olds. It was instant hysterics as soon as I got anywhere near; they would just scream, howl and pull at my clothes and hair.

Fortunately they weren't big enough or old enough to be allowed in the front doors of a hotel. Our fan base was mainly aged from twelve to sixteen, not grown-up gorgeous eighteen-year-olds – that didn't come until much later. These days a fourteen-year-old girl can look very mature, but back then the kids all looked like kids. There was an age of innocence that doesn't exist any more. Now we have S Club Juniors, back then it was *Junior Showtime*. There was certainly nothing sexual between us and our fans. That was never going to happen. It was all pure fantasy on the fans' part. Once we had done the concert and fought our way through the sea of screaming teenagers, I was back in my hotel room, left on my own, wondering what to do. Most of the time I'd end up watching *Starsky and Hutch*. We didn't have late-night television in Scotland, but telly went on until nearly midnight in England.

One other very good reason why there weren't any shenanigans going on during the Slik period was that I had a girlfriend, Addie – Alice Reilly. I'd met her because she used to come and see Salvation. Kevin McGinlay went out with her sister for a while, and we just kind of fell in together. She worked in a police station on reception – a very handy thing if you live in Glasgow. It must have been a weird sensation for her to see her boyfriend on the telly getting screamed at with girls throwing me their underwear. It never seemed to bother her that much, and she never complained. We were together right through Salvation and Slik to when I eventually moved down to London. That's when it fell apart. Addie and I tried to keep it going. I promised to come back to Glasgow to visit, but within a couple of months it had turned into a phone relationship. I didn't have a phone in my flat and I was spending what spare change I had calling her from the pay phone in the hall. Soon it was obvious to both of us that it wasn't going to last.

Today, the whole pop machine is much more controlled and rigidly structured than it was back then. They build an entire TV show to find the face: they've already made the record, and they don't care what the song is, as it's going to be a hit no matter what. The first thing I saw on *Pop Idol* was the big tour buses with faces painted on the side. The marketing is much more skilled and in the end that's what it's all about. The pop machine hasn't changed that much in thirty years. Today it's a slicker version of what happened to me. It's still about middle-aged guys writing songs for pretty boys to sing, though the audience is getting younger and younger.

In 1976 the process of creating a pop star was slightly different. Some of it was the same – write a pop song, find or manufacture the right face to sing it. But there was still an element of hit or miss: 'Push them out of the door and hope'. The Rollers had Tam Paton, who was more worldly wise than Unicorn Leisure, so they kept rolling out the hits. In Slik we didn't like the hit we started with. We aspired to be something much higher up the musical chain. We wanted to be Roxy Music, although we just didn't have the talent. These days that would only be a minor inconvenience.

It changed when Phil Coulter realised we were a proper band. Bill Martin didn't care whether we could play or not, but Phil was the musical one. At the end of February he came to see us play at the New Victoria Theatre in London and realised that we could actually do it. That's when we were allowed to play on the album. Phil stopped writing bubble-gum pop and tried to give us songs he thought were more suited to our capabilities. He wanted more input from the band, let us into the studio and we recorded the album in two weeks.

'Requiem', our second single, was quite a complicated song with a split personality. Phil tried to make it a bit moody and atmospheric to give us some cred. Then the chorus came in, and the song speeded up and got all happy and bouncy as if it was something for Cilla Black to sing at the Eurovision Song Contest. It scraped in at No. 24, though it did very well in Europe.

It's stupid the stuff you do as a kid. The first two proper shows we did after 'Forever And Ever' were at the Glasgow Apollo and the New Vic. Both were sell-outs so we were promptly booked into a fifteen-date tour in June. Although we were committed to doing these shows they weren't selling at all. The tour would have been a disaster.

It was decided I needed to break my arm in a car crash. Max and I drove up this country lane, pulled off the road and smashed the windshield of his car. I staggered back into his house holding my arm. Then I let him hit me across the arm with a truncheon. I had convinced myself I needed a bruise so it looked really bad and I wouldn't be pretending so much. I held out my arm and Max, who wasn't a violent man, had to steel himself to do it. The first couple of taps didn't do anything, didn't even hurt, so I told him to hit me harder. He did, and gave me such a whack my whole body went into shock. I thought I was going to throw up. It hurt so much I screamed, dropped to the floor and lay there writhing, clutching my arm, yelling and swearing. I thought he'd really broken it.

The record company knew something was in the works. I was promptly whisked off to see a doctor, who prodded me for a second, put my arm in a plaster cast and then wrote a note saying I was too badly hurt to go on stage. They needed that official document, otherwise we were liable to the promoters. The bad news was given to the papers, who all reported that as I had broken my arm in a car crash the dates were cancelled. The whole story was a con. I didn't like what I was being made to do but Frank and Max told me our backsides would be sued off if we didn't come up with some excuse to get out of the dates. It was about the band's survival and it was down to me to get us out of it.

Slik went into a rapid decline after 'Requiem'. The record company had thought we were the next Rollers and were going to keep churning out hits for the next couple of years. They didn't see what was coming. The hysteria lasted for six months until the Sex Pistols happened, then the Damned, and the Clash. Punk killed the whole teen thing dead – as it should have done. The straw that broke the camel's back was our final single, 'The Kid's A Punk'. The opening line was: 'Hey, Hey hear what they say/He looks just like James Dean/Yeah the kid's a punk.' It was just awful. I was listening to John Peel in the evenings so I knew what the New Wave sounded like. Maybe I should have accepted McLaren's offer to join the Pistols.

We held our hands up and told Bell Records, 'We're not doing this any more; we'll go out on our own.' We believed we could survive by performing live. 'Requiem' was a big record all through Europe, so we could go and play Germany and Finland.

Slik were huge in Finland for some reason. We drove there from Glasgow in a Ford Granada, four of us and the tour manager (that was typical Slik – we had a tour manager who couldn't drive). It took two days hacking across Germany, then onto the ferry over to Helsinki.

I saw a frozen sea, which was fabulous. It was completely frozen over but the ice moved so it was broken and there were these huge sheets of ice, massive blocks twenty feet tall. Beaver Jeans sponsored our concerts. We were staying in a big hotel and after the concert everybody came and stood outside the hotel with lighted candles. Three thousand kids screamed at me when I came out onto the balcony. It was my only Michael Jackson moment, and it came at a time when Slik were finished.

We were dead and gone, we just didn't know it. We struggled on for six months and then discovered we were a hundred grand in debt. After six months of flying up and down from Scotland and staying in hotels to do press and promo – all stuff the record company normally pay for – we found out that nobody had billed Bell back for it. Now that we were dropped they certainly weren't going to pay any of it.

I'm pretty sure 'Forever And Ever' sold over a million copies, but I never saw any royalties. Worse, we'd been advised to think that this was only the beginning, our first Number One record. I moved out of home and bought a house in Blackwood outside Glasgow. I paid £12,000 for it and I was going to put in my own recording studio. I lived there for less than a year.

The management had also said 'we needed cars', so we each got a second-hand car. They bought me a Granada. I had never had a car before. It was not a car of my choosing but it was a car, and that was fantastic. Within six months it had all gone wrong. When Frank told us we had to sell our cars, I bought a little motorbike to zoom back and forwards in. I was completely naïve. Some bloke phoned my house in Blackwood and said, 'I hear you're selling your car.' I went, 'Oh yeah', and spilled everything. He turned out to be a local journalist. The next day it was all over the Sunday papers – 'SLIK SKINT!'. That summed up my pop career in a nutshell: I'd gone from chart-topper to skint in nine months.

I had had a taste of success but without all the trimmings. I had had the promise but not the reward. I had been allowed to look through the window but not go through the door. Except everyone else thought I still owned the house: I'd been on telly, therefore I must be a multimillionaire.

It was too much for Jim. He was married with kids and needed to make a regular income, so he left to work in cabaret. We got in another bass player and the band limped on for a few months, doing showcases for record companies. They just weren't interested. We were dead, completely dead, and nobody would touch us.

Slik had been tarred with the teeny brush and it was never going to go away. Probably it never has. Very few artists survive that and go on to do anything with any quality. Robbie Williams, George Michael . . . and me. I can't think of anyone else who started off life in a teenybop disposable boy band who was allowed to grow into something else.

So there I was at 23, all washed up. I should have disappeared.

CHAPTER 5
NOT SO RICH KID

The first time punk was ever mentioned in a British music magazine was in an article about Slik.

Caroline Coon wrote for the *Melody Maker*. She saw Slik at a show we did at the New Victoria in the summer of '76. It was during the heatwave and even though the theatre was only half full she loved us. I think she fancied Jim, the bass player, but she hung out with the band, and wrote a huge article.

We were discussing the band's look and I said to her, 'It's a mixture of James Cagney, James Dean and the Bowery Boys ... American street punks.' She turned it around and described us as punk pop. The next article she wrote was about the Sex Pistols where she called them punk rock. So in a very roundabout way Slik coined punk. The term was derived from our look. It might not be what the punks would like to hear, but it's true.

In May 1977, while Slik were still staggering on, I got a telephone call from Al McDowell, who was a mate of former Sex Pistol Glen Matlock. When Glen was looking for a singer for his new band the Rich Kids he had talked about it to Caroline, who told him, 'I've seen the perfect front man for your band.' I was curious, so I went down to London to check the band out. I stayed at Glen's mum's house out in Greenford and met up with the other guys – Rusty Egan and Steve New – at Glen's squat in Stoke Newington. I strapped on my guitar and learned three songs. Later that night we went out for a few beers at the Hope and Anchor in Islington. It was tiny, a dirty, damp cellar, but one of *the* places to play. The Police were headlining with their original guitarist – it was before Andy Summers joined. The opening act didn't show so Glen asked if we could play. So we got up and played our three songs. The owner liked it so much – even though we had to pay to get in – that he gave us our money back plus a pound each for a few beers.

After the Hope and Anchor we went over to the Music Machine in Camden and played the same quick set before the Boomtown Rats came on. Then we headed to a private warehouse party down in the docks. There I was, coming cold from Glasgow, not knowing any of these guys and suddenly I was hanging out with all the bands I'd heard on John Peel or read about in the *NME*. Sid Vicious was over in one corner with girlfriend Nancy clinging onto him (later that night they were hanging out on a wooden platform when somebody pissed all over them). Siouxsie and the Banshees were on stage. I hung out with Mick Jones from the Clash. The only person who sneered at me was Billy Idol, who was more of a pop star than I had ever been. He thought it was so uncool to shake my hand and I nearly chinned him. To be fair, I bumped into him a year later and he apologised, and said he'd been a prick . . . which everyone knew he had been.

As an introduction to the punk scene it was a baptism of fire, but when I went back home I had serious doubts about whether I actually wanted to uproot my whole life. I wasn't going to move down to London without something definite, not like all those other Glasgow musicians who came down south, hung around, did nothing and just died inside.

The truth was when we were rehearsing and I'd listened to the Rich Kids' songs I'd thought they were bloody awful. Compared to Slik the band were pretty untogether. Rusty was solid, if not a little too fast, but Steve New was seventeen and straight out of school. Glen had bought him the first electric guitar he'd ever had, this great big Gretsch, and he couldn't tune it. He didn't know that when he wanted to do a solo not to walk over and turn up the amp. I showed him how to control the volume on the guitar, to play chords at 8, and turn it up to 10 for the solo. Steve was more interested in falling about and playing these really wild solos. Being more educated in the rock format, when it came to my turn to do a solo I'd play a tasteful kind of thought-out piece. Steve went all over the place; he was this bundle of nutty energy. When it worked it was great, but when it didn't it was horrible.

Ironically, although Slik were dying slowly, our songwriting was getting better. In July we had recorded three songs Billy and I wrote – 'Put You In The Picture', 'Pain' and 'Deranged, Demented And Free' – on a borrowed Revox in an empty pub. It cost us three quid to record and another two for cardboard and scalpels to make the artwork. We gave it to Zoom Records, a small indy company in Edinburgh (the other band they had was Simple Minds), who fell in love with it. We called ourselves PVC2, because we knew if it was Slik nobody would buy it – though it became pretty clear when Slik played the songs live. We sold 18,000 copies – not bad at all and the biggest-selling record Zoom ever had.

The Rich Kids courtship dragged on for another three months until I got the ultimatum phone call from Glen. 'It's time,' he told me, 'to make up your mind.' I went to Frank Lynch who, for all his faults, knew how passionate, how desperate, I was to do something. He was also sharp enough to see that there might be something in it for him – a way of recouping some of the hundred grand he had convinced us Slik owed him. Eventually a chunk of the advance (£20,000, I believe) the Rich Kids got from EMI went to Unicorn Leisure to cover my transfer fee down south.

Frank read me the riot act: 'You're stupid if you don't do it; there's nothing here for you. Just pack up, get your stuff, go. We'll sell your house.'

So I did. I was driving a green 1954 Vauxhall Wyvern that I'd bought for £200 after selling my motorbike. I packed it full of all my stuff and headed off to London. I moved into a bedsit in Randolph Avenue in Maida Vale. It was such a complete pit I never let anyone else into my room for a year.

I was petrified. I'd lived in Glasgow all my life. My family and my friends lived there; my girlfriend Addie and my current band were there. Kenny was the one I felt really bad about leaving, but the band didn't want to leave Scotland, so they brought in Willy Gardner, a very talented guitarist/singer, and turned into the Zones. Funnily enough, having just come off Bell, they were re-signed to Arista the mother label. After the Zones fell apart Kenny joined Simple Minds.

It didn't take long for my new environment to completely engulf me. I got to know the tube stations, and hung out with bands I'd never met before. It was a vibrant period. I'd pop down to the management office and sit in the pub with our agent, having great conversations about which bands were going to make it. Everyone in the business thought the Boomtown Rats and the Rich Kids were going to be huge in America. I sat there with 20p in my pocket, wondering, Is this true? Is this real?

It wasn't. The Rich Kids' moment had happened before I even joined the band, when they were on the front cover of *Sounds*, hailed as the saviours of British Rock and Roll before anybody had heard a song. That was a legend we couldn't possibly live up to. Reputedly the Rich Kids got an enormous advance from EMI, and people gossiped about it being a million quid – but it was probably closer to £100,000. There was a large lump sum followed by smaller ones. This was meant to cover four albums, but by the end of the first year there was nothing left. I don't know where it went; I certainly hadn't had it. None of us had: we were always broke. Glen lived in a squat up in Stoke

Newington, while Rusty had a room in Marylebone close to the office. We must have been on more than £50 a week, because that was my rent, but not a lot more.

The record company totally overdid it. We had to be twice as good as the Beatles at their peak to live up to EMI's expectations. We rehearsed for about three weeks and then, to break the ice, did our first gig. They sent *Melody Maker* to review us. The concert was dreadful. Half the audience were pogoing kids who used me as a target to spit on; the other half were teenybop fans who had grown up and put on plastic bags. Of course, the paper slated the gig and ripped us apart. It was downhill from that point on.

I was seen as the problem by the music papers. Coming out of the Pistols, Glen could have chosen any cool unknown to be in his band and got loads of cred. Picking me, a Scottish guy from a teenybop band, was asking for trouble. It was a very brave thing to do, and I'm not sure I would have done it.

Glen talked about the Pistols sometimes. There was no great love lost between them but he was more miffed with Malcolm McLaren than anybody in the band. The Pistols didn't like Glen because he liked Paul McCartney. Paul Cook was all right – I met him many times – and Steve Jones was OK. Johnny Rotten and Glen didn't get on at all, that was a serious hate–hate relationship – but that's what happens in bands.

Glen felt he was pushed out of the Pistols, and felt used because he was the musical talent who helped shape their songs. Then he was replaced by somebody who looked really cool, how the archetypal punk should look. Sid Vicious wasn't a musician – he was an idiot – but at that point it didn't matter: it was easy to learn what Glen had done on bass, parrot fashion. Glen had certainly earned some money from 'Pretty Vacant' because he bankrolled the Rich Kids before they were signed to a label. If it wasn't for that money the band would have never existed.

By 1978 punk had morphed into New Wave. Artists like Joe Jackson and Elvis Costello didn't really fit in with the punk ethic, or the punk look. That was always a strong part of what punk was all about; Malcolm McLaren and Vivienne Westwood needed a vehicle to sell their clothes.

The music industry likes to tag bands but they couldn't do that with the Rich Kids. We were described as 'power pop', a dreadful term. When Glen was asked what the band was all about he'd say, 'Good time Rock and Roll'. He was a big Small Faces fan, as I was. That was our musical link. He wasn't trying to look like a Mod, like the Jam; he had his own particular style. We fell on stony ground, between two extremes. We were individual with a sound of our own – we weren't the Clash but we weren't like the other pop bands that were around at the time. We could do everything: a BBC2 *In Concert*, appear on kids' TV shows like *Magpie*, and play a punk festival – rather like Slik, in fact.

I was one of the few guitarists around who could actually play – the others were Danny Kurstow from the Tom Robinson Band and Andy Summers in the Police. That was a bit of a drawback, because as a punk you weren't meant to be proficient, you were meant to struggle by. I was playing the same way I'd been playing in Slik, it was just more . . . erratic. Once I got used to the idea I really learned from Steve's guitar playing; I enjoyed the chaos. He had no rules and was forever playing bizarre things that I wouldn't dream of trying.

My songwriting got better. I had this huge realisation that all the songs I had written up to that point were nonsense, songs about nothing. Glen was an inspiration, and he made me aware that there has to be a reason for writing a song, that you shouldn't write a bunch of lyrics about absolutely nothing at all. He wrote about Burning Sounds, a record shop that he knew in the Harrow Road. 'Marching Men' was my first real song. It was inspired by the Anti-Nazi League, by all the tension in multicultural London between the punks and the National Front skinheads.

Within a year of being in London I had opened up, diversified and learned more than I had in the last six years. Rusty and I became friends straight away. It's funny, that band dynamic: when you join a band, the other members are strangers, then first they become your comrades and finally your friends. In the Rich Kids it was the four of us against the world. Rusty was an easy guy to like, as he is so gregarious and over the top, but, God, was he hard to live with. On the road we had to share rooms and we always drew straws to see whose turn it was to share with Rusty. He kept me up all night talking, showing me his new trousers – 'Look what I've got at the second-hand shop today' – and doing fashion shows. Whenever Rusty walked down the road he had twenty ideas before he reached the café on the corner.

'We're the soft boys' was a line in one of Glen's songs. If the Rich Kids had an image it was that, well away from the hard punk thrash. We were rather foppy, cuffs all undone, kind of messy but pretty at the same time, elements of the dandy but with no uniform look. Glen was into wearing very smart suits, Rusty his leather jodhpurs, neo-

Nazi look, while Steve had his own style. He was just a mess, dropping his books everywhere, his clothes hanging half on and half off, and his hair all over the place. By the end of the band Rusty and I were experimenting with a retro-50s, semi-military look, with ex-army shirts, forage caps, smart shirts with the tie tucked between the buttons at the top, cummerbunds, big wide trousers and lots of diamante badges.

The Rich Kids' graphics – backward Rs and sickles – were always really good. When the first single, 'Rich Kids', came out EMI wanted to do something different. I suggested coloured vinyl, because I remembered seeing it on kiddies' records. Nobody had ever heard of this. EMI went and checked it all out and we put the first 15,000 singles out on red vinyl. People bought the record straight away; it charted in the Top 30 and I was back on *Top of the Pops*.

That was the start of the whole coloured-vinyl revolution, and we started it. The floodgates opened and everyone brought out multi-coloured or see-through vinyls. It was a huge marketing ploy by the record companies. Unfortunately our single didn't build up enough momentum to carry on up the charts. Lots of others did.

It took us a lot longer to write enough songs to finish the album. I had three songs on *Ghosts Of Princes In Towers*: 'Marching Men', 'Young Girls', which was a real bit of nonsense, and we re-recorded the PVC2 song 'Put You In The Picture' properly. There were a couple of collaborations between Glen and Steve and the rest of the songs were Glen's. We recorded at John Kongos' Studio, in First Avenue, Barnes with Mick Ronson producing.

I was a huge Mick Ronson fan from his Bowie days. When we were talking about producers, we all came to the conclusion that Mick would be a great guy to do it. He was such a good arranger – the lovely piano playing that he did on Lou Reed's 'Perfect Day' – and a great guitarist, so we thought we'd get great guitar sounds. But it didn't work at all. Mick's idea of production was to walk up and down the back of the studio with a tobacco bag, smoking his little roll-up cigarettes. He wouldn't sit down at the desk; he'd stand over in the corner listening to the mix. That's not what a producer does. Mick was a lovely bloke; we had great conversations in the back of the car, but he was more interested in popping over the pub and having a few beers. At the end of the session he told me, 'You're probably a much better producer than I am . . . but I'm a better guitarist than you'll ever be.' Fair enough.

The Rich Kids did a lot of shows. We needed to, to keep afloat financially. There was a big college circuit at the time but we never really escaped beyond that. We played the Hammersmith Odeon once, supporting Mink deVille, and died a horrible death. For the first time in my life I absolutely hated playing live gigs. We all did. I had to be talked on stage every night.

All that spitting, all that punk shit – I never understood why I had to stand there and get covered in gob. I can't imagine anyone enjoying standing there, being covered in that stuff. There was one gig when somebody – I don't know what was wrong with them – spat at me. This gob of viscous green slime landed on my microphone and hung off the end like some luminous worm. There was no way I was going to sing anywhere near that. I thought I'd be really cool, jump up and kick the microphone over so that the crew would come on and replace the mike. Unfortunately the microphone was three inches higher than my leg could reach. I ended up doing a complete back flip, crashing onto the stage and looking a right tosser.

The crowds got increasingly violent. In February '78 we played at the Coatham Ballroom in Redcar. It was a Saturday night and the place was absolutely heaving, stuffed with a thousand kids going crazy. As we walked on, we got booed ... which was kind of interesting. Halfway through the first number a bottle hit the end of my guitar, and smashed all over it. I yelled, 'That's it, I'm off,' and stomped off the stage. Somehow the club management bribed us back on stage, as they were terrified the crowd were going to riot and tear the gig apart. As we began to repeat the first number, out of the corner of my eye I saw this full pint glass coming straight at me. I couldn't dodge in time. It hit me on the head and shattered, showering me with beer and shards of broken glass – there was blood everywhere. I ended up in Newcastle Royal Infirmary getting my head glued back together.

It wasn't just the Rich Kids, and it wasn't a statement that the Redcar punks hated our music. It was just another friendly night out in the Northeast. Everybody got the same treatment. Ultravox had played there three weeks before us and somebody on the balcony had hurled a table at the stage. It hit their singer John Foxx on the head, so maybe I was the lucky one.

It wasn't any better at Sussex University in Brighton. There was a bunch of dopey punks in the front spitting at us and chanting, 'Punk, punk, we want punk.' They shouted at Steve, called him a poof, and so he started camping it up, giving as good as he got. We didn't mind hecklers as long as it was fairly good-natured, but this lot were animals. They started throwing glasses and beer cans at the stage and halfway through our set a bottle smashed against my guitar, and we just walked off. It was a shame, because it meant the rest of the kids suffered, but there was nothing else we could do.

At times I felt I was back in the Glasgow gang wars. Guys stood there and they so obviously hated us: they didn't like the idea of the Rich Kids. We weren't true punks, we were softies. They just wanted to get their hands on us. At Barbarellas in Birmingham this guy down the front kept banging the mike stand so it crashed into Glen's face. Glen got so pissed off he said, 'Kiss my arse!' and stuck his backside out. The guy bit it so hard he was scarred for months. That's when things got out of hand. Glen and Rusty ended up down the front, fighting with the audience. The police arrived in time to save us. These thugs had razors and they ended up cutting two fingers off one of the cops.

Another time we were in Devon when a bunch of skinheads started pushing at the PA towers until they began to wobble. We knew that could kill somebody, so I stopped mid-song and the skins jumped on the stage. I was busy trying to be diplomatic, asking them to 'just back off' when a pair of feet flew over my shoulder and knocked this guy straight off the stage. That was Rusty taking direct action. He liked a ruck in those days.

By the end the gigs were getting worse and worse. Before we could face going on stage we all found ways to blank out the shit we had to take. Glen became a terrible piss head; Steve was doing too many drugs, although Rusty and I were more in control. At the time it never sat well with me. If someone is paying two quid to see a band, they should see some good music, not some drunk trying to tune his guitar. Unfortunately I haven't always followed my own advice. Music's a business. To do it properly you've got to take it easy at times, otherwise you crack up. Then you're finished.

There was one moment in Northern Ireland when Glen cracked. I still don't know why. I think he realised the whole thing was falling apart, and it wasn't where he wanted to go. We came off stage and he started screaming in my face, and then, totally out of character, he kicked me. It was pure frustration. The band wasn't working and he'd put his all into it. We had all put our all into it. To him it was going to be bigger than the Pistols, instead it was falling to pieces. The Rich Kids only did one more show after that. We split up in December 1978, though the split wasn't officially announced for another six months.

It was over long before Ireland. I had bought a synthesizer, and that's what really broke the Rich Kids up. Rusty and I were listening to this electronic music coming out of Europe – Kraftwerk, La Düsseldorf, Can in Germany and Telex out of Belgium. It was the most exciting music I'd heard for years. This electronic thing was screaming at me, just like guitars had when I was ten.

CHAPTER 6
LIFE IN THE BLITZ

There was a lot of violence on the streets . . . and all of us musicians were targets. After I went to see Jonathan Richman at the Hammersmith Odeon I was standing outside chatting with Joe Strummer when some 'Ois' spotted us and promptly dived into the pub to get all their skinhead mates. They rushed up yelling abuse; one hit the car with a bottle, then they started kicking and punching us. We piled into the back of the car and shot off round the corner. That stuff happened all the time.

What people forget – even some of those who were there – was how small the whole punk fashion scene was. Originally there was the Bromley Contingent, who followed the Pistols and shopped in Malcolm McLaren and Vivienne Westwood's shop, Seditionaries. People like Billy Idol, Siouxsie Sue, Steve December, Philip Sallon, Sue Cat Woman, a couple of hundred at most. By late '78 we were into the third and fourth generation of punk bands like the Members, Chelsea and 999. Punk had become high-street fashion, so the ones who had instigated the look, who were in at its very conception, didn't want to be punks any more. Their little sisters were doing that now.

Rusty realised those original style setters needed somewhere to go where they weren't going to get beaten up. He had started deejaying even before the Rich Kids disintegrated. 'Bowie Night' started as a safe haven for guys who liked to wear make-up and girls who wanted to dress like Marilyn Monroe. He and Steve Strange found this transvestite club at 69 Dean Street in Soho called Billy's. When it started in the autumn of '78 it was called Bowie Night, but was quickly rechristened 'Club for Heroes'. They charged 50p to get in and Rusty played the music he liked – mixing up the Only Ones with Bowie, Killing Joke with Roxy Music, Chic with Kraftwerk, Neu and la Düsseldorf. We kept the scene underground. It was a great place to go; style, image and look on a shoestring. I always made sure I had enough money in my pocket to buy a couple of cans of beer and get myself home on the night bus.

The club wasn't about making money, though Rusty was paid £40. One time when he was off touring with the Skids he asked me to fill in. Forty quid for playing records I loved, well, that doubled my income for the week. I went down, did my stint and the club was full. Then I had a fight over the cash with the club owners, who told me, 'You're not Rusty Egan, so we're not paying you.'

By the end, three hundred kids were trying to get into a place that could only take a hundred – provided half held their breath. Billy's cheapskate owners wanted to double the prices and when they tried to threaten Rusty he told them to fuck off and headed for Berlin. By the time he returned Steve had negotiated a new home at the Blitz, a themed wine bar on Great Queen Street (how apt) in Covent Garden. The décor was very 1940s, and as we all loved film noir it was perfect.

After Club for Heroes moved into the Blitz in February 1979 the whole scene took off. This was mainly because of Steve at the door, not letting anyone in who didn't look the part. There was no guest list and everyone had to pay a quid, no exceptions. Now we had a place to go but no music of our own to play in it.

I can remember seeing a synthesizer guitar on an early *Tomorrow's World*. It was a guitar that was also supposed to sound like an organ. It really appealed to me that there was this machine that could not only emulate other instruments, but also create new sounds like nothing else I'd ever heard before.

Back then people said synthesizers were distant and cold, not real instruments at all. That's crap. Part of it was due to the cold, clinical, mechanical image Kraftwerk had deliberately cultivated. When you first get a synthesizer, it's really easy to make funny, weird noises, so that's the way people think it always sounds. Trying to make music with a bit of feeling is a lot harder. Suddenly I had a machine that could make sounds that only existed in my head. I'd sit there, make a bass drum sound from a synthesizer, record that and then put a timed echo on it. It was a whole different spectrum of sound, but one which opened a new door to the creative world.

I bought my first synthesizer direct from Yamaha right before we recorded the first Rich Kids album. When I was in Slik I was one of the first guitarists in Britain to use the SG 2000 – which was their flagship model. I went to them and they sold me a CS 50, a polyphonic synth, for half price. For me to lay my hands on £500 was a major feat. But I needed it, because that was what I was listening to. It was a major investment, one of the best I have ever made.

I'd been fiddling around in the EMI demo studios where I'd recorded a punk pop cover of 'I Don't Want Our Loving To Die' – which they loved. I wasn't going to release it under my name so I got Kelvin

Blacklock (who'd sung with Strummer in the London SS and in Rat Scabies's band, The White Cats) to do it. I got £500 for producing it so I could buy my synth and he got £500 for singing it. (After the Rich Kids broke up Kelvin, Rusty and I rehearsed with a couple of guys from the Tom Robinson Band. We christened ourselves The Misfits, which was only too appropriate as we never gelled.)

I used the string machine very sparsely and the synthesizer on 'Marching Men'. When we went out on tour to promote the album, I took the keyboard out with me so that I could do my 'Marching Men' bit. Glen absolutely hated that – his thing was if you wanted a keyboard player you get Ian McLagan from the Small Faces. (Mac ended up touring with us.) Glen could never see the point of my dabbling behind the synthesizer.

To me, the very amateurism of the dabbling was what was exciting. I was creating noises and it was clear to me that if I could integrate that with standard instrumentation the results would be special. I saw the Rich Kids morphing into what Ultravox eventually became: electronics merging with rock. At our best we were a feisty power-house of a band. I saw how we could introduce the new technology, use that pop sensibility, that knack of being able to put a good melody together, and merge it with these amazing atmospherics.

That's how I saw it going, and that's how Rusty saw it going. As for Steve, I'm not sure where he saw it going, if he saw anything at all. It didn't work for Glen, who wanted to be in a proper band complete with brass section, kitchen sink and all – excluding synthesizers. We were divided, with Rusty and me on one side, going 'Let's get this electronic thing out, this is interesting,' and Glen and Steve on the other side saying, 'It should be a guitar band.'

I was completely skint as there were no wages coming in, and living in a one-bedroomed flat in Chiswick. When I couldn't stand the squalor of my old bedsit I figured out that with what I was paying I could afford to pay the mortgage on a flat, but it was pretty tight. Rusty had some money coming in from deejaying so most days he had to buy me dinner. We went to the Galleon Restaurant in Notting Hill where you could get a meal for a quid. We'd get into the Gate Cinema for free because Joe Strummer's cousin, who looked like the bloke from Eraserhead, worked there. Give him a nod and a wink and we were watching Bertolucci and Fellini movies all afternoon, munching free popcorn.

I had this idea to make some music to play in the club. We had to invent our own musical style because our points of reference were very limited – after Kraftwerk, Yello and early Bowie we ran out of influences. I wasn't into playing blues licks and rock chord sequences on guitars any more, but preferred using different sound textures to create music that was still built around classic song structures. The results would turn out to be very palatable and commercial – a huge worldwide hit – but that was never part of the equation.

I discovered that the Rich Kids still had time in EMI's 16-track demo studio in Manchester Square, so I went in and recorded a couple of tracks. I'd had at the back of my mind to re-record Zager & Evan's 'In The Year 2525'. I started it all on synthesizer and drum machine then I got Rusty in to play drums.

Then Rusty said, 'I've got this mate, you know Steve . . . he wants to sing.' Steve Strange was Rusty's roommate – well, he slept on the floor of Rusty's room when he had nowhere else to go – and manned the door at Club For Heroes. Steve desperately wanted to be a singer. He wasn't bothered about writing the music: he just wanted to be famous, and he didn't care at what. His major talent was having his face made up and choosing outrageous clothes. He worked in a cool clothes shop in Covent Garden and when we could scrape together enough money to buy something smart we'd go to PX. The first track Steve sang on was 'Tar', a dreadful song about smoking which he co-wrote. But it gave us a chance to develop the guidelines, and showed us the parameters of what my ideas could sound like. That became the template for Visage.

I came up with the name – it sounded very romantic, very European – and the logo. Actually it was something I was taught in art when I was ten: how to draw a face. I drew an oval, then drew the line across for the eyes, and a line down the centre, then I could start drawing. I drew that up, and that was our logo.

We were chatting away, Rusty coming up with his usual million ideas a minute, when he said, 'Wouldn't it be great if we had Billy Currie from Ultravox, John McGeoch, Dave Formula and Barry Adamson from Magazine and all worked together . . .'

'Stop right there, Rusty,' I told him. 'That's a good idea, let's progress on that.'

When we approached the musicians about it they were all up for it. Billy Currie was pivotal, as he was always one of the main writers; he brought his classical upbringing, that haunting air, a middle-European essence to all the tracks. Billy was a fantastic player; the noise he made with his synthesizer was incredible: he made it distort and drive like nobody else. At times the way he put together certain notes and chords sounded like an electronic Jimi Hendrix. Listening to Barry Adamson play bass was an education, while John McGeoch was a completely different guitarist to me and Dave Formula was another electronic pioneer. I learned from them all, all the time.

We all worked on Visage, even though we had no funding. Getting all these guys in one room together was a monumental nightmare, so we snatched bits of time when we had it. Fortunately we found a producer who believed in the project. Rusty played our demo tape to Martin Rushent, whose office was above the Blitz. Martin was a hot producer at the time, and he'd been really successful with the Stranglers. He fell in love with the demos because he'd never heard sounds like that. He said to us, 'I'm building a studio at home. It's not ready yet, but I've got an outbuilding at the back. I'll stick all the equipment in it and when I've got free time you can do some stuff.'

We went to Rushent's studio whenever we could, and virtually lived at the bottom of his garden. I was so skint that when I went down on the train to Goring and Streetley in Berkshire Martin picked me up at the station and we'd eat dinner at his house. It might have been great for us but it wasn't very conducive to a happy home life with six musicians hanging about, sleeping in corridors.

Martin was fascinated with the music. Every night he came down to see what we were doing. He couldn't believe the noises that Rusty was making using synthesizers and syn drums, sequencers and modern electronics. Soon after we finished the album, he went out and bought the equipment. His next project was *Dare* with the Human League. It sold millions around the world and Martin's always told me he learned it all from us.

Steve Strange wasn't the best singer in the world, but he was never meant to be. He was a brilliant front person for a band that didn't exist. We were all signed to different labels, so the idea was that Steve would sign the deal. We released 'Tar' as a one-off single on Rushent's label, Genetic, but as they had no clout with radio it did nothing. We all but completed the album, and got Ian Griffin – Strummer's cousin – to airbrush and paint over the cover photo, which was shot at the Blitz by Peter Ashworth with Steve and the model Vivienne Leigh dancing in front of the stage. It took another year before it was in the shops because of business cock-ups.

By then the Blitz was the hottest scene in London. Walking into the Blitz was like stepping out of time. Like *Bladerunner*, you never knew what period it was set in. Maybe the future, maybe the past. It was a mishmash of style, Batman, old cars, old suits, blurred genders, full make-up for boys and girls, film noir and modern technology.

Everyone looked forward to their Tuesday nights. There was a little clique of people I got to know and they'd be there every week; we were all friends, having a laugh. I think it was the last time I ever danced – I don't do dancing. I'd go down there and chat, drink my one beer and meet attractive girls . . . which was definitely part of the appeal. Rusty summed it up best when he said, 'The difference between the punk scene and the Blitz was that during the punk scene you might wake up next to someone who looked like a car crash. During the Blitz you woke up next to someone who looked like Marilyn Monroe.' I did wake up to Marilyn Monroe a few times. She was definitely wearing a pearl necklace and diamante somewhere else. I liked beautiful girls with their own particular sense of style, women who could make themselves look mysterious using their imagination with make-up and clothes, not just walk into a shop and buy it off the peg.

The Blitz was full of beautiful women, rich kids rebelling against their upbringing, as well as a lot of poor kids who just wanted to be somewhere other than where they were. Sabrina Guinness used to hang about down there. Steve collected these models, actresses, what-evers, at the club. It was like a casting call: 'We're doing a video shoot, and you're in the video, darling, we want you, and you, and you, you look fantastic; I'm not sure about you.' He'd show up with the entourage and then the director would ask Steve, 'Can you pout a bit?' Can a bear . . .

Perri Lister, who was Billy Idol's girlfriend, was a Visage girl – she danced and sang backing vocals. So did Chessie, a skinny redhead with frizzy hair, who went out with Steve for ages. I didn't know for years that her full name was Francesca Von Thyssen, and she was this mega-rich heiress. She's married to Archduke Karl Thomas of Austria these days.

The Blitz was a safe haven for all those people. The atmosphere was always great and the music was always interesting. At the same time down the road in Covent Garden the Roxy had third-rate punk bands thrashing away, with kids who had grown up old enough to be punk, but had missed the bus, still out there, pogoing.

Yes, in comparison to punk the Blitz was soft. It was a very non-aggressive, non-violent environment – the exact opposite of what'd been before. Music fashion goes in cycles. First heavy metal was all the rage, then everyone was into acoustic folk rock, then we had the mad punk thrash, where it didn't matter how ugly you were. While the Blitz was very glam, it was quite sedate and there wasn't all that punk testosterone flying around. Spandau Ballet, for instance, were a bunch of lads who were more interested in not getting their ties ruffled, in making sure the line of their jackets were straight and not creased so they could stand at the bar and pose properly.

I only remember one time when there was trouble. Jock McDonald, who was the singer in a punk band called the Four Be Twos, came along to the Blitz one night and wanted Rusty to play his new single. Rusty took one listen on his headphones and told him it wasn't the sort of song he played. They had an argument and Rusty, no stranger to the odd ruck, personally showed Jock the exit. The following week Jock and a bunch of his mates came back and picked a fight with some of the kids queuing to come in. However, just because they wore make-up didn't mean the regulars were soft – a load of them had been soul boys and knew how to handle themselves. There was a massive fight out on Queen Street but somehow the police didn't get involved.

It was never an overtly gay scene, more a little limp round the edges like an old lettuce leaf. The scene was androgynous – headed by Marilyn and Boy George. Most of the girls who hung around Steve were straight, they just liked being around him. I never saw him doing anything remotely sexual with a girl, as the entourage that surrounded him were into sharing make-up and clothes, not sex.

Going into the men's loos could be very dodgy. Girls walked into the gents and did their make-up when they couldn't get in next door. There were too many guys in one cubicle for me. I didn't know whether it was drugs they were doing or each other.

I was never hit on by men at all. Maybe I don't send out the right signals. It only ever happened to me once, way back when I was a kid in Glasgow. I had really long hair and was wearing a massive brass buckle I'd made. I was sitting on top of a bus in Glasgow bus station waiting for it to take me home when this older guy sat down next to me and said, 'I love your belt buckle.' I replied, 'Thanks, I made it myself.' We chatted for five minutes then he asked me, 'Do you want a lift home?' I wondered what he was on a bus for if he wanted to give me a lift home. Then the penny dropped. He got off the bus and that was the end of it.

I did spend a night in bed with Steve Strange. Once. It was late after a recording session and we stayed in some mews house in Notting Hill he and Rusty had borrowed. They always seemed to be able to blag somebody else's house or apartment to live in. I ended up lying on the bed next to him. I warned him that if he touched me I'd kill him. It was one of those occasions when the sheet went under him and over me. The threat worked, though I dread to think what are Steve's recollections of that night.

I never saw anyone doing drugs, though I knew blues was the drug of choice at Billy's – they were cheap and kept you awake. It got worse later when the fame subsided and Steve moved Club For Heroes to the Camden Palace. Coke and heroin started to appear.

The club closed at 3 a.m. At 3.30 we'd head to an all-night café and stay there talking until six in the morning. For a time the Rock Garden did an all-night breakfast, or there was Wichety's in Kensington High Street where Rusty paid the bloke not to play the piano as he liked to hammer out piano versions of current hits. Gary Glitter went in there and all the people who came out of Stringfellows. They had absolutely no taste whatsoever, a Rolex on one wrist, a tart on the other, and neither could tell the time. We just put up with their comments about how we looked different.

The Blitz really hit the headlines when Steve turned Mick Jagger away for 'being too old'. Whatever Steve says, it was a deliberate publicity move on his part. David Essex, who was as old as Jagger and far less cool, was a regular – his girlfriend worked behind the bar – and I had brought Phil Lynott a few times. It was different when David Bowie arrived. Bowie melted the cool at the Blitz just by coming in the door. I was standing at the bar and all of a sudden there was this huge buzz; all the cool people were just flapping about, bitching and bickering as to who could sit next to him. The Emperor, the king of cool, walked in and everybody realised they were not wearing any clothes. He got the kids for his 'Ashes To Ashes' video straight out of the Blitz . . . the boy in his hero outfit and the four dressed in black with the cats.

Once the media discovered the Blitz scene and called us New Romantics the scene changed. They described it as if it was all decadent nonsense, fluffy and disposable, full of bright young things flapping about for their fifteen minutes. They were wrong. The Blitz was an important moment in British popular culture. It was the inspiration, the place that spawned London's next ten years' worth of creativity, maybe its next twenty.

It was 1979, the beginning of the Thatcher era. London was a gloomy place, and everybody was skint. People had to rebel against something, but punk had dragged itself off into a corner on its dying legs. The Blitz was full of like-minded people. Those kids were brave: they got on a bus at night dressed like that; they didn't get changed round the corner because they were embarrassed about it. They wanted to project their identity as somebody different . . . and all those somebody differents went on to do something. Just for that little moment, it was a satellite, a trampolining spot for all of those characters to go off in a hundred different directions.

Inside the Blitz there was only one God and his name was David Bowie. It wasn't just the music but also his chameleon fashion sense. The kids were all influenced by him. During the week they'd be driving buses or working in shops, but on Thursday nights they could do their Bowie thing. The rest of the music played at the Blitz was faceless. The Blitz Kids were about to become fashion icons themselves. It wasn't just a revolt against the third-rate punk bands, but also they didn't want to ape high-street fashions because they were inventing their own particular looks. In the beginning, Spandau were more of a seed than a band, and Boy George was a clothes horse who hadn't tried his hand at singing. There was this bunch of kids who had come out of art school who hadn't yet evolved into what they eventually became. It was being invented in that room – the Blitz was a work in progress.

Rusty was one of the great instigators. There's a direct line from what he was doing in the Blitz to house. Rusty played records, but he also had a set of syn drums and he'd do live drum breaks over the top of the tracks because he didn't have the facilities to do a DJ mix. A lot of the stuff that he was doing back then – and we tried to do in Visage and Ultravox – was ground-breaking. We had to make our own sounds, our own atmospherics, our own drum effects. Derek May, a DJ at the Warehouse in Chicago, picked up on the electronic sounds that were invented at the Blitz, developed them and turned it into his own form of dance grooves which later became known as house music.

Boy George started out checking coats, until Steve fired him. The designer Judith Franklin's handbag disappeared and Steve blamed George, who denied it. He hadn't decided he was going to be a singer then. He just wanted to look different from everybody else – which he certainly did. We knew the Spandau boys before they were a band. They saw something happening, jumped in quickly, got involved with the scene and bought a synthesizer. I think they only used it on the first-ever single. For the rest of their career they were a soul pop band.

Spandau made music but other people made clothes, hats, shoes. The Blitz gave birth to make-up artists and stylists, photographers and video directors. Fashion designers like John Galliano and Melissa Caplan, and the hat maker Stephen Jones first flaunted their ideas there. Daniel James started Mute Records with Depeche Mode, while David Claridge invented Roland Rat. In the jargon of today, the Blitz was empowering.

They saw the people around them doing their alternative fashion shows, wearing their own clothes and thought, I'll have a go at that.

The Blitz scene was incredibly organic, so it was completely natural that I ended up with two different hits from two different bands in the charts at the same time.

CHAPTER 7
SEX AND DRUGS AND ROCK AND ROLL

I was in the middle of a Visage recording session, in mid-July 1979, when Phil Lynott phoned. He came straight to the point: 'I'm in Wisconsin on tour. Gary's not in the band any more. Can you get here tomorrow?' Phil and Gary Moore, one of Thin Lizzy's lead guitarists, had a notorious love–hate relationship. Gary had already joined and left Lizzy three times, but this time they were on a crucial American tour and Gary hadn't turned up for a couple of shows. Phil said he kicked Gary out, Gary said he walked out because Phil was being unprofessional. Who knows what really happened?

For me the timing couldn't have been better. I was finishing one of the blocks of recording with Visage, and had unofficially joined Ultravox, who had been dumped from their record label, had no management and owed a fortune.

After we'd hung out in Glasgow Phil and I had kept our friendship going. When Slik had headlined in London, Phil was in hospital with hepatitis, but the then guitarists, Scott Gorham and Brian Robertson, came down for the gig, and dropped off a book of his lyrics, dedicated by Phil. A year later I bumped into Phil in a tube station. He invited me back to his house and that was it: we were friends. I often hung out at his place in Cricklewood. One time he was strumming away and said, 'Help me do this song.' We had the chord sequence going and the chorus – 'Get out of here' – but when he played the verse he was singing the lyrics to a completely different song – 'Randolph's Tango' – over the top of it. It fitted because Phil ended up writing the same song over and over, recreating what he already had. 'Get Out Of Here' appeared on the *Black Rose* album; I got a writing credit and £1,000 from his publishing company. I was petrified to spend it so I kept thinking, I'll just leave it there in the bank, as a cushion if everything goes wrong.

The first time I met his managers, Chris Morrison and Chris O'Donnell, was after Lizzy's gig at the Glasgow Apollo in November 1977. I turned up wearing this striking red tonic mohair suit. After the gig we all went back to Brian Robertson's house. In interviews

Brian always claimed he had paid his dues and alluded to the fact that he was a child of the Gorbals. We went back to his parents' house in Clarkston, a very posh part of Glasgow with a bar in the corner. It was so genteel, like a vicar's tea party, all dainty sandwiches and polite conversation.

I still think I was an odd choice to replace Gary because there were a million great guitar players who could have done the gig. As a guitar technician I was pushed in Lizzy, though not by Phil, who was a very limited musician – as a bass player he was only ever a plodder. Even though he was in a hip rock band Phil was very fashion conscious. He always wanted to associate himself with what was going along, to have a foot in every musical pond. He started the Greedy Bastards, a jamming band with the Pistols and Geldof, and he could hang out with the best. He was cool in all areas.

Phil wanted me because I didn't look like the classic heavy-rock star; I was somebody different who could do the job and push some new influences into the band. All through the touring period we took it in turns to put on tapes; they'd put on ZZ Top while I, much to Scott's dread, played the Yellow Magic Orchestra, bits of Kraftwerk and Magazine, real music to slash your wrists to. While Scott screamed, 'Oh no, he's got his blips and blops on again,' Phil would actually listen.

I'd never been to America. The day after Phil's phone call I was sitting on Concorde with a ghetto blaster and headphones learning all the songs on *Live And Dangerous*. I had my first-ever taste of America in a limo from JFK to La Guardia and then flew to New Orleans. America wasn't what I expected. I did see Starsky and Hutch police cars during the limo ride, but that night I ended up surrounded by jazz and blues in Bourbon Street. I felt I was in the south of France. I went straight to Scott's hotel room to work out the harmony guitar parts. That was a tall order, because every song had one. An hour later we were at the sound check and 45 minutes after that I was on stage.

When we got changed into our stage clothes the others pulled their leathers on, ready to get down and shake their hair. Scott started twitching when I put on yellow peg trousers with stripes down the side and a bright red jacket with big, wide shoulders. He got really worried when out came my make-up bag and I started applying blusher to my cheeks. Phil had a word with Chris O'Donnell along the lines of 'Can you get Midge to tone the make-up down?' Except it was lot more graphic than that.

Then I was on stage in front of 10,000 people. Lizzy were special guests to Journey, a huge, corporate rock band fronted by guitarist Neil Schon. After the show I met this girl with the classic blonde cheerleader looks and a bright white smile, who loved my accent. Of course, I slipped into the whole atmosphere, got drunk and ended up pulling her. I didn't know who she was, simply thought she was my welcome-to-America present. The next morning, after I discovered she was Schon's girlfriend, I got really worried. She wanted to travel to the airport with me and I had to push her into Journey's limo before any of them suspected a thing. Lizzy thought it was hysterical. I'd just stuck my neck in a noose and I spent the next three weeks with these visions of Neil Schon sending his huge bodyguards round to our dressing room with orders to kick me to death.

Actually he was all right, though, suffice to say, a bit distant and standoffish. The rest of Journey were friendly enough. The drummer was funny because he used to watch our drummer Brian Downey play every single night, to watch his technique. He was still very much a muso, and the singer, Steve Perry, was fun. The odd day off, we would go out and try water skiing – Neil's blonde girlfriend was a brilliant skier – and stuff like that together.

There was an ongoing battle between the road crews. It's traditional that the main act makes life tough for the support. I knew what was going on, because Phil regularly had these huge rants, threatening to pull out of the tour if they didn't just leave the Lizzy set-up alone. We usually left the show by the time Journey were on stage, went back to the hotel and pulled some girls. Phil was particularly fun. We'd always go to a club, jam with the local band boys and get drunk.

Everything Lizzy did was excessive. They had a tour manager, a lighting engineer, a sound engineer, a monitor guy, all on permanent wages so if Phil wanted to go out and gig they were right there. It cost an absolute arm and a leg to keep that kind of machine running. Lizzy worked a lot but there were still periods where they were all just sitting about, twiddling their thumbs.

At times it was pure Spinal Tap. We had pyrotechnics and it was incredibly loud on stage. We had two Marshall stacks each and if I stood between my stacks I couldn't hear anybody else. I had to stand next to the drums to try and keep in time.

Lizzy went everywhere by limousine. They didn't want to drive on a tour bus because that was perceived as low-scale touring. We had to fly from city to city, which takes forever. By the time you've been rounded up in the morning, got into the limo, got to the airport, got to hang about before getting on a plane, flown from Chicago to Cleveland, got into a limo, to the next hotel and then on to the venue we could have done it quicker overnight on the bus.

The tour was fabulous, absolutely brilliant. I just loved it. I was a guitar hero, the stuff my boyhood dreams were made of. I felt I was in one of those Judy Garland movies where the star breaks her leg and Judy gets a chance to go on and shine, to show people what she can do. It wasn't hard work at all, it was a ball. If the band had a bad night or a downer, I didn't. They'd have a furious row with me sitting in the background, smiling, knowing it was nothing to do with me. I was on an all-time high, playing songs I'd grown up with in front of a huge audience that wasn't mine. There's a photograph of me two days into the tour. We're sitting by a pool in Shreveport: there's Phil who's black, Scott who's tanned and me who's puny white. I'm saying, 'This is the life, this is fantastic,' and they're looking at me in disbelief, saying, 'This is a crappy hotel in Shreveport!'

'The Boys Are Back In Town' – there has never been a lads' song better written or so brilliantly observed – had been a huge record in the States so Lizzy weren't fighting to be heard. We were special guests. The biggest venue we played was a baseball stadium in Cleveland with Journey, Ted Nugent and Aerosmith, where 80,000 people came to see us at the grandly titled World Series of Rock. They'd already done the West Coast, so I didn't get to do Los Angeles. My one serious regret was that I fell ill when we reached New York. My first time in New York, with a day off! Lizzy all went out while I stayed in bed, feeling sick and watching late-night telly.

Because the rest of the band never got up very early, Chris O'Donnell, who always accompanied Lizzy on tour, and I went for breakfast in New York. I sat there eating cantaloupe in disbelief – they ate melon for breakfast in America. 'This is the first time an artist has ever tried to buy me breakfast,' said Chris. That's how naïve I was.

I never wanted the Lizzy gig permanently, which was fortunate as I wasn't a good enough guitarist; I'm not fast enough, and I couldn't do the twiddly-diddly stuff. The album they were promoting at the time was *Black Rose*, and the title track was this mammoth epic. There was a section in the middle where Phil wanted to show off each of the individual player's backgrounds, so Scott, who's American, would play 'Shenendoah', and then Phil did 'Danny Boy' or something else Irish. Gary Moore often played an Irish jig. I couldn't do that, I couldn't even play the rhythm part to it. They were looking for an ace guitarist, not an all-rounder like myself. That said, I'm sure that, had I pushed, I could have joined, but I had a set-up back home that I was very excited about.

The band dynamic was interesting to observe. Brian was the quiet loner, who let it all go around him. Scott was knackered in the mornings because he stayed up all night, so he was inevitably grumpy getting in the limo. Phil was the one doing all the work, all the radio interviews, all the phoners for the next gig and he got pissed off with that so he'd drag me along to radio stations. Once he'd done his bit he'd say, 'Right, Midge, tell them about Ultravox' – whether they wanted to hear it or not.

I was on tour for three weeks, and came back with more money than I'd ever seen in my life. I had negotiated £500 a week, which was a lot back in the summer of '79, though most of it went to my soon-to-be ex-managers who generously gave me half. (After I told the Chrises what was happening they told them to fuck off and paid me direct.) Chris Morrison gave me a little word of wisdom, the first of many, before I went. He said, 'When they all go to the bar at night, don't go with them, you'll come back with no money. They'll be on per diems, you don't have any.' (PDs as we called per diems – the Latin being a bit tricky – were a daily living allowance for musicians on the road. Most people ate at the gigs and spent the cash on booze and drugs!)

After America finished, Lizzy hired me for a tour of Japan, where they were trying out a new guitarist, Dave Flett. I was relegated to keyboards at the back, and then came down and did the last five numbers on guitar. Phil wanted to put this keyboard element into Thin Lizzy, which was a joke because, over the sound of the guitars, you could never hear them. Japan had its moments. We walked into one hotel where all these young women were hanging around in the lobby. Phil's eyes lit up as they came rushing towards him. They ran past Phil and Scott screaming, 'Midgey! Midgey! Midgey! Lich Kids! Lich Kids!' You should have seen the others' faces . . . talk about put out.

The next year I did a Lizzy tour of Ireland with Snowy White on guitar. Snowy was the wrong man: he was a really nice guy, but all he wanted to do was sit in a pub playing the blues. He was quiet, not the rock-and-roller type, and he was conned into joining the band by Phil promising him 'some lovely bluesy solos'. Of course, he ended up playing heavy rock. Then they got John Sykes, who used to be in Tygers of Pangtang, and at that point Lizzy just lost their momentum. Phil had lost the plot. I saw that line-up playing at Reading Festival. I was a fan, but that night it didn't work at all for me. I'd seen them loads of times but this was cold: the magic had fizzled out, drifted away.

Phil had this great roguish charisma. He spoke so quietly in his thick Irish brogue that half the time I had to read his lips. He had an amazing ability to win people over. He was a gypsy charmer with a vagabond image. In his demeanour, his manner, he was magical to just hang about with. And he also taught me a lot about how the music industry works, how to stamp your little foot, when to stamp it and what for.

We turned up for this sound check in Japan where Lizzy were meant to have two lighting trusses, one at the front and one at the back. The tour manager came up and said, 'Phil, there's only one lighting truss.' He went completely mental. He just exploded at this Japanese promoter, screaming, effing and blinding and threatening, 'That's it, I'm on the plane out of here.'

I went to try to calm him down. 'Phil, are you OK? Is it all right?' He turned round and, quietly, so no one else could hear, said, 'That truss will be up by the end of the day.' And it was. He knew that the promoter was trying to pull a fast one and save some money on the gig, and he knew that it was in his contract to have the lighting trusses, and so he threw his stroppy rock-star act to get it. He was acting, but he was brilliant at it. I was conned, too.

The Ireland tour was a riot. There weren't many big venues in Ireland then – one in Cork, one in Dublin, one in Belfast – so Phil went out into the sticks. Thin Lizzy playing in village halls, now that was a hysterical thing to witness.

We were crossing the border when two unmarked police cars came screaming round and pulled over our two Mercedes cars. I didn't know what was going on. As I'd heard all about the IRA demanding cash donations for the cause, I thought it was that. It wasn't. The cops split us all up and took us to the police station. I always thought Phil's driver was a bit light in the thought department, a lovely guy but soft, and I knew that he used to carry Phil's drugs for him. I was thinking, This is it, I know that he's got drugs on him and I'm going to end up in some Irish jail and I've never touched the stuff in my life. We were pushed into different rooms, strip-searched and quizzed. Nothing was found. We were left standing in the foyer, which was crawling with drug-sniffer dogs. They let us go though, and before we got in the car one policeman had the nerve to ask if there were any free tickets for the show. Phil told him precisely where to go.

I thought Phil's driver must have swallowed the dope. As we drove off, the first thing Phil said to him was, 'What did you do?' He said,

'I got in there and there was the waste-paper bucket, so I got down to tie my shoe, dropped the drugs in, went off, got strip-searched, came back, tied my other shoe, took the drugs out of the bin and stuck them in my pocket!' My admiration for him soared. I was crumbling, even though I knew I didn't have anything on me, while he was as cool as a cucumber, even in front of all those dogs. He was obviously a lot more quick-witted than I'd imagined.

Phil might have been my mate but he was very capable of getting the knife out and slipping it in my back. I didn't know until years later, but after Ultravox signed with Morrison and O'Donnell it put Phil's nose firmly out of place. All of a sudden the focus wasn't on him, suddenly these new kids had come along and stolen a bit of his thunder. In November 1980, after 'Sleepwalk' had been a minor hit, he summoned Chris Morrison to Australia to discuss his managing 'other bands'.

Chris and Phil talked for two hours on a plane ride. Chris told Phil he didn't understand the economics of running a management office, that it couldn't exist without other income, that without Ultravox there would just be the two Chrises and a secretary, no accountants, nobody else. He might have been talking to himself. At the end of the conversation Phil said, 'I'll give you six months to make your mind up. Me or them.'

In February 1981, when 'Vienna' was at No. 2 and Visage had a Top Five hit with 'Fade To Grey', Phil called up Chris and said, 'Well, I'd be a right cunt if I tried to make you fire them now, wouldn't I? You had better carry on managing them.' It makes me smile because it was so typical of what he would do. With Phil it was always 'Me, me, me, me'.

When they were rehearsing the *Jailbreak* album, Chris O'Donnell sent out these itineraries. Everything was running very late and Phil wanted to change some rehearsal dates round. He phoned the office and said, 'What about the 25th and 26th? There's nothing in on those days.' Chris patiently explained that those two days were Christmas Day and Boxing Day. Phil completely lost it and started yelling, 'For fuck's sake, Chris, write down Christmas Day and Boxing Day. How do you expect me to know that if they are not on the itinerary!'

For all he hung out with the punks and wore PX suits Phil could only ever be a rock star. He actually believed that you woke up and pulled leather pants on in the morning, that was the only way to live. When the drugs weren't in charge, he was unbelievably funny, a hoot to be around. He could be outrageous – like the time he tried to seduce

Paula Yates. She went to bed upstairs while Phil stayed downstairs and got Geldof so wasted on booze and coke he was out of the way. Then he barged into her bedroom, woke her up and, ever the gentleman, offered her his services because Bob couldn't. Paula just laughed.

Yet underneath his rock-star exterior Phil was very insular. I only ever saw him sit in a restaurant once. He didn't like eating out because he had no concept of how to deal with it; he had no social skills at all. He was always at his house, in a club or a hotel. At times he was quite scared by stardom, because he feared it might go away. It wasn't until Lizzy actually split that I saw that was his big fear. After his Grand Slam project didn't happen and his solo records didn't sell, he relied more and more on drugs.

Phil always had a breathing problem; he was bunged up: congested, and his voice was throaty, but whether that was drug-induced or not I'm not sure. He was very protective of me, like a big brother. He never did drugs in front of me because he knew I wasn't into it, maybe he didn't want me corrupted. I knew he was into heroin and cocaine, everybody did.

Why do musicians do drugs? Because they can. It might sound trite but it's like dressing up, you're doing what you do. You can do it because being in a band you're supposed to be an outrageous, hotel-wrecking, rock-and-roller who can stay up all night snorting coke. There is a template for what a rock star should be, and that template is the excessive poet . . . Jim Morrison, Jimi Hendrix. But all those great geniuses need to feed the genius somehow and there's always a lopsidedness about it, a dark side that has to be fed, a piper who must be paid.

Phil was a classic example. He thought that's what rock stars did, and he ended up the way he ended up because of it. There was a self-destruct side that took over. Phil was constantly surrounded by these shadowy hangers-on who were there to share in it with him only because he'd got the money to pay for it.

He was notorious for his excess. There was something obsessive about his character. Drugs was part of that, though whether it helped him write the songs or not I don't know. When I wrote a couple of things with him he was dead straight. I never saw him in the drug-induced mess that killed him in the end.

Phil played a game with the press. There was a lot of messing around, tricks that went on. He was going to play the lead role in a Jimi Hendrix movie that never existed; there was the time that he nearly lost his eyesight – utter nonsense – and Lizzy did at least two 'Final Tours', because they sold out. Eventually he got bored of the whole thing and pulled the plug.

When we were sound-checking in Japan I used to play around with this riff on the keyboard. Phil obviously clocked it, because when we got back home he started working on his album, *Solo in Soho*. He suggested we work it up and record it, and asked me to bring Billy Currie in. I got Rusty to put drums over the original drum-machine pattern. As I remixed it Phil was still inventing the rhymes in his head, but there wasn't anything actually written on paper. He just went in and scat sung, insisting on trying to get every word to rhyme, which is why some of what he sang was absolute rubbish. It wasn't really a song, just a jam that made it onto vinyl.

Phil might never have finished 'Yellow Pearl' but it still became a solo hit. *Top of the Pops* loved the tune and it became a little bit of 80s history. It ran for three years as the theme tune, earning £350 every time it got played, and paid my mortgage.

Phil had built his home studio at the bottom of his garden in Kew. It was the only seven-track studio in the history of the world (he could never get one of the tracks to work). Being Phil, he had it put up by Irish builders. It was so badly built that you could hear planes flying overhead on the way to Heathrow. Phil always insisted that that didn't matter, because the sounds he made couldn't get out. When I built my own 24-track studio just over the river I'd invite him over to have a dabble. I had an engineer working there full time, so he never had to worry about how to get the technology to work.

Phil wanted to be a musical chameleon, but eventually it backfired. When he was doing his solo records and his Lizzy records at the same time it got very grey in the middle. I couldn't tell what a really good Lizzy track was, or what a good Phil track was; he just ended up doing some weird soft things on his solo records. The lines got very crossed. And not just in his music.

One of my biggest regrets is that I never asked him to put Thin Lizzy together again for Live Aid in 1985. We asked the Who to get back together so Phil should have been up there doing 'The Boys Are Back in Town'. Why that never struck Geldof or me I don't know, but not for one nanosecond did it cross my mind. I don't like to think what went through Phil's mind, with two of his best mates putting the whole thing together and we'd never asked him to do it. I'd seen him that year and by then he was bloated and out of condition. Perhaps subconsciously I knew it was too late.

Whatever he did, whatever he took, somehow Phil almost always got away with it. He got himself in trouble, but he always came back. I knew there was something serious going on at the end of 1985 when Chris Morrison told me, 'Phil's looking absolutely dreadful. I'm worried this time.' I was on my honeymoon in Montserrat when I got the telephone call saying that he'd gone. The doctors said it was liver, kidney and heart failure and pneumonia, brought on by a heroin overdose. He was in a coma for eight days. That was it, he couldn't pull it off that time. I wasn't there for his funeral; I wish I had been . . . but in the end there was nothing any of us could do for Phil.

I sometimes wonder how I have managed to avoid taking drugs. I've seen a few people destroyed by them. Steve New was heavily into it: he was only a kid who got himself embroiled. Steve and Phil . . . I think that's what has scared me off drugs. I didn't want to go there. It's probably due to abject fear, and I have quite an addictive personality, I'd hate to do it and find I liked it, that would completely kill me.

It was one of my taboos, one of the things my mother always told me. 'Never do drugs, never marry a Catholic girl and never be tattooed.' (I went against that last one – I got tattooed just before I hit forty. I thought I had to do something, so I now sport a Celtic star on my right upper arm.)

I have never smoked cigarettes, so smoking pot wasn't interesting. It's not down to my squeaky-clean character, but drugs have never held any fascination for me at all. I can't imagine anything worse than being completely out of control. I didn't come from a drinking culture either. My father had a glass of sherry at Christmas and a beer once in a blue moon. By the time I was old enough to be out in the pubs drinking I was already on the stage . . . and, as any musician knows, the best drug of all is the audience. The applause, the clap on the back, now *they* are truly addictive. It's when they stop that the drinking starts, and I've had more than my fair share of those times.

My only drug experience was a long time coming and very short-lived, but at the time it felt like forever. I was doing a dinner for a bunch of friends at my house and I'd spent all day preparing a Thai oriental banquet. My bass player at the time was a bit of a smoker, and he thought it would be really funny to make some dope cakes. He made up these little fairy cakes decorated with Beano characters on top and ground in his stuff.

Being the forty-year-old rebel that I was, I thought, I'll try one of those. I munched into Dennis the Menace thinking he couldn't do me any harm. I started feeling very odd; I could feel that my hands were getting further away, and my head was getting further away from my hands. I put all the food into the dining room, and sat down to have dinner. One of my friends had brought their dog, a little spaniel, and I sat talking to the spaniel, rubbing its head and playing with its ears for what I thought was just for a minute or two – actually it was half an hour. Then, during dinner, the giggles kicked in, and I was just laughing hysterically, I don't know what at.

I started feeling really, really odd. It was only ten o'clock at night, an hour since I had eaten this cake. Eventually I just said, 'Finish, have the meal and close the door when you've finished. I've got to go.' I went upstairs to bed. Nobody had told me this stuff when ingested could be hallucinogenic. I lay on the bed holding onto the sides, and when I closed my eyes it was just like every freaky trip movie that I had ever seen, lights flashing, objects zooming through my head. I couldn't close my eyes, so I was lying in bed, and the bed started to move, and I had to hold onto either side of this big double bed, because it was lifting off the ground; it was moving, wobbling about and I was lying there, wide awake with every sound I could hear amplified a hundred times, really loud. I could hear voices laughing downstairs, glasses chinking like church bells. I heard people saying goodnight until it went completely silent, and they had all gone. I lay there with my eyes open for six hours.

So my ultimate nightmare of actually trying a drug and having a horrible experience finally came true. I never did it again.

CHAPTER 8
ANOTHER FIFTEEN MINUTES

Life-changing moments should not happen on freezing cold, wet Tuesdays in January. Certainly not in a dodgy rehearsal room with a dirty carpet covered in cigarette burns.

Rehearsal rooms are always in grotty parts of town, places where they don't care how much of a racket you make. But this was a hideous, scummy area, up beyond Kings Cross, worse than Blythswood Square in Glasgow. The shagging strip stretched up the road past the gas tanks. Every morning I walked past the detritus of the night before: used condoms, broken glass, puddles of vomit, sometimes bloodstains, everything congealing everywhere.

The only people out on the Caledonian Road were the local prostitutes turning blue in the biting wind. They never spoke to me because I didn't have a car. The girls were all young, most still in their teens, runaways I guessed, very skinny, almost emaciated. They dressed in skimpy outfits even though it was icy. All hours, day and night, they walked up and down the street hugging their jackets tight around them, waiting for the kerb-crawlers. Cars drove up and down constantly, moving very slowly until they stopped by a girl and the window rolled down. I saw the girls jumping in and out of the cars on my way to rehearsals and wondered who the hell needed to buy sex at eleven in the morning.

Ultravox didn't need a big room because we still didn't have that much equipment. It was an empty space, pretty grimy, full ashtrays and empty cans everywhere. Madness were next door and some heavy-metal band on the other side. Trying to have a conversation while someone is tuning up their bass guitar at 200 watts was impossible so we worked in a semicircle, a jumble of wires, makeshift keyboards and a drum kit facing each other. That way we could talk as we wrote songs. We could only afford one roadie, Dave Hughes, who spent most of the day sat in the corner with a soldering iron making leads.

It was mid-afternoon on 20 January when the two Chrises turned up. We all chorused, 'What the fuck are you doing here?' It was unusual to say the least, the mountains coming to Mohammed. Morrison and O'Donnell never showed up at rehearsals; when we wanted to see them we went to their offices in Putney. They liked their bands to get on with it, and anyway we were way below Thin Lizzy in the popularity stakes. After my stint on the road with Lizzy I knew what being a rock star meant. And in January 1981 it wasn't me.

Ultravox were only a middling successful band. The first two singles had done OK but the album had trickled out, selling just a little better than previous Ultravox albums had always done, maybe 40,000 copies. Exactly what you might expect from an art-school band, but disappointing because we all believed that in *Vienna* we had created something special.

So there was Morrison breaking the habit of a lifetime, braving Kings Cross and clutching two bottles of champagne. Being Chris, it was expensive champagne. 'You're in the charts,' he explained. 'Twice. Both charts – singles and albums.'

I was absolutely gobsmacked, not really believing that I'd done it, that finally my records had done it. It wasn't just 'Vienna' – all six minutes of it – that was a hit. 'Fade To Grey' had also crashed into the Top Twenty.

The celebrations meant we didn't get any more work done that afternoon. 'We warned you not to buy that flat,' was O'Donnell's parting shot, as I stumbled out of the rehearsal room. 'We told you things were all going to change.' I might have had two new chart hits but I didn't have car keys or any more money in my pocket. So just like every other day it was back on the tube to Turnham Green, back to my maisonette above the estate agents. I'd bought a two-bedroomed place because I thought I could ease up my finances by renting out one of the rooms. All of us in Ultravox were on a weekly wage of fifty quid, enough to keep us bread-and-watered and cover the rent/mortgage. Things were that tight.

I staggered back to Caledonian Road station. Somehow I got on the Piccadilly Line but thanks to the champagne I crashed right out and missed my change stop. I woke up at the end of the line on a siding somewhere in Uxbridge, feeling very fuzzy. I got home eventually and had to go straight out. It was Blitz night. I wasn't going to miss seeing Steve play the superstar and hear Rusty play 'Fade To Grey' as many times as he could get away with.

I counted the money in my pocket. I'd got a few pounds, a quid to get into the club, enough for a beer and the night bus home. I had my own particular, peculiar dress sense, dead man's clothes, 1940s double-breasted suits, with button on braces to match my pencil moustache and pointy sideburns. I bought my suits for two quid in Oxfam, or other second-hand shops, but in the Blitz I looked as smart and cool as everyone else.

I was the same bloke I'd been on Monday morning. I hadn't done anything different. 'Vienna' had been available to hear on our album for six months. Yet suddenly the world had shifted on its axis. I realised how much it had changed when we were doing *Top of the Pops* with Genesis the next week. Phil Collins came over and said, 'You're Midge Ure.' It should have been the other way round: it always had been before. That was when the penny dropped.

My life dissolved from the routine of anonymity into the chaos of celebrity. All of a sudden stardom came along and landed on me. Having got it wrong so many times before I had this overwhelming sense of finally getting it right. It was like a rush of blood to the head, a feeling of elation and satisfaction. I'd never had that before. Something had changed in my little world, but it wasn't something tangible I could put my finger on. It was all very well feeling great but I wasn't going to see any money for a year. I was still travelling on the tube; the difference was I was getting recognised on it.

'Fade To Grey' made the Top Ten and started to sell all over Europe. 'Vienna' went to No. 2 and stayed there for what seemed like forever. John Lennon had been murdered in December so we could live with being kept off the top spot by 'Imagine' and then by 'Woman', but by the end of February it was slipping and we were still selling 30,000 singles a day. We never made it to Number One. Instead some Aussie barber called Joe Dolce came up behind us with a novelty record called 'Shaddap You Face'.

Overnight stardom comes with a reality gap between public expectation and private living conditions. There is a fiscal delay too. Months pass between hitting the charts and the royalty cheques hitting the bank account. My new flat had no phone. In those days it didn't matter who you were or how much you needed a phone, it took three months to get one installed. So twice a day, every morning and every evening, I had to call the office to see what was happening. I walked down to Chiswick High Road and queued up outside one of the red boxes. I never had enough change, so God knows what the guy in the paper shop thought was going on. He probably thought I was some sad bloke arranging dodgy deals, pretending to look like that pop star off the telly.

It was worst in the mornings. If one of the boxes had been trashed I might have to wait half an hour in the cold. Nobody spent long in them, though, because they stank of piss, as in the evening they doubled as public toilets. I wanted to spend as little time in there as possible, but the news I was getting was so good I needed to hear more.

It was surreal at times. I'd be standing in Chiswick, a hand up to my nose to keep out the smell, stamping my feet to keep warm, asking, 'What's happening today?' The *Vienna* album was selling ludicrous amounts – it sold 150,000 copies in two months – while Visage was flying out of the shops. The singles were hits in Europe. In Australia they went crazy for the 'Vienna' video . . . and for the song. My publishing was free so every day a different publishing company was offering a bigger and better deal.

Everything was different. Instead of letters saying I was overdrawn at the bank, or informing me that my credit card had been cancelled, I had conversations with my managers telling me the opposite. 'You've got all this money now. You have to think about buying a car, about buying a house. Otherwise the taxman will take it.' By the time I finally got the phone installed I had already sold the flat.

It was a crazy period but one which I absolutely relished. I had already touched success once, and seen it all taken away from me. Exactly five years later I had been offered another fifteen minutes of fame.

CHAPTER 9
FADING TO GREY

I was really peeved when we couldn't get a record deal for Visage. For a year we had this finished record from the hottest club in the UK, and nobody was interested in releasing it.

Record companies thought that the Blitz was all about Spandau Ballet. Everyone wanted to sign Spandau. In those days there were groups and there were singers, who made records and toured in a never-ending cycle. There were no 'projects'. Not surprisingly people fought shy of the whole concept of Visage: they couldn't grasp the idea of an invisible group, a band that wasn't a band. Visage was seven people, five of whom were signed to other labels, fronted by a very strange gay guy.

After Morrison–O'Donnell (MOD) started managing Ultravox, I took the Visage tapes to them. Morrison grumbled about an artist collective being 'a bloody recipe for disaster' but agreed to become the production company, the front organisation for our collective, and to take a 20% management fee. Martin Rushent's record label had gone tits-up due to some business problems. As he was having family problems he was happy to bail out for ten grand – it had probably cost him closer to £500 and the electricity bill for his empty studio, but it would never have happened without his help. MOD took it to America of all places, where Jerry Jaffe, who ran Polydor in New York, completely fell in love with it, didn't care about the concept, signed it for the world and gave us an advance of $125,000. It was finally released in the UK in 1980, two years after its first conception.

The album was 90% complete so I went into Mayfair Studios to clean it up and finish the mixing. There I realised it didn't stand up, that we were a track short. I remembered Billy Currie playing me 'Toot City', a tune that he and Chris Payne jammed at sound checks when they were on tour with Gary Numan's Tubeway Army. I'd always thought it was a fantastic bit of music so I asked Billy for his tape. I went home, sat up all night, came up with the top line (the vocal melody) and wrote the lyrics. 'Fade To Grey' became the most successful track Visage ever had.

Chris and Billy had already done the backing track, so all I had to do was stick on Steve's vocal. That was harder than you might think. It was very time-consuming when he couldn't – or wouldn't – sing what I asked him to. There were specific melodies he had to do and he found it very difficult. I recorded the vocal myself and then piped it into his headphones as loud as I could get it. Somewhere in this process out of his mouth came something close to the right notes. It took a lot of patience and trickery. Steve was intimidated by me as I certainly wasn't the easiest person to be in the studio with, and he was never a singer and I knew that. In hindsight it was a bit unfair that whenever I lost my temper I bawled his head off.

Rusty sang the deep 'Fade To Grey' responses. He had a little Belgian girlfriend, Brigitte Arendt, who had accompanied him to the studio. I asked her to translate the lyrics into French and to speak over the mid section. She had this breathy tiny voice which sounded beautiful and it just made the track. However, she came back to haunt us after we paid her a session fee – her brother turned out to be a lawyer. He called up saying, 'Incidentally, the cheque wasn't cashed . . . but did you know that if you translate lyrics you are entitled to fifty per cent of the song?' We had to pay her off with £7,000 that we didn't have.

The concept of an artists' collective was radical. It went right against the rock and roll grain of the time. Promoting Visage could have been a logistical nightmare but as it was a studio/video project we never performed anywhere live, and never did a TV show as a unit. There was only one photo session where we were all together. The joy was we sent Steve, accompanied by two dancers, off to deepest, darkest Europe to do all the telly shows. Visage went into territories Ultravox could never reach. The French loved Visage.

While Steve was never a great singer, he earned his share. His role was to be in the magazines, do all the TV shows. He wanted the glory and that's what he got. Steve, who came from a little town in Wales, was always a camp lad who loved dressing up, loved make-up, loved the glitz and the glam and being the centre of attention. He was a pied piper with an entourage that used to hang round him, and they all looked outrageously fantastic. Steve's input made Visage tangible: he was the face, the front man, the image, out every night, in every newspaper; he represented the Blitz.

Every so often I'd have to slap him down for getting way above himself. The video for 'Damned Don't Cry' was a night shoot at a privately owned station down in Tenterden, Kent. There was a big party going on in this steam train with all the old Pullman carriages packed with Blitz kids, all Steve's mates dressed up to the nines, desperate for a chance to be seen on the telly. That was what so much of it was about – the pursuit of celebrity through image.

I don't know exactly what he had been doing but Steve was way off his face. He was showing off, mincing about being the centre of attention and I was trying to direct this video in the freezing cold. (I think I got frostbite, because three months later I was on a beach in Australia and I still couldn't feel my toes.) 'Steve, I have to talk to you,' I said. 'I don't know what you have been doing and I don't care. But you are way off your face and you have got to finish the video.'

By this point his face was melting: all his make-up had started to droop. 'Midge,' he said, 'I haven't touched a thing. I promise.' At that moment he slipped on the ice, did this amazing back flip, and lay there moaning in a designer heap. I put my head in my hands and walked away.

Every so often when he threw his little tantrums I had to pull him back. He demanded his boyfriend go with him on one promo trip to Europe, which I thought was pure brat behaviour. The rest of us had earned our place in the music industry and we didn't go around demanding limos and hotel suites. So why should he, a clothes horse, a front person for other people's talents?

Although Visage made good money for everybody, it got to the point where it wasn't worth the headache. I did the second album, *The Anvil*, but by then Steve had started to believe his own publicity and he was getting smacked out all the time. It got sillier and sillier, until one day when I was sitting in Chris Morrison's office. Steve was in New York promoting the Visage mini-album at the Chase Park Club. Chris was talking to Jerry Jaffe who told him the camel had got stuck in the midtown tunnel.

'What camel?' I interrupted.

'Steve wants to ride up in front of the press on this camel.'

I flipped. It had just got so ridiculously over the top. Visage had ceased to be fun any more, and fashion and pomp had taken over. Now everything was for the cameras.

'The moment he puts his arse on the camel I will leave.'

Steve climbed onto the camel. The camel crapped on the sidewalk. Steve's make-up ran. He burst into tears. That perfectly summed up Visage's future. I quit.

I originally did Visage to be recognised as a producer by my peers. To the public it might have been the Steve Strange band, but the industry knew where the sound was coming from. Steve was the not-very-good-at-singing head. Up until that point I was never allowed behind a mixing desk to experiment and try out the ideas I had. It was like being back at school where the boy next to you has his hands round his homework so you can't see what he's up to. The engineer engineered and didn't tell you what he was doing; the producer produced and didn't tell you what he was doing – which wasn't much.

I had got it into my head that you got more respect if you produced the music as well, created it from scratch. The first two albums say: 'Produced by Visage & Midge Ure'. That little credit led to a huge ruck with Rusty, so huge we fell out for years. He wanted it to read 'Produced by Visage'. Rusty's production contribution was when he turned up for twenty minutes in the evening before he nipped out to the clubs, said, 'Oh, I like that,' and then disapppeared. That pissed me off.

I was the one working my backside off sixteen hours a day. I didn't want any extra points – though as producer I could have asked for 3% – or any extra money. It was a collective, and I didn't want any more than anyone else had. All I wanted was what I had earned: the producer credit.

It became the main bone of contention. It niggled me because Rusty couldn't see I was handing it on a plate to him. Fair enough, he'd come up with the original idea, but I had made it happen. If I hadn't he would have gone on to his next twenty ideas. All the musicians worked hard but I was contributing music, lyrics and production, and happy to be splitting it with everybody.

By 1982 Rusty had decided he wanted respect, to be seen as a businessman and not just a drummer. Except it wasn't really Rusty sounding off about me having a credit: the words came out of his mouth but there was this other person living inside his head. He met a French guy called Jean-Philippe Iliescu, who hung out with him 24 hours a day, alternately whispering honey and vitriol into his ears. 'You don't need Midge. You write the songs. You're not getting what you deserve. It's your idea but you're just the drummer. Look at the way you they treat you. Why aren't you running it? Why aren't you getting a production credit, you go down to the studio every day?'

There is a sub-species of people inhabiting the music industry who don't create anything. They watch for success, then dive in on vulnerable people and tell them, 'I could have got you this, I could have got you that.' I never liked Jean Philippe. I thought he was always making promises and then delivering precisely nothing. I never understood how he had wriggled his way in with all these creative people to become part of the scene, but he always managed to squeeze a good living out of it.

Rusty and Steve decided they wanted to be represented by Jean-Philippe and an American lawyer called Marty Machat (one of whose many claims to fame was that he introduced Phil Spector to Leonard Cohen). Fair enough. Chris Morrison managed me – Chris O'Donnell left in 1982 and the company changed its name to CMO – and looked after Visage as a whole; the other guys were all in working bands. Whenever Machat came over to London he summoned Morrison to his flat in Grosvenor Square where he would pronounce, 'Let me tell you how it's going to be, Chris. I'm going to get a solo recording deal for Steve Strange.'

Chris just nodded and said, 'Fine, go and do it. I have a contract and when you have done the deal we will address it. Until then I won't lose any sleep over it.'

After *The Anvil* Polydor had taken up their option and owed Visage money for the next two albums. I'd left and Chris wanted shot of the whole deal. At the next meeting he told Marty, 'No, Marty, let me tell you how it's going to be. You are getting Polydor to pay CMO Productions $55,000 – which is our share of the next two albums. You are also going to get Polydor to account separately to me, to Midge and to Billy – without taking any future costs to recoup against. You do that and you can have it all.'

Machat did just that. The initial outcome was that, being in charge of their own destinies, Rusty and Steve went off and buried themselves in two seconds flat. Visage made one more album, *Beat Boys*, which was such a mess that Billy left halfway through the recording. They made two videos for the same song, didn't tell Polydor they were making one of them, and then tried to get them to pay for it. They drowned themselves in debt and Visage fell apart at the seams. Chris, Billy and I still get paid our royalties today. Nobody else gets anything because it all goes into paying off the debt.

I feel bad about that because everyone did pretty nicely to begin with. But after too many people got embroiled in Visage it all got nasty, no longer what it set out to be. It was never meant to be deadly serious, just a side project full of dabbling and experimenting but having a laugh at the same time. Look at the song titles – 'Moon Over Moscow'? 'Malpaso Man'? – they're all jokes. At the time a lot of people got it all wrong: they viewed us as serious artists. We were serious about what we did, but we weren't incredibly intense. Well, not all the time. Visage started off as pop Oscar Wilde, a touch camp, a little gay, but knowing. It moved further and further out there until when it finally imploded the songs and imagery were about fisting (the last single was called 'Love Glove'), sado-masochism and bondage in bath houses.

Rusty and Jean-Philippe bought Trident studios. For a moment it buzzed, and kids were coming off the street with tapes . . . but Rusty was a butterfly who could never sit still long enough to pollinate anything. Within two years he had lost the lot. We met a couple of years later in the Hiroko, a Japanese restaurant in Shepherds Bush where I appear to have met most of the important people in my life. Rusty had just got married and he sent a note over. Visage was old news by then – I was still with Ultravox and he was into some new venture, managing clubs – so neither of us cared. We've been friends ever since.

I was happy to leave when I did, as the bubble had burst. Anyway, by then I was much more involved with Ultravox. Ultravox was the real thing, Visage the bit of fun that led up to it.

CHAPTER 10
THIS MEANS NOTHING TO ME

It was Rusty, of course, who first suggested I join Ultravox. During the Visage sessions Billy went off to do a US tour. Ultravox came back a broken band: John Foxx had left and the guitarist Robin Simon fell in love and went back to the States. Billy, Warren Cann and Chris Cross returned home to find a letter from Island Records telling them their services were no longer required – and also that they owed them a huge amount of money.

One day Rusty said to Billy, 'You've got the right man standing over there: he's a songwriter, he's a singer, he plays the guitar, he can do keyboards. Midge is the guy.' The penny didn't drop with Billy at all, but Rusty had sowed the seed. He already knew how much I would like to have a bash at working with them. The idea of joining a band like that was just incredibly exciting. I hoped it would satisfy my lust for the keyboards and the technology.

I was waiting to be asked, hanging outside waiting! Ultravox had already been going for five years; they had built a solid fan base in the colleges, and in John Foxx they had a charismatic frontman. I thought that on their third album, *Systems Of Romance*, they had found themselves. I loved that album. Rusty used to play 'Quiet Man' and 'Slow Motion' down at the Blitz, where they were one of the key musical influences. It was just rather unfortunate that they promptly fell apart . . . Well, actually it was very fortunate for me.

Billy finally got the hint and arranged for me to meet the other guys in a pub in St Peters Square, Hammersmith. I was very keen to impress so I made loads of grandiose, sweeping statements like 'If I can't write a hit record for the American market, nobody can . . .' I never did.

I clicked with Chris Cross, the bass player, instantly. Warren, the drummer, was always easy, so he wasn't a problem. I thought I already knew Billy but he turned out to be harder, as he could be a moody so-and-so. This was at the time I was planning to get a two-bedroomed flat, and I had offered Billy one of the rooms to rent. Chris dragged me aside and said, 'Don't do that. You'll end up killing him in three months . . . and that won't help the band at all.'

The first time I plugged in and made a noise with Ultravox was in April 1979 at a rehearsal room in the Elephant and Castle with Richard Burgess working next door. Right from the first minute I knew I had come home. This noise was what I had been searching for, not only could these people make that noise, but they also could teach me how to make it. It felt so right I drank it all in.

What we were doing was radical and new: synthesizers, drum machines and electric guitar mixed together, synth bass with regular drums playing on top of it, the electronic and the organic. It had never been done before. Our sound was massive, this weird crossover between Kraftwerk and the guitars, bass and drums that belonged to every rock band in the world. I learned a lot about melody and structure from Billy, a classically trained viola and piano player. He brought in these influences that reeked of Berlin and Prague, while I was the guy from Glasgow who was into the Small Faces' 'All Or Nothing'. In Ultravox I could become the art-school boy I never was, making fantastic weird noises, building songs from sounds.

From the outset, outsiders got it twisted. They thought Billy, with his classical training, was the dark, serious, mid-European guy, while my pop sensibility made Ultravox a hit band. Just like in the Rich Kids, I was the pop villain. In fact, it was the reverse. Billy was the one who wanted huge success, Top Ten records and to be on *Top of the Pops*. Billy wanted success so he tended towards making it more commercial. I wanted the cred, to work with Conny Plank.

That is the irony about Ultravox. I might have been a one-time teeny-pop guitarist but once I was behind the technology the music that made me famous was the darkest, most serious stuff I'd ever done. Those early days in Ultravox were the best time of my life. The result was a complete crossover, maybe that's why it worked. The music came from all of us: everyone contributed, and we split all the songwriting credits four ways. The classic example of all of us working together was 'Vienna'.

One night I was sitting having a conversation with my old manager, Gerry Hempstead, who had co-managed the Rich Kids with Pete Walmsley, when his wife, Brenda, said to me, 'Midge, what you need to write is a song like that "Vienna".' I looked blank and she went, 'You know, the Fleetwood Mac song.' I looked blanker.

'No, it wasn't "Vienna",' said Gerry, 'it was "Rhiannon".' That night I went home with 'Vienna' lodged in my brain.

The next morning it was still there. I walked into the kitchen in my little flat and said to Billy, who was staying over, 'I've got a line running around in my head I can't get rid of, "this means nothing to me, this means nothing to me, Vienna".' We built the song from that one lyric. Every component element came from all four of us. It wouldn't have been 'Vienna' without Warren's heartbeat drum sound, and it wouldn't have been 'Vienna' without the bass synth notes and Billy's eerie viola.

Every other song we had the music first and had to write the lyrics later. Generally we'd jam, and suddenly I'd have a chord sequence, Chris chipped in with a bridge and Billy conjured up a Central European melody. We were very prolific. We wrote a good chunk of the *Vienna* album immediately but we had money problems: the equipment we needed was expensive and even the cheapest rehearsal rooms cost £50 a day. We had to pool whatever we earned. Fortunately Billy got to record and tour with Gary Numan and I did the Thin Lizzy stint, which enabled us to buy some of the gear that we needed.

At the same time as I was doing the Lizzy gig, the other guys were talking to Chris Morrison about management. Ultravox had been one of the first bands to play on the club circuit that Ian Copeland had set up in the States. Ian was Miles and Stewart Copeland's brother and he'd started it to give the Police somewhere to play after they got sick of being spat at in England. Clubs in America had their own lighting rigs, their own sound systems, so Ultravox didn't have to hire any of that. They simply took their back-line equipment out on Freddie Laker Airlines and came back with $10,000. It really impressed Chris Morrison that a band without a manager could do that.

Chris agreed to help the band get their next US tour together, and loaned them some money on spec to see if anything might materialise. Three months later he asked one of his employees, 'By the way, how much have we loaned Ultravox?' On learning that it was £20,000 he suddenly decided to take an intense interest in our career. He took their three Island albums home (for years his offices didn't have a stereo and we had to show him our latest videos in the local branch of Radio Rentals) and listened to *Ha Ha Ha*, which was far and away their most left field. He hated it. The next day he stumbled into the office in Putney moaning, 'We're done for!'

I only learned that later. For us MOD were great, a big management company who had dealt in America. Most musicians seldom know what is going on in the business side and I've never been the sharpest Scot at sorting out my deals. In 1979 I was in a mess: to get out of my original publishing deal with Martin–Coulter I had given them the rights to my Rich Kids songs. We couldn't say anything about my having joined Ultravox for six months until my contracts with EMI and Pete Walmsley were sorted out. While the Rich Kids got good money up front, the terms were heavy. When the Chrises went to discuss getting out of my deal, the EMI MD Brian Shepherd told them he had me signed for ever and he wanted a percentage override on any of my future earnings.

I'd have folded then and there, and agreed to anything, but fortunately Morrison–O'Donnell were made of sterner stuff. They told EMI it was restraint of trade and they would be going straight to court. They argued that if Rusty, as the drummer, had as much chance of getting a solo deal as the man in the moon, why should I, as the front man, be penalised. The EMI legal affairs bloke was spluttering defiance but Brian Shepherd agreed to tear up the contract and wished me luck. Like most of the record industry, he probably thought Ultravox was a dead end.

I offically joined the band on 1 November 1979. Once I was legit we did four dates in England. The Boat Club in Nottingham was jammed and, when Morrison saw 500 kids watching this band, the cash register went off in his head, and he realised it could work. We had most of the new songs up and running and we padded it out with the key songs from the first Ultravox – 'Slow Motion', 'Quiet Men', 'Hiroshima Mon Amour'. I loved those tunes so I didn't mind doing them. Mind you, when I sang them it was quite different from the originals. The hardcore fans seemed to accept I was there, rather like Phil Collins singing Peter Gabriel's Genesis songs. It was quite seamless although, given my chequered background, it could have hiccuped badly. Hearing the new material, old fans saw I was bringing something to the party, rather than detracting from the band. I brought some fans of my own too.

When I went out on tour with them in America it was a completely different ball game, and we came back having lost £10,000. As we had this big bee in our bonnet that we wanted to procure an American deal we ended up in Los Angeles doing five nights at the Whiskey a Go Go on Sunset Strip.

The shows were great but on the final night, New Year's Eve, I was introduced to someone who would become my constant companion for the next twenty years. Somebody in the dressing room handed me a Jack Daniels and coke. 'Try it,' they said. 'I think you'll like it.'

I did. Oh yes, I thought, that's quite nice. I can remember how it tasted. Up to that point I wasn't particularly interested in alcohol. I got pissed but it always tasted foul and I hated having hangovers. But this was different. It was good; it was smooth. I liked the taste of Jack Daniels. It became my drink of choice.

The idea behind the Whiskey shows was that all the record companies would come and see us, but they were all on holiday. When we came back Chris told Chrysalis, who were our only real suitors in London, 'If you don't sign this week, we will sign with A&M.' It was a classic management scam. There never was an American deal. The closest we got was when we spent five days in front of an American record company exec. He watched us piece 'Vienna' together like a big jigsaw and then he didn't sign us. He heard the final thing and walked away.

It didn't help that we refused to make demos. We said they could come and hear us at rehearsals, and record us on cassette machines but we refused to do a demo, because we knew that sometimes a band can capture something – a really good drum track or an amazing atmosphere – that it cannot recreate later. That was the way of thinking in those days: a demo was a demo, inferior. These days it's a digital recording, so it doesn't matter.

Chrysalis got so fed up that eventually they just said, 'You've got two days in our studios, do what you like.' So we recorded 'Sleepwalk'. No producer, just recorded it, gave them the finished single, and they signed us on the strength of that one song. It was our first single.

For a band that already had three albums out and had lost its lead singer and front man, getting any deal was major. This was a good deal, a 16% royalty on the retail price, which meant my quarter share was more than *all* of Slik had been offered five years earlier. Chrysalis had the feel of an Indy record company, and the sensibility of an Indy, but they were actually well connected.

We were a more self-sufficient unit than Thin Lizzy, with a defined idea of what we wanted to achieve, so we didn't use the management office in the same way. We did a lot of the decision making on our own. We knew the sound we wanted to create, the technology we had to have to make it and who we wanted to do it with. We booked ourselves into RAK Studios, hired Conny Plank as a producer, did the recording in three weeks, then flew over to his place for ten days to mix. In four weeks we had recorded an entire album for under forty grand.

Conny Plank had co-produced *Systems Of Romance*, and I thought we should stick with him. He was a great character, this affable, massive man with a bushy beard who looked like a bear. He had started in radio engineering in Hamburg, then he worked with all the classic German electronic bands: Kraftwerk, Neu, La Düsseldorf. He engineered 'Autobahn', one of the seminal electronic records of all time, and worked with Brian Eno, Bowie and Robert Fripp.

Conny talked in sounds. His English wasn't great but he could describe images in sounds. When we were about to record 'Vienna' he listened to us rattling through the tune a couple of times. Then he said, 'What I see when I hear this is a man sitting at a piano in a big empty ballroom. He's playing the same tune he's played for forty years . . . and he's tired.' We looked at each other and raised our eyes to the ceiling.

When Billy went in to play his part Conny had made the piano sound exactly as he had described it, haunting, distant and sad. He put things through little electronic boxes he had built, and he'd distort sounds, so I didn't quite know what he was doing. He could put an orchestra through his boxes, which gave it a peculiar distortion that made it sit right up in the mix.

Because we had rehearsed so much we knew all the parts, and the album was all there before we went into RAK. We used the studio as an experimental area, recording the drums out in the marble hallway to get an ambient sound. 'Vienna' only took a couple of days to record because there's not a lot in there: piano, a couple of synths, drum machine. Warren's syn drums looked like flying saucers with knobs sticking out of the side. The viola solo probably took the longest to actually get the sound right. To get a decent sound Billy had to play in the studio toilet – and he did it all on a ten-quid fiddle.

Technically it was a nightmare. Because the synths did not talk to the drum machine and the rhythm tempo kept changing, the drums had to be recorded in sections. The tempo was marked on the drum machine with a Chinagraph and Warren turned up the tempo to get the speed up while Chris was playing synthesized bass. The tempo for the mid-section was different and in order for the synth to be played in time with the drum machine, the tape had to be cut, edited and glued together by hand. All the other parts had to be played on top and we had to get our parts in time. Conny was really good at that; he wasn't fazed by chopping tapes up and gluing them back together.

The album was originally going to be called *Torque Point* and there are still some sleeves in existence with that title. That was Billy's idea, because he didn't want to focus on any one track on the album. Chrysalis turned round and said, 'No, the album is called *Vienna*.'

'Sleepwalk' came out in the summer of 1980 and it was mildly successful, skimming into the charts enough to get us on *Top of the*

Pops. By the autumn Spandau Ballet had their first hit with 'To Cut A Long Story Short' and everyone was talking about the New Romantics. Suddenly synthesizers were the new cool thing. We had synthesizers so obviously we were New Romantics. As a result we kept being offered slots on Saturday morning kids' telly, and for that we needed videos.

Although MTV had not yet been invented, the pop promo was all ready to change. Bowie had borrowed Steve Strange and some of the Blitz kids to shoot 'Ashes To Ashes' in glamorous Southend. Ultravox's first video was shot in a grotty club in St Alban's and featured us playing live. It looked very boring. We had some very different ideas for 'Passing Strangers'.

In February 1980 I was at Phil Lynott's wedding to Caroline Crowther, when Chris O'Donnell introduced me to Lexi Godfrey, who produced great videos. 'We'd love to work with you,' Lexi told me. 'I know this fantastic director, Russell Mulcahy, he'd be perfect.' Russell had hardly directed at this point, and was still an editor with ambitions. He wanted to direct Hollywood movies . . . and now he has. Chris Cross and I sat down with Russell and told him what we wanted. 'Everything we've seen that's been done is shot on video,' we said, 'We want to shoot on 16mm film, to crop the top and bottom of the screen, to go from grainy black-and-white to colour; we want shadows on wet cobbles . . .' We gave him a list of all this imagery, so when we shot 'Passing Strangers' it was like a rehearsal for 'Vienna'.

Even when we wrote 'Vienna' we knew it was something special. It was like nothing I had ever heard before. We played it at the end of every day's recording because we all got this huge buzz hearing it. It was so unique with the big overblown powerful ending. It was everyone's favourite track, yet the record company didn't want to release it as a single – especially as we insisted on it going out in its complete uncut five minutes and forty seconds grandeur.

That was much too long. Forget 'Bohemian Rhapsody' and 'Macarthur Park' – it didn't fit in radio formats. Chrysalis kept saying, 'We'll need to edit it, and we need to do a remix.' Matters came to a head when Chris Wright, the head of the record company, came down to see a sold-out show at Hammersmith Odeon. The audience was pretty calm until we played 'Vienna', then the crowd got up on its feet and never sat down again. Afterwards Wrighty came backstage and told us, 'Hands up. You're right. Just put it out the way it is.'

In 1980 nobody bothered to release a new record just before Christmas. The Radio One playlist shut down; the charts froze and they kept on playing the same old crap for weeks. 'Vienna' was taken to radio ten days before Christmas. They lapped it up, played it all the way through January. The single came out and it climbed up the chart and went to No. 2.

Having a Number One was really important back then. It mattered. At the time Lou Reizner's orchestral 'Tommy' was in the charts, and Chris O'Donnell thought if we did a full-on 'Vienna' with orchestra it might give us the final push we needed. We went up to De Lane Lea in Wembley and hired the Royal Philharmonic Orchestra. Unfortunately, the guy we hired to do the arrangement was doing a film score in Rome until the last moment and then turned out to have an attention deficit problem. We had a 75-piece orchestra sitting waiting for half a session while he 'put the finishing touches' to the arrangement. When he finally came in they were all sitting there reading the paper; they had lost all respect and he couldn't get them to do anything properly. The arrangement was a piece of crap. We had assumed it would follow the record, all low resonance and bass strings, but he made it pizzicato with lots of bells. It cost £5,000, but I took a razor blade to that tape.

I did end up doing an orchestral arrangement of 'Vienna' a couple of years later for German TV. They had this huge show called *RockNacht*, a stadium TV show and the kids got in for next to nothing. There were 50,000 people waiting to see Ultravox, Robert Palmer and a bunch of other acts. Because Ultravox were so loud we had to go into a studio to record our backing track that afternoon, because otherwise we would have blown the 75-piece orchestra and 100-piece choir off the stage. Eberhard Schoener, Germany's equivalent of George Martin, did these fantastic arrangements of 'Vienna' and 'Hymn'. It was just unbelievable, full of choral flourishes that made the hair at the back of my neck stand up.

People always wonder what 'Vienna' was about. We lied about it at the time. In interviews with the *NME* I talked for hours about the Secessionists and Gustav Klimt, all the stuff that was going on in turn-of-the-century Vienna. That was all rubbish designed to make us sound interesting.

It was a love song, the story of a holiday romance, about going to a beautiful place and meeting somebody special. You have this huge holiday romance, that you vow is going to continue forever, but, once you get back home and start living your nine-to-five job again, it just fades away. A week after you're back home it's slipped back into the shadows. You say, 'It means nothing to me,' but you're lying, harking back to Vienna, to a fabulous moment in time. I'd love to have it, but it's all gone – forever. It wasn't real life.

The whole idea was made up. I'd never been to Vienna, never had a holiday romance. I'd never been on holiday until after Slik had that Number One record. When I went abroad for the first time, I went to Ibiza with Addie.

What turned 'Vienna' into a worldwide hit was the video. Our contract only allowed for two videos per album, and initially Chrysalis rejected the idea for a video flatly. They didn't want to spend any money on a song that was already at No. 2, as they didn't think it would make any difference. They didn't have the foresight to see that if we gave them a ground-breaking video it was going to bounce all round the world.

O'Donnell and Morrison had a private meeting and agreed they had to make the film. Chris told us, 'If we have to break the bank, so be it. This is something different.' They lied to Lexi and told her it was all confirmed. The first filming was a midnight shoot in Covent Garden when she went up to Chris and said, 'A word, please. I've just spoken to the record company and they don't know anything about this.' There was some fast negotiating and in the end Lexi and Russell agreed to temporarily waive their fee. They knew they might get paid, or they might not, but if they didn't make the film we'd all miss a great opportunity.

We shot most of the film in the Gaumont State Theatre in Kilburn. It was a bingo hall at the time but the baroque decoration and the staircase was just incredible. We also shot in Searcys, a deb hangout behind Harrods and then we ended up going to Vienna. Instead of paying airfares, hotel bills and per diems we hired a small plane from Gerry Bron – it was so small that Russell had to sit on the toilet – and did the whole trip to Austria and back in a day.

The weather was foul. It was bloody freezing when it wasn't hailing, and there was snow everywhere. Our coats didn't keep out the winds that had come all the way from Siberia especially for us. It didn't appear to bother Warren, who slept for most of the day. Every time he woke up he kept boasting to Paula Yates, who'd come along to cover the shoot for *Record Mirror*, that he came alive at night. The scenes we shot in Vienna – at the piano-maker's gravestone in the cemetery and this enormous house – made the video. We did the whole thing for £18,000.

Russell was a brilliant director. We didn't know it at the time, but we were making a template for every video that was going to come afterwards. Until that point promos were all shot on video and so squeaky clean they looked like an episode of *The Bill*, with no atmosphere. All those styles that are now looked on as video clichés came from us. I suppose the Orson Welles movie *The Third Man* was the subconscious inspiration for 'Vienna', though I didn't realise that when we did the video as I hadn't seen the movie for years.

Mind you, it would all have been very different if Russell had got his way. At our first meeting to discuss the shoot he went off on his personal vision. 'Vienna ... fantastic ... I can just picture it, the gondolas, the arches, the little bridges.' He'd got his geography wrong, but then he's a camp Aussie, so maybe it was deliberate.

I can see that clip right now. Me in the back of a gondola with my dodgy moustache, a flat sombrero and a striped T-shirt, poling through the canals of Venice. God knows what that would have done to my career.

Instead 'Vienna' changed the course of my life.

CHAPTER 11
LIVING THE HIGH LIFE

It isn't the money that changes people, it is the acclaim. The success I had with Visage and Ultravox was sudden and that sort of success can make a musician very arrogant. While I hope I never was, others may remember it differently.

Second time around I was surprised by what stardom brought with it. This time it came with all the trappings and all the temptations. All of a sudden I was incredibly attractive to women; I was in demand, not just as a musician but as a person. This door had been flung open and there they were. Girls. Lots of girls. Where had they been hiding? They certainly weren't there before 'Vienna' was a hit.

Ultravox's first world tour began in September 1981 and lasted nine months. The band members were mainly single. When we got to Australia we were greeted by what seemed to be a conveyor belt of women – I'd have one in bed with me in the morning, and there'd be a knock on the door and another girl was waiting there to come in and take me. It was like shift work coupled with a very tiring form of gymnastics. This went on for the whole nine-month tour.

It was a brilliant time to be in a band, and Ultravox were a brilliant band to be in – we were just doing what any young man would do. It was a lot of fun, and there was nothing dark and subversive about it. It came along with the fame and glory and the rider in the bloody dressing room. At the end of the show the road crew went out front cherry-picking, armed with backstage passes. They chatted up pretty girls using the traditional lines – 'Do you want to go back and meet the band?' And they did.

It was the perceived fame I had that made me attractive. I didn't change. I wasn't any different from that day in the Kings Cross rehearsal room when the records went into the charts, and I didn't look any different, but the hits turned everything around. I became somebody who was sought after both as a sexual partner and as a musician. I can't explain it. A successful singer becomes an icon, something (not someone) sought after as a sexual prize. It's not just a rock and roll thing, as it goes back much further; look at Sinatra, look back to Paganini. The allure also spills over from the band to the crew, to anyone connected with the whole game. It's like the old joke about the guy in the circus who shovels up the elephant shit – he's still in show business.

There is something attractive about a successful man, whether it is Formula One racing, golf, acting or being in a band. Girls see musicians on stage standing in a halo of light, portrayed as some kind of rock demi-god. If they can get their hands on you they will.

I saw many more girls in spandex trousers and cowboy hats backstage at Lizzy gigs. Ultravox never really had that kind of following, no head-banging groupies for us. I never encountered many groupies – certainly never the traditional ones like Cynthia and the Plastercasters. Mind you, I'm not sure I'd have liked anybody going near my bits armed with a bag of plaster of paris. There was one in London, a very pretty little girl, who bonked quite a few pop stars; she did a big exposé in the papers about how badly all the guys had treated her, how she had got her fingers burned. According to her, and to the paper, I was the love of her life. That was news to me. Then there was a woman in Detroit who walked into the dressing room and announced, 'OK, who wants four minutes of head?' She was quite happy to oblige.

Japanese girls were very odd, and very polite. It was all very by the book, very polite, hardly a word said as if they had read a manual on how to fuck a rock star. They knocked on my hotel-room door and let themselves in. Literally it was: 'Ah, Midgey san.' They bowed, walked in, took their clothes off, did the business and then left. There was no polite after-chat.

If anything we were the ones being used. I was a notch on the bedpost, targeted, sought out, hunted down . . . and a very willing victim. Men are rubbish at resisting. I had nobody waiting for me back home; I wasn't saving myself for the schoolgirl crush I was going to marry, so it was very difficult to say no – why should I? But when I did have a girlfriend I didn't do any messing around, and all the time I was married nothing ever happened. It wasn't fair. I always found it incredibly demeaning when all the band and the crew knew guys were busy bonking other people but kept it quiet from their girlfriend whenever she turned up. It was tricky, because the temptation was always there, but I have always thought if you were going to do something then do it properly.

I was a lad doing what a lad does. It wasn't using, and it wasn't us manipulating. I never said, 'You are the love of my life,' or made any promises I wasn't going to keep. The girls all knew the score, that we were off to Brisbane the next day, and they still chose to come and find us. In Sydney we stayed at the Sebel Town House, because all the bands stayed there. There I was, three sheets to the wind, having a nightcap at the hotel bar when some gorgeous girl came up and started telling me, 'I love your music. I think you're fantastic.' What was I supposed to do? Talk to a roadie about guitar strings? Next thing I knew I'd be upstairs, where maybe they had been the week before with somebody else, I didn't ask. It was a naïve period, before we knew anything much about AIDS. The worst thing you could catch was a quick trip to the doctors. I was lucky, I didn't.

In a roomful of girls I'd see the one I was attracted to. If she wasn't into it I went to bed alone. For me, no has always meant no . . . but no was not very often. At the same time, I can see how easy it would be for things to turn nasty. As a star you get so used to everyone doing your bidding you start to expect it, to believe you can have anyone you want.

However, as quickly as that stuff comes it goes at the other end. Fame is fleeting, and the novelty of casual relationships wears off. By the end of the *Quartet* tour I was tired of it and looking for something more substantial.

I met Donna Blackman at the Lexington Queen in Tokyo. She was a beautiful south London model who was working in Japan. Advertisers in Japan like to use European and American models and they'd all hang out in the Rappongi clubs. One of the great bonuses of going to Tokyo was that we got into all the clubs free. So did the models, who were fed up with Japanese men, and wanted to hang out with someone who could speak English.

Donna was a great character, lovely, really funny and when she came back to London we started going out. She was young, bubbly and full of life – exactly what I needed at that moment in time. But I was so busy writing, rehearsing, recording and touring and when I wasn't I just felt Donna wanted too much from me. She wasn't living with me and I didn't want to be pinned down. After we split up she went back to Japan, where Chris Morrison heard on the grapevine that she was getting more and more upset. He sent her the money for an air ticket to come home. Chris claims that he did it to protect me, as Ultravox were going on tour and he didn't want her chasing me all over Japan. But then at heart he's a softie.

After Donna I didn't think I was ready for settling down. But there's only so many evenings you can sit in your nice little house in Chiswick on your own, and only so many numbers you can call up in your black book.

The video storyline for 'Lament' was pretty basic: four lads up in Skye meet four girls, go to a ceilidh and holiday romances follow . . . except one turns into something else and becomes a long-lasting relationship. Pretty prophetic the way things turned out. We needed four models so we each got to pick one girl, choosing from dozens of modelling cards. I was struck by this one card. The girl looked stunning, very sophisticated. Her name was Annabel Giles . . . of course, at the airport up turns this girl in jeans, no make-up, with her hair tied back and little granny glasses. I wasn't so impressed.

During the two-day shoot I changed my mind. Annabel was so funny. She was a smart upper-class girl, but there was an edge to her, and she was very feisty. She tap danced, she told stories, she sang, cracked jokes; she was just plain witty. When we got back to London I invited her to the video edit. She came along. I didn't know it was the night before her wedding.

I was really taken with her. It's not often you meet somebody you're instantly relaxed with, but Annabel was just so easy to get on with. After the edit we went to the pub next door, sat out in the garden and got completely wrecked. After a few drinks I said to her, 'You shouldn't be getting married: you should run away with me.'

Annabel didn't get married the next day. She did go on the honeymoon with her fiancé to try and sort it all out, and then decided it wasn't happening. We started seeing each other. There was this wonderful madness about our relationship. It was romantic but I was also absolutely, utterly, bemused by the entire thing. It was something I didn't see coming. It snuck up behind me and whacked me over the head and for a long time it was wonderful.

I was never much good at spending money sensibly. My old maisonette was above an estate agents' in Turnham Green Terrace. It suited me fine as I was out all day and at night I could make as much noise as I wanted because there was no one below me. Art Deco and Art Nouveau has always been fashionable with rock musicians. I'd always loved the style, the clean lines, the angular aspects, and even though I could never afford it I had always collected bits and pieces of Art-Deco furniture. I was on a bus in Hammersmith when I saw an old green and cream Art-Deco three-piece suite with the classic flower-shaped back and big rounded arms. I bought it for seventy quid.

I had a little black Art-Deco ship's piano I'd bought after I made £500 doing a production job for an Irish band called the Atrix. I spent it all on the piano; it had chrome stands going up the side with lights at the end of the keyboard, the most beautiful thing I'd ever seen. It was my pride and joy and sat in the corner of my flat along with my suite, my portable colour telly and a few other bits and pieces I'd picked up in junk shops.

My first big royalty cheques from Visage and Ultravox came in late 1981. They amounted to well over six figures. Suddenly I had everything I ever wanted. I bought a house in Grosvenor Road and furnished it the way I liked. The house dated from the 1930s but it was built by a local builder to live in himself, so it was a lot better finished than the other houses he built. The bricks were feathered and the interior was all parquet floors. The house wasn't huge. It had three bedrooms with a dining room and I put a sauna in the basement, but its main selling point was the granny annex where I could put my studio – that was how I saw the future unfolding.

The house had a very long sitting room with a bay window at one end and French windows into the garden. The room, the walls and fireplace were all painted grey with chrome radiators. It looked fantastic so all I had to do was furnish it with the right things. I took great delight in going to very expensive designer shops and buying classic pieces – like two Le Corbusier chrome-framed black leather sofas which are so timeless I still have them in my house today. Being a good Glaswegian I've always loved Charles Rennie Mackintosh's furniture. I couldn't afford the originals so I went for 'Mockintosh', remade and redesigned by an Italian company under licence. I bought a pair of black ladderback chairs and eight Argyle chairs as a dining set. Everything in the sitting room was black, chrome and grey: there was a black Chinese rug, black velvet curtains and my ship's piano. It was very stylised, very laddish – no frills. I had a variety of cleaners who kept it tidy for me.

While we were recording *Rage In Eden* in the middle of Germany, Chris Morrison found me a mint-condition, red 1966 Porsche 356. I flew back, found the car outside the office, got in, started it up and drove back to Germany. It was a very cool car to be seen in: a glorified Volkswagen basically, there was nothing flash about it, but it looked fantastic. I wanted something that showed what immense good taste I had.

I ended up with a collection of classic sports cars. Cars were both an extravagance and a passion. I lavishly poured some of my new-found wealth into the old beast, the Vauxhall Wyvern which I drove down from Glasgow. Because you couldn't buy the parts for it – it was a 1954 car, built the year after I was born – I had wings hand-beaten. But because I had all these other cars I never drove it and it sat in the garage. I bought a white Jaguar XK 120 ragtop. Any time it rained I had to clip on these windows and pull up this flimsy, flappy top, but water still poured in the sides as I drove along. In hot weather it overheated all the time. If I got stuck in traffic I'd just watch the temperature gauge go up and up, the needle would go right past full temperature and keep going. The next thing steam would erupt out of the bonnet and I'd get towed away again while everybody stuck behind me either cheered or laughed. I swapped that for a red Jaguar XK 140 drophead. The windows wound up so it was much more practical.

I didn't buy cars as an investment, but because I liked them. I didn't care about how fast they went or how uneconomical they were. All the cars I had were classic objects. I bought another Porsche, a 356 cabriolet, as a pile of parts. There was the basic shell and a load of bits and pieces, and I paid mechanics to build it up like a great big Meccano set. There was an Aston Martin DB6 which I never got round to doing up. I traded that in to buy another classic, a Sunbeam Alpine cabriolet with white leather upholstery, whitewall tyres and matching steering wheel, all very Grace Kelly, as a birthday present for Annabel. The week after I traded it in Aston Martins went through the roof, so a car worth five grand suddenly became worth thirty grand – another classic Midge move.

I had a Mercedes G Wagon jeep and eventually I bought a Golf Gti convertible, which I had to have so there was one car that actually started in the morning. The office got tired of me phoning up and announcing, 'I'm going to miss my plane because the cars won't start.' Eventually they told me, 'Buy a real car, will you.' The idea of driving about in a 35-year-old car is wonderful until you have driven a new car and you discover that the heater works when you want it to and the wipers actually wipe when it's raining.

The car that gave me most pleasure to buy was a Ford Fiesta. When I was playing in Glasgow on the *Vienna* tour my parents came along, but I could see my dad was really upset. He had just had his fifteen-year-old Ford Escort stolen; it was only worth £500 but he didn't know how much he would get from the insurance and whether he'd be able to replace it. I asked him casually what kind of car he'd like. 'I'd love one of those little Fiestas,' he said, 'but we could never afford one.'

I didn't say anything, just went out and sourced a Fiesta. The day before Christmas Eve I took the train up to a garage off the A1, picked it up and drove it up to Glasgow, going very slowly because you still had to run in new cars in those days. Christmas morning I gave Mum and Dad their presents, lovely gold Dunhill lighters which they never used. Everything I ever bought them, the Cartier watches, the Burberry raincoats, they kept for best – which meant I never saw them again. I slipped out, took the Fiesta through the car wash, tied a big ribbon to it and parked it out the front. 'Dad,' I said, 'I've got another present for you.' I gave him this little cardboard box with a key in it. My mother went, 'Oh, that's nice,' thinking it was something else weird to keep for best. My dad got it at once and his eyes started to well up – and he was never an emotional man. We went outside and there it was, only a £6,000 car, but to them it was unbelievable because they had never owned a new car.

It was such a hectic time I didn't see my family much. Mum and dad were still in Glasgow. I went back home every Christmas or New Year when I could but they didn't like coming to London. Whenever Ultravox played in Glasgow I'd send a car for them to come and see the show. Bobby was in East Kilbride working for Rolls Royce, Linda lived in Milton Keynes and they were busy raising their families. I caught up with them whenever I could.

I treated myself to a Harley Davidson, an ex-Belgian police Electraglyde. I'd never ridden a Harley but I'd always wanted one, so I went down to the Kings Road and tried it to make sure my little legs could touch the floor. The great thing about Harleys is that they are very low, so even if you are short like me they are easy to drive. I drove it to rehearsals, which made Warren extremely jealous.

Later that year Steve New, who was fairly *compos mentis* at the time, and I drove the bike to Venice. On the way back we stopped off in Cannes, where I was spotted by a bunch of Hell's Angels who wandered into the car park, unlocked the panniers, nicked the helmets and took off over the Italian border with my bike, never to be seen again. I still had my passport and money so we came home on the plane. I couldn't claim the insurance because I had no bike-driving licence. My theory was that if you were driving about on a Harley you should have a licence and nobody was going to bother you. That was £3,000 down the drain.

When we were in Australia we had a couple of days off in Sydney lounging around on this glorious boat. I came back home thinking I needed a boat. I bought this 28-foot twin-engine power cruiser in

Poole for 25 grand. I had these brilliant images of me popping over to France at the weekend, sleeping on board. The year and a half I owned the boat I was on it once, and I learned that boats are just a hole in the water you throw money into. After realising that it was a complete and utter act of folly, when I came to sell it water had seeped into one of the engines, so the guy offered me 15 grand. That was an expensive day out on a boat.

And then there was my grand folly. Montserrat. I owned this beautiful plantation home on a paradise island. Once. Open rooms, big ceiling fans, wooden slatted floors, dark wood shutters and windows overlooking the sea. When Ultravox had recorded *Quartet* at George Martin's Air Studios I had fallen in love with the island. When I bought the house for £125,000, the survey was a handwritten piece of paper which failed to tell me it was infested with termites. Instead of having to change the shingles on the roof, the whole thing had to be rebuilt, except for the stone walls, which were two-foot thick. All the woodwork from the roof to the basement had to be replaced, then I had it reassessed and reinsured for the full value.

Two years later I was staying in Los Angeles, watching CNN, when I heard that Montserrat was directly in the path of Hurricane Hugo. I phoned up my friends on the island, who had shuttered my house up and were preparing to sit it out and see what happened. The hurricane didn't just hit once: it went over the island, turned round and went back over again to give it a right good kicking.

I rushed out to the survival shops in Los Angeles, stocked up with meat, water-purifying tablets, batteries and a one-man tent. I wasn't sure if my house was going to be there or not. I booked a plane to Miami, island-hopped to Antigua, then got the first flight out at five o'clock in the morning to Montserrat. Luckily when the hurricane hit there was a British warship nearby. They cleared the runway and opened some of the roads. I grabbed a taxi straight to Air Studios and went in there expecting to be greeted like I was Indiana Jones, the hero coming to save the day. 'Great, you're here,' said Yvonne, the studio manager. 'Do you fancy coming up for dinner? We're having duck à l'orange.' The Stones had just left and, as there was no power, anything they hadn't eaten or drunk was going to go off unless we ate it. The first few nights we ate like kings – we were brushing our teeth in Evian.

For the second time I had to rebuild my entire house. I had just doubled the insurance so I was well covered. The guy who came out from the insurance company turned out to be Scottish. While his son swam in our swimming pool, he said, 'Right, let's haggle.'

I said, 'I think the damage is . . .'

He wrote down another number and said, 'That's what I think you're going to get.'

We had a drink and it was resolved. Or so I thought until the volcano started smoking in 1995.

The mountain smoked for about a year and a half before it blew. Long enough for my insurance to be declared null and void. By then the termites had eaten everything again. Not many people can say the government ate their house, but I can. Next door was Government House and it was their termites that lived in the adjoining wall inside the cavities. The authorities spent a million pounds refurbishing Government House. Within a week of being finished the termites were back in again and back in my house. The last time I saw it, it was a shell, and I could poke my finger through the roof.

I've still got what's left of my house – a bottle of black volcanic ash and a brass door knocker – in my studio at home. Occasionally I look at the bottle and I have to laugh. That is God's way of reminding me that I am a working-class boy from Cambuslang.

It was a stupid place to buy a house. I did love it, but my head was up my backside in the 80s. Fancy buying a house in the Caribbean – it was a difficult place to travel to and took an age to get there. Why not buy a place in Spain? But that's logic. Montserrat goes hand in hand with the boat . . . needless things.

What seemed to be my greatest extravagance actually turned out to be the shrewdest investment I ever made. I'd always wanted my own studio and my new house in Grosvenor Road had a separate building in the garden. Chris Morrison advised me not to do it because he knew artists are notoriously flaky and there is always a great studio in Malibu where they want to do their next album. Everyone thought I would blow 150 grand on a studio and never use it. But I wrote a lot of hit records in my studio, and it was there that Bob Geldof and I recorded a song that changed the world.

I had met Bob on my first night in London with the Rich Kids – though Bob can't remember it and claims, 'You obviously made no fucking impression on me whatsoever.' The Boomtown Rats had let us open for them at the Music Machine in Camden where we played our three songs and blew up one of their speakers. It wasn't a great gig for Bob. Halfway through the lead singer of Skrewdriver leaped up on stage and punched him in the face. He sang 'Looking After No. 1' with blood streaming down his face.

I met him a few times at the usual bars and clubs, backstage at gigs but we weren't really mates, though we were both good friends of Phil Lynott's. I'd played with Lizzy and Geldof and a couple of the Sex Pistols were with Phil in the Greedy Bastards. I got to know Bob through Paula.

Paula Yates was very bright and lovely with it. She wasn't a classic stunning beauty, but she made the most of what she had. She was manipulative in a very good way; she had a presence, this character who she could just turn on and off, if and when she wanted to. She did the whole flirty thing, fluttering her eyelashes and baby talk, with every boy that she ever met, charming the pants off everybody. She switched on and off her Marilyn Monroe, little-girl-lost act all the time. She was very good at it. It made us boys feel like someone special, and we loved all the attention. Men are pretty simple really. If women treat us nicely, pat us on the head and make big eyes at us we're quite happy. Paula knew that.

When Bob wasn't around she'd get bored and phone up her boys. Paula loved hanging out with pretty boys, and she had a whole clique, Martin and Gary Kemp, me, Glenn Gregory, whoever was around. 'Do you want to come over and have some dinner?' I'd go and hang out with her, or she'd turn up wherever I happened to be. Bob didn't seem to mind at all. She was very funny, with a witty, very PG Wodehouse sense of humour. She had a lovely knack of recalling stories and coming up with great one-liners.

There was nothing, absolutely nothing, between Paula and me. It was all incredibly platonic. I didn't have many women who I thought of as friends, and she was with Bob so I wasn't going into that territory at all. One day she came over to my flat in Turnham Green Terrace on her scooter. When I got back there was a note on the door saying 'I'm in the burger bar next door getting something to eat.' She was wearing a sweatshirt which she'd cut the sleeves off and she was leaning forward eating a burger with her tits all exposed. 'Paula,' I yelled at her, 'put them away, it's only four o'clock in the afternoon.' She had no idea; she was just being completely natural.

Paula befriended all these guys in bands. They were her mates: she knew everyone who was young and going for it, the glue who stuck it together. When Paula came along with Ultravox for the video shoot in Vienna I took pictures of us all crammed into the little plane. I took this wonderful shot of Paula in silhouette, a goddess playing the little girl.

She was ambitious and smart and soon she was writing for the national papers and doing TV. Because she was pretty, Geldof's girlfriend and presenting *The Tube*, Paula was newsworthy in her own right. Sometimes she played up to it, but usually she behaved normally. Normally for Paula. One brilliant Paula moment came when she was presenting her first show for London Weekend. She was chatting away live until she got really hot, so she took off her jacket and threw it over in the corner with the microphone pinned to it. She kept on talking but no one could hear a word. Another was when she was lying on the shag-pile carpet, interviewing Patsy Kensit, two over-the-top sex kittens trying to out-pout each other like something out of *Austin Powers*.

The best side to her was when she was just Paula as opposed to when she was playing Paula the Vamp. Paula the Vamp was all tipsy-wipsy, touchy-feely and squeaky; Paula was this really clever girl who was great fun to hang about with. She could snap out of her lost Marilyn thing, and the next moment there was this big laugh and she was back to reality, frying sausages, making bangers and mash and trying to deal with her kids.

In the early days Bob and Paula had a house in deepest, darkest south London, somewhere off the South Circular. Paula decided she wanted to have a dinner party and asked me and my girlfriend of the time. She also asked Hazel O'Connor because she wanted to fix us up together. Bob, who knew she couldn't cook an egg, was nervous, convinced there was going to be a culinary disaster. Paula served grilled trout covered in breadcrumbs. It looked amazing, just like in the book. Unfortunately, instead of grating bread over the fish she'd bought a packet of breadcrumbs – which turned out to be apple crumble mix. She served half-raw trout with apple crumble liberally sprinkled over the top. It was deeply disgusting.

'Don't worry,' I said smugly, 'I'm not hungry. I had a McDonald's before I came over. Just in case.'

Bob got his revenge later when I was bragging about my car: 'I've just bought this beautiful old Porsche 356.'

He looked concerned. 'Maybe with better luck you can make some more wedge and buy a new one. You'll have to write some fucking decent songs first, though.'

Paula's matchmaking worked up to a point, as I did go out with Hazel after that dinner party. Hazel was like a cloned Paula: she acted the same way, did the same little-girl-lost thing – but not as well. She was great fun but never a long-term girlfriend. She definitely seduced me but, as usual, I acquiesced graciously, without a struggle – 'Sure, take me home.'

We didn't make a big song and dance about it. It sneaked into a few of the gossip columns (mainly the one in *Record Mirror* written by Paula) but it certainly wasn't Posh and Becks stuff. We hung out, did dinner, went to gigs, all that sort of stuff for a few months. It was no great romance, just two individuals who drifted together. The *Breaking Glass* movie had just happened and she'd had a couple of big hits. A lot of time all we did was sit and talk about the business and that's not what you want from a partnership – 'Oh, you think you have problems with your record company, wait until I tell you my problems with mine.' I wanted to talk about something else and the excitement soon wore off. I took my usual coward's way out, suggested we take a break from each other and never phoned again.

Bob and I did a couple of things together. He is convinced that we were the Nancy Boys, providing Clint Eastwood-style backing vocals, for Paula's version of 'These Boots Are Made For Walking'. Martin Ware and Ian Craig Marsh asked her to sing it on their first British Electric Foundation album. It was suitably ridiculous: she'd lisp, 'I just got me a brand-new box of matches' and we'd go, 'Strike, strike!' Silly stuff. We certainly appeared together at the Secret Policeman's Ball, a charity concert for Amnesty International, standing at the same backing mike while Sting was singing 'I Shall Be Released'. I learned then that when standing next to Bob it's best to try to block out whatever he is singing.

Our friendship developed slowly. He wasn't my best mate but, every time we met up, it was easy. I'd say hello, sit down and chat like he was an old friend I hadn't seen for years. I spent lots of time down at their place in Faversham, an old priory with the church still attached and Tudor gardens. It was a nice ride. I'd jump on my Harley, and go down for weekends. I'd hang out with him and Paula, go for walks, or sit and read the Sunday papers, which Bob does religiously. I've never seen anybody read so many papers in my life; he absolutely scours them.

Down in Faversham they had an open house – Sunday lunch and chill out – full of friends. Jools Holland was part of the scene because he and Paula were working on *The Tube*. They invited Simon Le Bon to come down and open the Faversham fete because they had the rights to the village green and they used to donate it for the fete.

I was horrified when Geldof was sent out to go and buy nappies for Fifi one Sunday morning. I went with him as moral support, because I had no idea what fatherhood was like. No one else had kids then, but now I know it is part of what you do. They were a very domestic family; it was all about the kids, the babies. She doted on those kids, and she was a really good mother.

That's the way I choose to remember Paula.

CHAPTER 12
HEAVY METAL WITH SYNTHESIZERS

For almost five years Ultravox were running blind, hamsters on a wheel. Rehearsing, writing, recording, touring. Straight after the tour we'd be back in again rehearsing and writing, recording and touring again. Plus we had to squeeze in all the promotion – flying off to Germany to do three days of fifteen interviews a day. Between July 1980 and Christmas 1984 Ultravox released four albums, a Greatest Hits collection, played over 400 concerts in eighteen countries, made fourteen videos (seven of which Chris Cross and I directed) and a live film. I also produced two albums with Visage, a bunch of singles for other artists, made a solo single and directed eleven other videos.

I loved every minute.

It's funny what the right hit does to a career: it gives you the opening but you have to be strong enough to capitalise on it. 'Forever And Ever' had catapulted Slik from the Scottish circuit into concert halls but we didn't have the material to sustain the momentum. Ultravox were different. At its peak the band was big just about everywhere . . . except America. Japan was one of the first countries where our music was used on a TV commercial. Suntory Whisky used 'New Europeans' and credited the music in the bottom corner of the screen like they do on MTV. We were headliners at the Sweetwater Festival in New Zealand in 1982 in front of 36,000 people. We constantly toured Europe, though France wasn't a great market for us, which was a puzzle because the French always like really odd things.

Ultravox were the heavy-metal kings of the electronic era. Most of the other synth bands were lightweight, but Ultravox rocked, especially on stage. We were a serious rock band: synths can make a powerful noise and we sounded stonkingly good played through big speakers; it thumped, like a bass drum hitting you in the chest. There was just as much guitar as there was synthesizer but people don't remember that: they remember the keyboards, the videos . . . and the stage sets.

Our touring costs were astronomical. We'd go on tour, and come back down £100,000. That's not good business, except it was selling records and the wisdom of the time was that, if you impressed live, people would buy the album. Chrysalis paid a certain amount of the touring costs (which were not recoupable against our royalties) because it was deemed incredibly important. That attitude no longer exists.

It was the stage sets that cost so much. We were always supposed to do a UK tour with the full stage set then cut back, get rid of half the lights, the backdrops, all the heavy stuff that meant extra crew, and go out and do a skeleton version of the show around the rest of the world. But no, we did the whole thing, took it to Germany, America, Australia. We couldn't work for a month before or a month after a different leg of the tour because we were freighting the equipment – by boat it cost £26,000 or £100,000 by plane.

It was never about the money, but all about the quality of what we could actually do. None of us ever looked at the figures . . . I never knew how much we got for a date, never asked, never questioned it. Chris Morrison got really frustrated with us because he'd negotiate the best possible prices and calculate a profit that had evaporated by the time we'd finished. He told us frequently, 'It's a no-win situation. If you can only do what you are doing using this equipment why do you do that . . . because you can't do it.' There was one moment when it struck me that although we were losing seventy grand on a tour CMO would still take 20% of what we were earning. I said to Morrison, 'Hang on. You insist we go out on tour with this but if we lose money you shouldn't take twenty per cent of what the intake is' . . . and he agreed, which was very nice. He didn't have to.

We did it because nobody else did it; it was all about standards. Nobody else had stage sets so we did stage sets. Everybody else had huge stacks of amplifiers so we got rid of all the amps, had a really clean stage set without any clutter and played through the monitors. We wanted to convert the same tired old venue into something completely different just for that night. The curtains dropped at the beginning of the show . . . and there'd be another curtain behind it with a great big painted head or the UV logo. As the music started to play the front lights went down and the back lights went up so you would see the thin wall. Open up the thin wall and you'd see right through, then that curtain would drop and we'd be off into the show. We used big theatrical tricks, like scrim to create special effects with light. If you light scrim, which is basically a transparent fabric, from the front it is just a solid curtain, and if you alter the lighting from the rear it becomes transparent.

The *Quartet* tour set was a massive 30-foot structure. The album sleeve was an architect's views of a building, the horizontal, elevation and plan. I'd just been to see a play with Paula – she wanted to see her friend Rupert Everett who was starring – where the entire stage was painted grey, and had grey furniture on it. I thought it looked fantastic, because, when you hit it with a white light, it was all grey, but, when you hit it with a coloured light, it took on that colour. We had our entire set, stage floor, backstage, screen, the instruments, the amplifiers, the monitors all painted grey and then used spotlights to light it from behind. We wore black.

When it came to the first night in November 1982 we weren't ready. We'd had a month to rehearse and nothing went right. It wasn't that we weren't trying – though it didn't help that Warren liked to come in when the rest of us were leaving because he couldn't get up – but we had run out of time. It was a logistical, technical nightmare. We spent so long programming the show and getting the equipment working that we hadn't done enough stage rehearsals, so we only had four days to do the lights.

Both Chris Cross and I called Morrison the night before and told him we had to postpone the tour. 'No you can't,' he said. 'It starts tomorrow as planned. If I give you another week you still won't be ready. Don't worry, I'll be there with you.' As if his presence would help. I was absolutely furious about having to go ahead. I expected everybody to have the same standards that I did and this was way under par. I knew we wouldn't be able to pull it off.

There is one recurring dream I have as a musician. I am standing on stage, usually playing a song I don't know. Suddenly I realise I don't know the next chord . . . I freeze and watch the audience walk away. The next night in the Francis Xavier Hall in Dublin my nightmare came true. It was one of the worst shows Ultravox ever gave; only half the PA worked, so the sound came out in mono, on one side only. We had to stop and start one of the songs again it went so wrong. The audience hated it and started walking away from the front of the stage.

It was a crap gig but our next show showed a thousand per cent improvement, and the one after that was better still. That baptism of fire really pulled us together. It ended up as one of the best tours we ever did.

In those early days the machines couldn't talk to each other. Warren was pretty technical, and he understood a lot of things about gates and pulses and spikes, and we had Pete Wood, a lanky boffin, who looked like a cross between Eno and Wurzel Gummidge, travelling with us. Every instrument was altered in some way, so we had to carry a spare of everything. One time when we were in Boston, and Chris's mini-Moog went down we borrowed one from the Cars, but it couldn't do the job.

We were paranoid about people thinking we were miming. Bill Wyman was quoted in the papers saying, 'I went to see Ultravox in Hammersmith; the music was coming out but nobody was playing anything.' It did look that way with Warren using a programmed drum machine, playing clap traps, and I'd be standing back from the mini-Moog because a lot of the times I just hit the key. In fact we always played every note. It was cheating to use tapes.

We always used the best PA systems – it sounded like a record on stage – and the best lighting engineers. I had Alan Wild, the lighting man, in tears during rehearsals. I knew exactly what I wanted to happen at any particular spot; we had talked through it all so, if he missed a lighting cue, I stopped the song, went back to the beginning and did it again until he got it right. It was rigorous. Our standards were devilishly, ridiculously high. How people accepted it I don't know. Every night after we came off stage I would know exactly who hadn't done what. They would have to come in and admit 'We missed that lighting cue' and I'd tell them, 'You missed that bit' and 'That was late' – though not always in the politest language.

After I saw Phil Lynott throw one of his tantrums I had told both Chrises never to let me get like that, to force me back into reality. There were moments when they both had to throw that back at me. I was probably pissed, and O'Donnell might crack one of his jokes and that would push me over the edge and I'd be flying off on one – 'Fucking record companies, follow spot was late, blah blah blah' – until he would click his fingers and bring me back to earth.

My emotionally disturbed moments usually occurred either directly after coming off stage, whenever Morrison told me the album had dropped, when I was drunk or all three. One night he came up to my hotel room in Sheffield and something had been going wrong. I was not happy, and I had also consumed a fair amount of Jack Daniels. I told Chris I wasn't happy. I told him how and why I wasn't happy for two and a half hours, repeating the same thing over and over.

When I came down to London a few days later he said to me, 'Listen, Midge, I'm quite happy to listen to your complaints. I only need telling once, though. Now here's the deal. If it is you telling me what all your complaints are, I will sit and listen. If you bring Uncle Jack along, you and Jack can sort it out between you. I will not listen to Jack repeat something thirty times.'

I heeded his advice for a while but, hell, I was a rock star. Rock stars are expected to behave badly and I only drank after shows when I needed to unwind after the high of the performance.

I can't remember ever signing a deal with Chris Morrison. It was all done on a very informal agreement: 'Let's try it for six months and see how it goes.' After 25 years he's still my friend and adviser. Chris is different from many other managers, and he's very easy-going. He sees that artists are artists and if they don't want to do something you can't make them, and that includes people leaving his management company.

He's dedicated to his acts. On the first day of our Canadian tour Chris got very flustered and insisted he had to be there. He flew halfway round the world and got there in time for the opening show in Vancouver – because that is what Phil Lynott would have demanded. We were all set, and the place was sold out. The dressing room was in a narrow corridor right behind the stage. There was a mattress in the dressing room which Chris spotted, so he lay down on it for a minute and announced, 'I'll see you out front in a second, boys.' When we came off two hours later he was fast asleep, having missed the entire show.

It was crazy that we never cracked it in America but because of the technical aspects – our sound checks took five hours – we couldn't open up as a special guest for someone in the big stadiums as I had with Lizzy. The biggest show we ever did in England was at Crystal Palace when we had Madness as our special guests, otherwise we were limited to 3,000-seat theatres – we could sell out five nights at Hammersmith Odeon.

Ultravox never played the bodyguard game. That was a Spandau/Duran Duran thing where they tried to outdo each other. We only ever had a tour manager and a personal assistant who looked after Billy and Warren because they were notoriously bad at getting to sound check. He was their mum because they had to be woken up twenty times in the morning. They'd be hungover and sleeping in the car, and Chris and I would go skiing for the day. We just jumped into a car and drove ourselves to the next gig, having little adventures on the way. Driving up to Scotland, I said, 'Have you ever seen Hadrian's Wall?' So we pulled over and when we found Hadrian's Wall went for a long walk along the ruins. We did that sort of thing all the time.

Then there was 'The Amber Light of Tuscany'! Danny Mitchell and Colin King, the Messengers, who were opening up for Ultravox, travelled with us because they couldn't stand the nannying. Danny opened up the guide book and read out the bumf telling us how every evening the mountain towns were bathed in amber light. That was another diversion we had to make.

I enjoyed Japan, but Billy hated it. It was so high tech it felt like a completely different culture. It was absolutely ideal for Chris, who described it as Tottenham Court Road and the British Museum rolled into one. At the end of our Japanese tour there was a week-long gap before Australia. The other two flew home, but we stayed on to explore. We visited traditional Japanese inns out in the country, went out to a fantastic restaurant and drank too much peppery sake. We bought a couple of flagons and went back to our hotel room, which had paper walls. The next room had some businessmen with three geisha girls singing to them. We slid the doors a little bit, not to watch them, just to listen. We sat there, in our kimonos, completely zonked.

Chris had a very understanding girlfriend, and I didn't have one. When another tour ended in LA we rented a couple of motorbikes – without licences – and drove up the Pacific Coast Highway to William Randolph Hearst's place. We couldn't resist visiting San Simeon, Hearst's grand design. In the 30s and 40s Hearst was the most powerful man in America. He owned newspapers across the country and could make or break careers – he was Orson Welles's model for *Citizen Kane*. He decided to spend some of his fortune building this ludicrous castle on the Pacific Coast. He would send his people out to buy an ancient Italian ceiling and then would build a room around it. Hollywood stars would come and hang out for the weekend. It didn't matter how big a star you were, if Hearst called you tugged your forelock and went out to him. It's now a museum and Chris and I spent an afternoon wandering around taking photographs. When it rained we rented a U-Haul van, put the bikes on the back of it and drove around listening to country music. Death Valley was brilliant and riding a bike through a ghost town felt like we were in a cowboy movie.

I was in permanent overdrive. At the same time I was doing Ultravox I was making records with Visage. I was constantly in the studio, constantly working. I was hot to trot, the in-demand talent at the time, but by the summer of 1981 I was rapidly heading for burnout.

Morrison realised that and freaked; he cancelled four days' studio time and booked me a holiday. Chris Cross came to keep me company and we left for Majorca on the day Charles and Diana got married. It was a terrible place, a tiny hotel in the middle of nowhere where the only other guests were German geriatrics. Within the space of 24 hours we'd found a topless beach and Chris and I were walking around posing as two photographers from the *Sun*. The film never came out because the batteries were flat. Another night we were both paralytic. I was driving and I skidded, nearly killing us both. We were spinning round and round in the car with me howling, 'Fucking hell, I think we're going to die.' Amazingly the car didn't have a scratch.

Billy Currie was the excessive one. He got a bit crazy or so neurotic that at times I thought he was schizophrenic. One moment he was perfectly sensible, then five minutes later he'd become this aggressive monster. Billy's got a great sense of humour, but it could suddenly turn to the dark side. We could hear it in his voice: he'd be happily chatting away and then he'd say, 'You fucking wanker, you cunt.' As soon as we heard 'cunt' we knew he was off and there was trouble brewing. So it was 'See you later, Bill.'

Drugs were all right, and booze was all right, but drugs and booze together were a disaster. Billy was a free spirit, deeply passionate about the band and music, but he was volatile and I never knew which side of him was going to turn up. In the early days his bark was worse than his bite. When we were mixing 'Vienna', Chris Cross and I were giggling in the back of the studio, and Billy jumped up, right in our faces, really antagonistic until I called his bluff. I just said, 'Outside, let's sort this out.' He bottled it and walked away, which was a good thing as I'm a coward at heart.

Billy could never get up in the morning, which drove our tour manager Laurie Small – a placid, unflappable vegetarian – to distraction. One morning in Sweden we had to leave early to catch a plane but Billy wouldn't get up or answer his phone. Laurie was hammering on his door until Billy finally opened up and started to mouth off. Laurie punched him straight in the mouth. We caught the plane and Billy never said another word about it, though he did have a grumble with Morrison.

Billy was prone to getting carried away . . . and getting into trouble. In May 1984, when 'Dancing With Tears In My Eyes' was in the Top Ten, we were touring. After a show at the Southampton Gaumont Billy decided to celebrate by streaking through the lobby of the Post House Hotel, leaping into the pool and shouting obscenities at all and sundry. Something else must have gone down because Billy ended up being chased by the hotel chef brandishing a cleaver, threatening to chop his dick off. He got up to some flaky stuff, our Billy, which he used to tell us about in graphic detail, usually in front of somebody who had nothing to do with the band.

Warren was Canadian and had his own foibles. He always reminded me of Gregory Peck, a real gentleman; he was very quiet and just got on with it. He was like a machine in lots of ways, but one that came to life at night, a truly nocturnal being who turned into Vlad the Impaler after 2 a.m. He'd sit in the studio reading *Guns and Ammo* and other magazines all about the velocity of bullets, studying pin-up pictures of The Weapon of the Month. He kept a little armoury, with Uzi machine guns, Colt 45s and Winchester repeaters out in Los Angeles where it was legal to buy them. He went out into the desert to shoot at targets . . . and gophers. He really wanted to buy a tank.

In Montserrat one day George Martin asked us all, 'What is your ultimate ambition? The one thing you'd like to do before you die.' We all came up with the usual clichés about visiting beautiful places. Warren didn't say anything until everybody else went back to the studio leaving him and Morrison drinking beer at the table. He leaned over and said quietly, 'I got to tell you, Chris, that my real ambition is to off somebody . . . and get away with it.'

My first US tour with Ultravox was pretty basic: the equipment went in a van and we all crammed into a station wagon, taking it in turns driving. The only way to stretch out was to clamber into the boot. For the second tour we went up a bit in the world. *Vienna* had been successful so we had an RV, a mobile home, not huge but big enough that we could play cards at the table or lie down on a bunk. By the time we reached the Everglades we had done so many miles that it broke down.

The Florida law is you can't tow a vehicle with people in it so we were hanging about by the side of the road next to this pool, waiting to be picked up. I found a gun lying in the grass, a real pistol, a snub-nosed Magnum revolver. I picked it up. It was a bit rusty and one of the wooden handles had broken off. Warren saw me brandishing this gun and rushed over. He grabbed it out of my hand, checked the safety was on, pushed out the chamber, checked it was empty and looked down the barrel.

'Should we take it to the police?' I asked, all innocence.

'No,' he said, giving me a look. 'I think we should put it where it was meant to go in the first place.' He chucked it into the water. Obviously a few months earlier some guy had been shot with the gun and the shooter was driving along the road looking for somewhere to dump the weapon. He saw the water coming up ahead, opened the car window and just tossed it out. It had never landed in the water.

Warren had more fiancées than anybody else I've ever met. One night at Hammersmith Odeon he had three turn up backstage. Morrison pushed them each into different rooms and organised it so they didn't bump into each other. It didn't faze Warren at all; he was very cool about the whole thing, never got flustered. We'd turn up at a hotel in Germany and Warren would walk up to reception and ask them, 'Do I have any mail or messages.' He always did, and there'd be letters, notes and phone messages from girls living nearby. Somehow he managed to keep them all going all the time. I guess that is what you can achieve if you stay up all night.

When we opened our tour in Vancouver Warren sent a limo to pick up his family. Backstage after the show he came up with this woman and introduced us. 'Midge, I'd like you to meet my mom.' We shook hands and chatted for a bit. A few days later we were in LA and he came up with a completely different woman, a bit younger this time. 'Midge . . . this is my mom.'

I was speechless for a second then I gulped and went, 'Uh, OK, nice to meet you.' I felt like asking, 'And how long have you been Warren's mom?'

I later found out that he had been brought up by the lady in Vancouver. He thought she was his mother but she turned out to be his grandmother who raised him because his real mother left to live in LA.

I think Warren suffered from narcolepsy, though Paula always claimed he'd been bitten by a tsetse fly. On the *Quartet* tour we sometimes did two shows a night to try to make more money, with a ninety-minute gap between shows. Warren came off stage first and he'd be asleep before the rest of us got into the dressing room.

Being Ultravox, as soon as we got a bit of success we got a bit too fancy for our own good . . . too arty. After *Vienna* we turned up at Conny Plank's studio in Neunkirkin, just outside Cologne, without one idea in our heads. It was a fairly radical task that we set ourselves – live there for three months and write the entire album in the studio. We ended up with a good but incredibly dark album – *Rage In Eden* – with no potential hits anywhere. Not surprising really. Imagine the state of our heads, having lived for three months in the German countryside. In hindsight we could have done it differently and would probably have maintained the level of success that we'd achieved. But we weren't happy doing that at all. We had to go off and experiment.

Conny liked using his own tools, and he didn't like being plugged into another studio;, he had built his own desk with its own character. Although Conny was German, he was not overly serious. When we were recording *Rage In Eden* we used to pray for care packages coming in from the UK, and the office would send us magazines, videos, anything to alleviate the boredom. Conny watched the videos at night with us. He thought the 'don't mention the war' *Fawlty Towers* episode when the Germans came to stay was hysterical. He got all of Chris's humour.

We were so bored that Conny invited us to a party in the local village hall. We thought it would be funny to dress up as British soldiers. We used to go into second-hand army shops all the time so we had the clothes – some half-arsed fashion statement. We were all paralytic, pissed as farts, but we thought it would be hilarious. After we grabbed all the drums off the stage I don't know how we got out of that place alive. Luckily the locals thought we were squaddies.

Chrysalis really didn't know what to do with Ultravox. Groups like Orchestral Manoeuvres in the Dark and Soft Cell were successful, so it was like anything could be a hit. They didn't necessarily want a pop album, but what they did want was *Vienna* parts 2, 3 and 4. Which we didn't want to give them. The French hinted that 'Paris' was a good name for a track and our Japanese record company actually said, 'Can you write a song and call it "Tokyo".' Looking back that was a pretty good idea. Except if Ultravox had done it we'd have chosen some place that not even the Japanese know is in Japan.

We recorded *Vienna* and *Rage In Eden* differently but we were still using the same producer, so the basic sounds were the same – very atmospheric, but not so good in a disco. When we were discussing a producer for our third album we wanted to get a harder sound. We were interested in Chris Thomas, who'd done the Pistols and Roxy Music, and we talked to Chris Hughes, but when George Martin's name came up, all four of us agreed it was off the wall. We hadn't heard anything he'd done for ten years but we were all Beatles fans.

I knew George from the first Prince's Trust rock concert at the Dominion Theatre. When we asked him first he turned it down – primarily because his hearing was going. So we begged him. George was never brought in to give us any commercial edge at all; we thought it was going to be more experimental than it was. We had all read stories about when he was producing the Beatles with him throwing tapes up in the air and cutting them all up. *Quartet* turned out to be a very commercial record.

It was totally different working with George. Conny worked alone; his version of production was engineering, getting good sounds – nothing to do with arrangements. He was strictly technical, and left everything else to the band. With George, when we were trying to take it too far, just waffling around, he stopped us. He was very much a hands-on musical producer and helped a lot with the vocals and harmony structures, especially on 'Hymn'. He spent a lot of time standing round the piano, throwing things out, going, 'If you hit this . . .'

Working with George confirmed all I'd ever heard about him. He is the godfather of modern British production. He broke the mould when it came to producing guitar bands – he introduced them to strings and classical instrumentation – and is brilliant at what he does. He was a cross between my father and my favourite school teacher, a mine of fantastic information and brilliant anecdotes. Just like the rest of the Beatles he started from a very working-class background but he took himself off to sea in the Merchant Navy and came back with a posh accent.

He was the first guy to bring multi-tracked recording systems over from America, which meant we could have stereo music. Until then it was mono, one track bouncing onto another over and over. He gave our other ears something to listen to.

George was a wonderful raconteur. In the seven weeks we spent in his studio in Montserrat he told us some great stories. Like the time John Lennon wanted to be hung upside down by his feet with a microphone put either side of his head, and then spun round so that he could let his head go and sing. When we got into the studio the first thing he said was: 'Geoff, have we got John's Neumann?' John Lennon's microphone was reverently produced.

George never touched the desk. That was a hierarchy thing dating back from his days at EMI. There was George, Geoff Emerick his long-time engineer, and right at the bottom of the pecking order there was the tape operator, Jon Jacobs. George would say, 'I'd like to use the compressor, Geoff.' Geoff would go, 'Good idea, George. Jon, just patch up . . .' and Jon would adjust the machine. It was funny watching the old school at work.

Warren refused to lie out in the sun. He took pills to turn himself brown, but instead he turned orange and looked like a Jaffa. Chris and I really got into sailing Lasers; we'd rush out of the studio and straight down to the beach. We were getting really cocky, flying about the waves, capsizing, the whole bit. One day, after Chris shot out to sea, I had a few problems as the cleats to hold the ropes were broken – everything was broken in Montserrat. I was about fifty feet out into the bay, so I dropped the keel and started pulling the rope in.

When I looked up there was a fin in the water coming straight towards me. I could see the dorsal fin and the tip of the tail, and they were twelve feet apart. I sat there paralysed, bobbing up and down in a Laser, which is notorious for flipping, watching this fin until it disappeared right underneath the boat. There was nothing between me and a giant shark except a few millimetres of fibreglass. I closed my eyes, shivered and waited, then I turned the boat round very carefully and sailed it to the shore. Danny, who ran the water sports on the island, had always told us you couldn't get sharks on that side of the island. That's why there were no cages to keep them out.

When Chris came back he found me sitting on the sand with an ashen face. I only had to say one word: 'Sharks'. That was the end of our Laser sailing.

When we were mixing the album, George, Geoff, Billy, Chris and I worked all day and all night. Warren slept. At eleven the following morning we went in to hear the finished mix. Warren had actually got up so we held off until he came over. At the end Warren paused and announced, 'I'm not sure I'm happy with the drum sound.' There was a moment's silence . . . then he was leaped upon from a great height by everybody in the room. Billy was quite prepared to kill him. 'Warren,' Chris Morrison said, 'if you want to make comments like that, be there at the mix, you cannot come in afterwards.' It was George Martin who smoothed everything over, and his reasoning was spot on – either a record sounds right or it doesn't. Changing the drums would alter the overall mix, so to do that differently we would have to go right back to square one, start at the beginning. Nobody wanted to do that.

After the George Martin album we decided to do it ourselves and recorded *Lament* at my place in Chiswick. It didn't matter to us who hit what or who played, who came up with melodies, as long as it added to the music. There were songs in all our heads and it was very much just walk in and play with the keyboards. Warren didn't really like anybody else messing with the drum machines so it could get a bit boring after he had been playing with them for three days.

There were some really good musical ideas on it, which came about because Chris and I went up to Scotland to write the lyrics. That usually consisted of me coming up with verses and bouncing them off Chris, who'd come up with better alternatives and corrections. We went up to Harris and Lewis where we came across the standing stones of Callanish. They are all fenced off now.

We lived in a huge Winnebago, covered in lights so it looked like *Close Encounters of the Third Kind.* People stood and gawped at it. One Sunday I got told off for filling up the water tank – I'd forgotten about how strictly some of the islanders keep the Sabbath. They don't work on the Sabbath and you certainly can't get a drink until after church. Our days started late and we weren't always that together, because most nights we sat up writing with a bottle of Jack Daniels.

One afternoon we were sitting on a jetty when I spotted a sperm whale. We were whale watching for about an hour and a half before we realised it was a rock. Then we tried our hand at fishing. These dodgy guys – they all looked like Phil Mitchell from *EastEnders* – got out of a huge estate car and came over to chat. 'How are you, lads?' It sounded like they came from Bermondsey. We decided they had done a bank job and were up there hiding.

Later that night we went to the pub and they were in there too, so we chatted away and they turned out to be riggers, cabling the islands. One asked us, 'What do you do?' just as 'Reap the Wild Wind' played on the jukebox.

I said, 'That's what we do, that song is us.'

He said, 'Really? We thought you were a couple of thugs hiding out up here. You obviously couldn't fish as you were sat there chatting to us with your hooks dangling a foot above the water!' From then on they sent postcards from all over the world to the office with messages like 'We're in Oman and just saw you on the telly.'

Even though we involved ourselves in everything we weren't always right. 'One Small Day', the first single from *Lament*, wasn't very successful. We wanted to release 'White China' as the second single in the UK and 'Dancing With Tears In My Eyes' everywhere else. Morrison went to a meeting at Chrysalis and called me up to say that he was worried that there wasn't enough time to do two videos and Chrysalis really wanted to release 'Dancing'.

'You will have a big hit with it,' he said. 'The record company will kill for this because you are holding it back from them.' There was a long silence from my end and then we had what can best be described as a heated discussion. Chris finally said, 'I really believe in this.'

I snapped back, 'Right, well, if it's not successful, I'll have your Porsche!'

'If it's not successful,' he replied, 'I can't afford for you to have my Porsche.'

There was always a bartering involved if Chris tried to change my mind. 'Dancing' went on to hit No. 3, the second-biggest hit of our career.

Another little revolution we made was in putting one new track 'Love's Great Adventure' on *The Collection* and releasing it as a single. It was the first hits collection to cross a million sales. Otherwise it might have only done a couple of hundred thousand. We were the first act to do that. Everybody does it now.

CHAPTER 13
THE LOOK'S THE THING

Even though Billy and I were heavily involved in the Blitz house band – Visage – we weren't New Romantics. We became so only by association. Ultravox never wore the frilly shirts and the headbands like a lot of the New Romantic bands. Spandau wore some really silly stuff – even kilts – while Steve Strange was very camp . . . all make-up and outrage.

In the early 80s Ultravox were fashion statements. We had a definite, distinct look: we were into dead men's clothes; we bought old 1940s double-breasted suits from second-hand shops, wore shirts with a pair of braces. It was a film noir look, based on that mean and moody, mid-European imagery that complemented our music. We never did the ridiculous 'let's go down Kings Road and spend a grand on a Jean Paul Gaultier suit', though a couple of hits down the line I found myself about to pay really silly money for a leather jacket. I confess all – by then I, too, was a fashion victim.

After the *Quartet* album I went for a paramilitary look, combat trousers tucked into army boots, which was fine for photographs and walking about the street but not on stage. I wanted to keep the look, so I bought a pair of Lonsdale boxing boots and dyed them black. I thought they'd be lightweight and good to wear on stage but it looked pretty poncey, as if I was wearing ballet slippers. Warren used to wear some odd things on stage, classic German dark-green felt jackets with piping, and jodhpurs with knee-length boots.

We never sat down and planned what we were going to wear, as we were all individuals. The looks evolved naturally. After the 40s suits I moved into plus fours – actually they were plus eights because they went down to my ankles – a big cocked flat cap and tweeds that veered into pseudo-country gentleman. That was my take on John Wayne in *The Quiet Man*. By the time we got to 'Love's Great Adventure' we were into Katharine Hamnett designer army trousers.

My dodgy-facial-hair period began just before 'Vienna' was released. I was on a train coming back from Glasgow where I had been producing Modern Man – Danny Mitchell's band. I was bored and I had a week's growth, a sure-fire recipe for disaster. I got this Bic disposable razor, cut away the plastic around the edge to leave the blade exposed, then I sculpted this little pixel moustache and the pointy sideburns. Actually that moustache was something we'd tried in Slik when Max had tried to get Jim into a double-breasted suit with hair slicked back and a pencil moustache. It didn't work at all back then.

Everyone thinks my pointy sideburns came from *Star Trek*. Actually I nicked the idea from Glen Matlock, who in turn had nicked it from Ian Dury, who was born with those London barrow-boy sideburns. To be honest I felt a bit of a prat to begin with, but once Ultravox started to happen it became my trademark and was very hard to shave off. People have various periods of my life mixed up, so they've got this mashed-up conglomerate image of what I look like: pointy sideburns, the moustache, the raincoat and ponytail. The ponytail came four years later.

As we travelled around Europe Chris and I were forever looking through fashion magazines – *Uomo*, *French Vogue* and the like. We were directing videos for other artists, including Visage, Fun Boy Three and Bananarama, so we were always on the lookout for ideas. Phil Lynott's trademark was always having his jacket collar up and I wanted to make him look different for 'Yellow Pearl'. In a fashion shoot I saw this picture of a guy in a big long coat wrapping bandages round his hand like he was about to enter a boxing ring. I got Phil to do that.

Long hair was starting to become cool and trendy again when I saw this model with his hair pulled back. At the time my hair was growing longer so I tied it back in a ponytail with Beau Brummell velvet ribbons. That's where the look came from for the 'Love's Great Adventure' video: we were all dressed in white, hacking through the jungle looking like Harrison Ford crossed with the Four Musketeers. Or was it PJ Proby meeting the Scarlet Pimpernel? Having a ponytail then was a very cool thing, though within a year it was considered dreadful.

Ultravox were seen as a guys' band: we wore a bit of make-up but we weren't a bunch of ponces. We had a large male following but we definitely appealed to girls as well. The girls fancied me, so the guys dressed up as me which meant playing concerts could be really unnerving. I'd look out into the audience and see dozens of me. Whatever look I had from a particular photo shoot, there it was: a guy with a flying jacket with his trousers tucked into his big army boots, next to a bloke in a dodgy 'tache and a raincoat. Weird.

Graphics and music were the only things I stood out in at school. I was a frustrated art-school boy. When I joined Ultravox there was this vehicle to let all these ideas out . . . and not be laughed at. Chris and I were the artistic creatives in the band, and we worked hand in hand with Peter Saville, who designed the sleeves. We came up with the concepts and ended up directing the videos, and wrote 90% of the lyrics. We didn't believe that once the record was finished the band should hand all the artwork and the videos across to outsiders. The image was an extension of the music and I believed that I should get involved, learn how everything worked then do it for myself.

Billy and Warren weren't fussed by that side of things. They were bothered about how much they appeared in the video. Warren timed his appearance on 'Love's Great Adventure' and told me that he'd only been on screen for a total of 23 seconds. I didn't really have an answer for that, so to appease him we let him carry a gun.

The graphics on our album and single sleeves were very important. A lot of it was sideways thinking. When we did the first single sleeve for 'Sleepwalk' nobody was interested in the artwork. We wanted to have a particular finish on it but we couldn't afford it because we were still unknown. So we asked them to make the sleeves up inside out so the printing was all on the rough side. People were going, 'Feel that, it's great.' A simple idea, but it didn't take a lot to get it happening.

It was Chris Cross's idea to bring in Peter Saville. He was really impressed by the whole Factory ethos, all the stuff Saville was doing up in Manchester with Joy Division. Saville didn't actually do the 'Vienna' sleeve – a long, oblong, black-and-white photo inside a white background – but when we met up the first thing he said was 'You've nicked my ideas' and showed us the sleeve for Joy Division's *Closer* which was very similar. He wanted to come on board because he saw that to us what was outside the sleeve was as important as what was inside it. The sleeve had to work as a graphic.

The industry was steeped in the tradition that the album cover had to have a picture of the band and the ad that went into the music papers had to say, 'NEW RECORD OUT NOW' inside a starburst. We agreed with Peter's ideas that it was all about telling something, about using the right reference points and subtle imagery to get the message across.

We'd give Peter a brief about the album and the songs and off he'd go. For *Rage In Eden* he found an old 50s cinema poster with a head and a screen where the eyes would be, which he used as inspiration for the album cover. Unfortunately the wife of the original designer saw it in a record shop in France and, believing we'd used elements of her husband's idea, tried to sue us. We changed the sleeve instantly. Luckily, enough got out there so that the head remains the image everyone remembers. Saville changed the sleeve to show horizontal perspective lines going off into the sky with cut-outs of wooden laminates that looked like a face. It was very 50s futuristic, a bit Dali-esque.

We geared him up and he produced these concepts. Peter had great taste, a little flaky sometimes but his standards were every bit as high as ours. The music always came first, but he was notoriously slow and we had to keep the release date of album floating until he finished the sleeve. We learned after the first time and after that we'd always lie to him tell him we needed it for March even though we didn't have a release date until June.

We were mixing *Lament* at Mayfair Studios when I announced I wanted to have a plain black sleeve. Nothing else on it. The image was to be a black square that went into all our advertising with no mention of Ultravox on it. Chris Cross was equally insistent, telling Morrison, 'It'll be like Benson and Hedges . . . you just see the gold block and you know.'

'Yes,' pointed out Morrison, 'but they have spent thirty million pounds and twenty years getting the gold block across. You will have somebody in a record store doing a Saturday job pulling out the sleeve and going, "Who the hell is this?" '

When I saw *This Is Spinal Tap* a year later and they came up with a completely black sleeve I cringed and wanted to vanish under my seat. Morrison does like to remind me of that.

The eventual *Lament* sleeve was matt black with a small picture of the standing stones of Callanish – high-gloss black squares were printed over it with 'Lament' written in the corner. If you didn't catch it in the lights it seemed plain black. The sleeve was gorgeous but hideously expensive – instead of 15p per sleeve it cost over a pound – and they would only do a run of about 10,000. That was important because those sold out quickly and we got a good chart position. When they changed the sleeve it was not the same at all, grey squares instead of shiny black on matt black.

For *U-Vox* we went right over the top – probably trying to make up for the music inside the sleeve. We wanted to have a special label, but in order to get the logo onto the label it had to be printed and then baked. We were told it was impossible – 'You can't bake a label' – but told them to change the boundary again. It looked wonderful and then the Chrysalis art department was harassed by all the other artists saying, 'We want what Ultravox had'. That sleeve was another classic. It was carefully designed with a plastic outer rather than a cardboard sleeve. The inner sleeve had 'U-Vox' in large horizontal-striped lettering like a bar code, while the outer sleeve was also covered in horizontal lines. In the rack it looked like a plain sleeve with no writing, but as you slid the sleeve apart 'U-Vox' was revealed. It was a great idea, except that all the lines had to be horizontal and somebody forgot to tell that to the ladies who packaged the album. They put them all in wrong so it ended up with red-and-silver tartan squares all over the sleeve.

Just before *The Collection* came out I insisted on reading a market survey that Chrysalis had done. They had asked a thousand people about Ultravox and most of them saw us as completely humourless. The photos, the album sleeves, our image, everything was perceived as if we were a bunch of pó-faced technicians who were up our own backsides. It was fascinating reading.

After that I wanted to make fun of our image, which was one of the reasons that the 'Love's Great Adventure' video stopped in the middle. We were out in Kenya in the bush and I suggested: 'What if we stopped the music for a second, held up the whole shoot, took a breather, went "phew", wiped our faces, then shouted, "Let's go!" Run off and the music starts again.' We did that and gave it to *Top of the Pops*. Except they didn't watch it first. It went out live and when the music stopped they were all running about like headless chickens thinking something had broken down. It gave them a heart attack. That video won lots of directing awards.

Chris Cross had got me into photography when we went to Germany to mix *Vienna*. I bought a little 35mm Olympus and started taking photographs to alleviate the boredom. I loved it and had lovely black-and-white prints printed up by photo labs in Cologne. Then I got into video, but back then you couldn't make the videos I wanted to see with a domestic camera. Video always looked electronic and unnatural so we never did that much with it and we lost all the footage we shot at Conny's studio. Which is a shame because it means Chris's David Bellamy impression has been lost to posterity. Conny was remodelling his studio and there was Chris spluttering, 'This is where we are mixing our new album,' standing next to the cement mixer.

Videos were very important to Ultravox. Rather than just have a lovely sleeve, a piece of music and leave the rest up to your head, video carried the whole concept into a new dimension. Whether that is a good thing or a bad thing I still wonder. Once you make a video, that seals the image in the public's head for all time. When I was a kid listening to Bowie's 'Moonage Daydream' I had my own interpretation of the song, a seriously fantastic image of space inside my head, whereas 'Bohemian Rhapsody' will forever be the four heads of Queen repeated over and over again.

Video was both a blessing and a devil. It was a blessing that I could carry on my interpretation of what my song was about, use my imagery. On the first couple of videos we gave Russell key pointers but no storyline ran through it. It annoyed me at the time but he was right, which I learned to my cost later. You don't use a literal storyline because more often than not the punchline comes at the end of the song, at which point the TV company has already faded out the video and it never gets shown.

Most bands making videos had no idea what they were making. They'd be told to turn up at seven for make-up, and then act out someone else's fantasy of what their song was about. Ultravox saw video as the ultimate extension of writing a tune; we created the atmosphere for the lyrics, then the next step was to visualise it. 'Dancing With Tears In My Eyes' was about a nuclear disaster, what you do after the four-minute warning sounds. That's what we filmed, dancing with a girl, pulling the sheet over your head waiting for the end of the world, dust going everywhere. People couldn't understand what we were doing, why we didn't make this fluffy video of us singing and dancing. We carried the original idea to its logical conclusion.

Video wasn't that expensive originally. I don't think we ever spent more than £25,000 – except 'Love's Great Adventure', which cost forty grand as we filmed in Kenya. When Chris and I were directing we didn't charge a fee, which helped the budget. We had a great producer in Lexi Godfrey who wangled great deals. In the early days a lot of the companies who rented cameras, lenses and lights saw the potential and encouraged it. Instead of sitting there with the stuff idle in the warehouse waiting for the next commercial TV show or mini-movie there was this new income. They didn't know what a pop promo was but it rented the equipment for two days.

Ultravox gave me the platform to be creative. After our first mini-movies Russell took off in a big way and every other band wanted to use him. We were scripting and storyboarding all the videos so the natural conclusion was to direct the next one ourselves. Directing was another little box I could live in, something that wasn't just making music. When I went to Polydor in June 1981 and said I wanted to direct the third video for Visage they went, 'OK, we trust you.' There were no questions asked for me to make a £25,000 video. Because I was successful on one platform it was OK to jump over to another. We cut our teeth making that video. Nowadays there'd be no chance; record companies don't trust anybody unless they have a huge track record. It is a complete and utter waste of money if you don't get it right.

In an amateur way we did push the boundaries. We certainly did things, and asked other people to do, very dangerous stunts that make me shiver now. If anyone had died I'd have been sued for every penny and probably still be in prison. The most dangerous was 'Love's Great Adventure'. The script was all Indiana Jones action stuff. The four of us ran off a cliff on hang-gliders, landed down on a plain and carried on running through the jungle. We got four guys from a local hang-gliding club, amateurs not stuntmen, who ran down a hill and took off over some flamingos. I never thought for a second that they didn't run off cliffs every weekend. A couple of the guys actually got as far as the edge, while another half jumped then crashed into the side of the mountain and had to be pulled up by ropes. The crew were tapping me on the shoulder and saying, 'This is a bad idea.' Then this little French guy said, 'I'll do it, I'll just keep running.' Dressed up as me, he ran right over this 2,000-foot cliff, flying out over the plains. It was a fantastic moment. It was also incredibly dangerous, and stupid to even contemplate asking somebody to do that.

Something always happened on our shoots. On 'Passing Strangers' we managed to set fire to an extra's hair. We had painted a tree with petroleum jelly so that it would ignite properly and used a bit too much. In 'Hymn' we had the actor Oliver Tobias (I'd met him when he lived in the flat below Rusty and Steve) in a panic after we fitted him with fluorescent contact lenses. When we finished filming he couldn't get them out – he panicked and we did too. It's hard to explain to someone who is obviously in pain how to get contact lenses out.

For 'The Thin Wall' I got into a car filled with freezing water at four o'clock in the morning. The car was sealed to keep it from leaking and the seats were weighed down with lead weights. It looked dangerous but they did cut a hole in the roof so I could come up for air. When they wrenched the door of the car open I was thrown out along with all the lead weights. I wouldn't do it now but back then I didn't give the risks any thought. We deliberately did two versions of 'Visions In Blue', the one that got shown on *Top of the Pops* and the one that didn't and was shown on late-night telly because it had topless girls in it.

One of my favourite locations to film was the Western Isles in Scotland, though the weather conspired to turn the shoots into Arctic expeditions. We did a recce up in Skye for 'Lament', and we found all these great locations, lots of pretty pictures to cover up a pretty thin storyline that gave us an excuse to each pick a stunning model. My choice was Annabel – but, as you know, that is a different story. We went back a week later to do a two-day shoot. The night we arrived it was beautiful, and we could see the islands in the distance. The next morning the rain was battering down, and it was so foggy we couldn't see two feet in front of us, just grey mist and loads of rain. We tried to shoot that day, but at the end all we had on film was some pebbles and a bit of water. So we shot the whole thing in one day, the ceilidh scene, meeting the girls on various parts of the island.

For 'One Small Day' we went to the Isle of Harris and Lewis to film at the Callanish standing stones. We set up all the equipment, huge stacks of it, drums and keyboards in the middle of the stones, and helicopters for tracking shots, but it was January, and bitterly cold with snow everywhere. The plan was one very long day shoot, but it was so miserable that by four o'clock I called time. We retired to the hotel for a couple of stiff brandies and a chance to defrost our fingers.

Chris and I were asked to do videos for some other acts, which was both a compliment and a challenge. We did Banarama's 'Really Saying Something', which was dreadful, as we only had 24 hours to shoot and edit it, so it had to be shot on video. They had this idea that it should be brightly coloured and cartoony. We edited in Battersea on the night of the Brixton riots and there were cars going up in flames a few miles away. I had my little Porsche and I wasn't driving that near any riot so we edited all night and had it ready in the morning. By the time I got out the riots had calmed down.

We did Banarama's 'Shy Boy', which was much better, and 'Yellow Pearl' for Phil. My favourite was the Truth's 'Stepping In The Right Direction'. We shot it in classic Mod style, drum kit falling off the roof into the camera in slow motion, columns of colour like in 60s movies with the singer right up front, the drummer way in the background. It took me back to watching *Top of the Pops* as a teenager.

'Fade to Grey' has managed to remain both my favourite and the worst video of all time. It was incredibly cheap and groundbreaking at the same time. Godley & Creme did it for £1,500, most of which went to the makeup artists for Steve whose arms were painted like snake-skin. It's the worst because Princess Julia, who mimed the French lines, couldn't speak a word of French and it is blatantly obvious that she is out of sync.

These days when I switch on MTV or any of the other dozen channels showing pop videos I often think that Ultravox helped to create a monster. When we started it was with the seed of an idea and a very small budget. We'd knock something together and because there were no rules it was fairly ground-breaking stuff. Unfortunately the ideas started to burn out very quickly and more money got pumped into promos to cover that lack of imagination.

Twenty years later the only people who can afford to make a decent video are multimillion-selling artists with a budget to match. Other-wise, most videos look dreadful: they are either all full of the latest tricks or a room full of girls gyrating their backsides.

Fortunately the technology – cheap computers and software pro-grams – has turned it around again so anyone with an idea can make a video on a very low budget. It has got back to how it started, which is a lot more exciting than going out and doing a million-pound shoot for a video that might never get shown. I used to think a hell of a lot of money got wasted making music until I entered the film world. The wastage there is simply frightening.

CHAPTER 14
DON'T THEY KNOW IT'S CHRISTMAS?

I missed Michael Buerk's first TV report from Ethiopia on 15 November. I can't remember why, but I was probably tinkering in my studio or getting ready for Ultravox's appearance on *The Tube*. It was our last performance together to promote *The Collection* and then we were going to have a six-month sabbatical. It lasted two years.

After the show I dropped into Paula's dressing room for a natter. She was chatting on the phone to Bob about something domestic. 'Do you know where the front-door key is? I can't find it,' she said, then waved to me. 'Oh, I'm talking to Midge.'

Next thing she handed me the phone. I was chatting away about nothing much when Bob interrupted, 'Did you see that report about the famine in Ethiopia on the telly last night?' I confessed I hadn't. 'It's just horrific.' Bob went on in great detail about how he wanted to do something about it, and ended up saying, 'I want to do something to raise some money for Ethiopia. Will you help?'

'Count me in,' I said, knowing you don't say 'No' to Bob. 'I'll ring you tomorrow when I'm back in London.'

Bob was going to Ireland to visit his family over the weekend so we agreed to meet up on Monday for an early lunch at Langan's Brasserie in Mayfair. Over the weekend I made a point of watching the reports from Ethiopia. They were all over the box so I couldn't miss it. I found it horrific that we should be seeing images like that in this day and age, but I also couldn't escape the feeling that anything I did would be nothing more than an empty gesture.

At Langan's Bob and I talked around a bunch of bizarre schemes, before coming to the obvious conclusion that the only thing we could do was make a record. The quickest option – covering somebody else's song like 'White Christmas' – was out of the question because almost half of the monies earned by a record go to the writer. There we were, two songwriters sitting at the same table arguing over which old chestnut we could cover, when eventually we realised that what we had to do was to write and record a new song and that we only had a few weeks left before Christmas. Initially we calculated that if we came up with something, invited our friends to sing on it and managed to get a hit we could raise a hundred thousand pounds.

Bob might have had the bones of a song in his back pocket, but he was embarrassed to admit it, so he didn't tell me about it. 'We can do something,' I said, 'but who's going to write the song?'

'I thought you might have something lying around.'

'I'm up to my neck. Why don't you write something?'

'I might have a bit of a thing . . . but if you've got something?' This wasn't like Bob: he was sounding a lot less self-confident than usual. Bob was a songwriter, a bloody good one, so why was he being so reticent? He waffled on a bit more, kept telling me, 'Think Lennon. Think "Happy Xmas, War is Over".'

'Fucking hell, Bob –' I had got a bit irritated by this point '– get a grip. You come up with something. I'll come up with something – if I've got a moment. I'm sure we'll be able to cobble a song together.'

By the end of our meeting I was feeling a little bit insecure, too. Not about the music but about what I was getting myself into. I'd never done something like this, had never actively joined a campaign. I was committing to something for the first time in my life. I felt very nervous about it, worried I was getting myself into this way too deep. Once he starts, Bob's very intimidating and he was driving this, dragging me with him. Bob's an educated man whereas I had left school at fifteen. I was concerned that I didn't see the big picture.

What I didn't realise was that it was Bob's confidence that was way down, not mine. When the Rats were in their heyday he'd have written the song himself and harassed all his friends for money. But in 1984 the guys having the hits were Sting, Duran Duran, Paul Young, Spandau . . . and me. Not Bob. His career was in the sewers and the Rats were broke. It's impossible to imagine now, but he was too embarrassed to call up Sting and ask him to help. Sting, being Sting, would have said yes without a moment's hesitation, but at that time Bob didn't believe in himself enough to even pick up the phone.

I was the first person he spoke to and because we were friends he wasn't embarrassed. Of course, I didn't know any of this for years. Artists don't confess weakness and self-doubt to other artists, even if they are mates. As Bob puts it (with added obscenities), I kicked him up the backside when I told him, 'You are a songwriter, just write a song.' I was his backstop, his credibility; once I'd agreed to write with him he could tell people, 'Midge and I are writing the song together.'

As Bob was broke I paid for lunch. The moment we left the restaurant he went into overdrive. He phoned Sting, who said yes, then he left his house in Chelsea and walked up Flood Street to the Kings Road to look in the window of the Pushkin Gallery. He saw Gary Kemp inside, collared him and soon Spandau were primed and ready to go. By now he was a man on a mission. His next stop was to be the Picasso Bar, where quite a few musicians hung out, and there was Simon le Bon walking down the street towards him. He told Simon about the record. 'Midge is writing the song. I've just seen Kemp, they're in. Sting's said yes.' Simon was a bit taken aback as Duran were due to play some dates in Europe, but quickly agreed they would be back for the recording. That night Bob bumped into Martin Kemp at a party. The word was out and soon people were calling Geldof. We had artists but what we didn't have was anything close to a song.

When I got back home I didn't go out to the studio. Instead I sat at the kitchen table with a little Casio keyboard, just messing around, thinking 'Christmas'. I came up with this bell sound, a little third harmony part that made it sound familiar and added a touch of 'Jingle Bells'. I played it really slowly on my little portable keyboard, recorded it and messengered the tape round to Bob.

On Tuesday morning I rang him to get a reaction. 'What do you think? I thought it sounded very jingly and Christmassy.'

'I think it sounds like fucking *Z Cars*. *Z Cars* done on a stylophone,' he said sarcastically. 'That's great, very Christmassy.'

'It is not *Z Cars*,' I snapped back. 'If anything it's "Jingle Bells" mixed with the *Dambusters* theme. Anyway, what have you got?

'I've got some words,' he mumbled. 'Something I tried for the Rats. But –'

I interrupted him. 'Have you got a tape of it?'

'Of course I don't have a fucking tape. I'll come round and play it to you.'

'Get round here, then. I've got the gear and the equipment. You'd better hurry up because I don't have the time.' Then I added sharply, knowing that if I didn't tie Bob down he'd get caught up in a hundred phone calls, 'You need to be here by three.'

He was in Chiswick within the hour. First Bob explained his song was based on 'It's My World', something he'd written for the Rats but they had rejected. 'What are the words?' I asked him.

He read them out starting with 'It's Christmas time, there's no need to be afraid / At Christmas time, we let in light and we banish shade.'

'Not bad, that works.'

'It's a bit fucking corny,' he grumbled. Bob is the opposite to me. He has always been confident with words and he was obviously a bit embarrassed by these lyrics. 'You can change the words, just do what you want, I'm really not sure.'

'Yes, it's corny, but it's an anthem. Anthems are all corny.'

'Yeah, you're right.'

'OK, now play me the tune.'

Bob had brought his guitar, a 12-string which only had seven strings on it. He plays a right-handed guitar left-handed, so all the chords are upside down, which is a really weird thing to watch. Bob's not the best guitar player in the world because he's got no timing at all. You could see that if you watched the Boomtown Rats. When he jumped up in the air he was supposed to hit the floor just as the song finished, but generally he either landed five seconds before it ended, or three seconds after the band finished.

The song was in his head but he couldn't play it. He hadn't worked out the chords yet and had to have the guitar there because that gave him confidence. He started bashing away on those seven out-of-tune strings. I stared at him, half in amazement, half in horror.

'Bob, will you please tune that . . . that thing.'

'No, it's fine, This is just to give you an idea.' He played two verses.

'What the fuck is that? Do it again. Try changing the key. Take it up from A to C.'

We did that for about half an hour. Every time he sang it, it was different – the lines, even the melody were changing constantly. The song was partly formulated in his head, but hadn't been nailed down. The choruses were different lengths, the verses seemed to change, part of it he seemed to make up on the spot. Most of the lyrics were there but it hadn't got a mid-section and there was no anthem for the end.

Eventually I decided to tape him. After I recorded the bones of what he'd got I said, 'OK, let me work with that. I can work out what the chords are, just leave me to come up with the music. I'll do the arrangement.'

Originally Bob had wanted Trevor Horn to produce the record. I agreed with him because Trevor is brilliant, maybe the best producer Britain has ever come up with. When they spoke Trevor told Bob that he needed at least six weeks to record and mix a single, by which time it would be January and we'd have missed the bus: the whole opportunity would be gone. 'Sorry, Bob, I can't do it,' Trevor said eventually, 'but I'll give you a day in my studio.'

Bob turned to me. 'We don't have Trevor Horn. We do have twenty-four hours in SARM West on Sunday. You're the producer.'

It was Tuesday. We had four weeks left before Christmas, but just one week to get this song written, recorded, mixed, pressed and into the shops.

We took on our different roles without further discussion. I had the studio, as Bob wasn't interested in being in the studio. That didn't work for him, it never has – he goes in, sings his song and somebody else works all the faders. I'm the opposite: I'd bought my own faders. It took my engineer Rik Walton and me the next four days to landscape the whole piece, to block out the backing track, to pro-gramme the drums and play the instruments.

Most of the original lyrics were Bob's. I had a bash at changing them, but I couldn't come up with anything better than he already had. My only major alteration was where he originally had 'and there won't be snow in Ethiopia this Christmas'. It just didn't scan at all, no matter which way you looked at it. A rap artist might be able to squeeze five syllables in but singing it just doesn't fit and sounds ungainly. I changed 'Ethiopia' to 'Africa'.

I did a guide vocal on top of a sketchy backing track. The song still wasn't there, and there was a lot missing. We had the two verses, but we didn't have the coda at the end nor the middle eight. The 'Do they know it's Christmas' line was not part of Bob's original lyrics. I don't know which of us came up with that line because by then the song was a true collaboration.

Bob calls it discursive songwriting. It was a discussion, pinging back and forth between us, which was very odd. Both of us have written with other great songwriters but neither of us ever had that John Lennon–Paul McCartney connection. Not before or since. We were just looking at each other, thinking, Where are we going with this? and letting the song take us there.

I was playing the guitar – the chords were very simple, a three-chord structure with a shift – when Bob asked, 'What's the middle eight? It has to be classic pop, a hook riff, easy-to-understand lyrics but with a turnaround at the top.' I kept strumming away and looked at him hopefully.

'What do you do at Christmas?' he said. 'To celebrate.'

'You make a toast . . . you know . . . Cheers. Here's to you, then everyone raises their glasses. So what's our toast?'

'Here's to you. Raise a glass for everyone . . . that's us here in England.' He paused. 'But this toast has to be embittered . . . Here's to them . . . underneath that burning sun.'

'In Africa they won't even know, let alone care, that it's Christmas.'

'They don't know it's Christmas . . .'

Once we had 'Do they know it's Christmas time' we knew that had to be the line that repeated. I did the arrangement and played most of the instruments on it. The song started all dark and moody but it needed to finish big and bright and Christmassy. It wasn't until the third day in my studio that it made linear sense. I'd done the bass and the basic drum pattern, and all of the ominous opening bars on keyboards. To make that haunting beginning I took a drum sample from Tears for Fears' 'The Hurting'.

Bob sat there listening to the clang of doom that began the song and said, 'We need something for the ending, something that we can sing over and over and over. We need some kind of anthem, we've got to get that "Happy Xmas, War is Over", "Give Peace A Chance" chant in at the end.'

By this stage Bob had already convinced Peter Blake, the artist who did the *Sergeant Pepper* album sleeve for the Beatles, to do the cover for the single. He had also drawn up a logo, the globe with Africa highlighted in white, flanked by a knife and fork with a banner saying 'Feed The World' over the top. I have no idea where the final spark came from, either of us, both of us, but we took 'Feed The World' and I fashioned that into a melody.

A few people came to my studio to lay their parts down on the Saturday. Most of the bass was synthesized, though John Taylor from Duran Duran came down to play bass guitar. John is a nice guy, a good character, and although I was never a fan of Duran's music he could certainly play. Paul Weller came down and played some guitar but it didn't fit with the keyboard-heavy backing track I'd already done and we both agreed to leave it off. Paul does take himself far too seriously – I've never seen him smile. Ever. Bob had always thought the Jam were 'shite' and decided I shared his opinion. He didn't like Paul because he was an old-fashioned socialist, which Bob found old hat and deeply irritating. It was mutual, but for this issue they were happy to put aside any petty grievances. This wasn't a political issue any more. It was a moral one.

My answer machine was full of messages. I should have kept them all for history but they got wiped away in the chaos of the moment. 'Hi, it's Sting here, I'm just on my way. Do you turn left after Chiswick roundabout?' He had phoned me from his car, and I was very impressed: 'Wow, he's got a mobile phone, very flash.' Sting sang his harmony parts – 'and there won't be snow in Africa at Christmas time' and 'the bitter sting of tears' – to my guide vocal. But when we changed it, whoever it was that sang the line – Glenn Gregory, Bono or George Michael – Sting's harmony still fitted perfectly. It was electric. Simon Le Bon came and did his line in Chiswick but then redid it at SARM because he wanted to be part of the moment.

While Rik and I laboured on the music this human whirlwind blew in and out of the studio. Bob had been managing the Rats' affairs for a few months from a desk he'd commandeered in the Phonogram press office, so he knew some of the right people to talk to. I just left him to deal with all the business side, the retailers, the legal bits. He was doing all of that stuff, running up massive telephone bills, while I was going, 'We need a good bass line on this part.'

I left getting the artists to Bob – though I did call my mate big Glenn Gregory up in Sheffield and told him, 'Get your backside down here for Sunday morning.' Bob used any phone he could find – usually mine. I'd hear him on the phone in my studio: while I was working on the track at the mixing desk, he was in my other ear shouting at people down the phone.

'I know it's early,' he yelled at Boy George, while I was grappling with a drum sound. 'Get out your scratcher, talk to me, get your arse on the plane, get here on Sunday, you've got to be at the studio.' George was jet-lagged out of his brains and it was five o'clock in the morning in New York. Whatever. To Geldof it didn't matter. He wouldn't let anybody get away with it. He was electric, impassioned, utterly driven by what he believed in.

It only worked because Bob got straight through to people. I don't know how he got their telephone numbers, but he did. He wasn't dealing through managers and agents: he was talking artist to artist. Or rather he was telling his peers what they had to do. If they tried to wriggle out of it Bob had no conscience – he promptly resorted to intimidation and blackmail. 'I'll tell the world that you've fucking turned it down, that you're not doing it because you can't be fucking arsed.'

There was a lot of that going on in the background. He wasn't taking no for an answer. But, even when he got a yes, we still weren't sure who was going to turn up . . . and who wasn't.

It was late on Saturday night before I had finished the backing track, phased all the bells, knitted the programming and the keyboard parts together. On the Sunday morning Bob and I pitched up first. The studio was just off Portobello Road. At eight o'clock in the morning the whole area is usually empty, filthy and damp, suffering from a Saturday night hangover. On this Sunday the world's media were standing outside, TV crews and photographers poking cameras in my face, journalists waving microphones. There was no one else inside the studio. Not a single star in sight.

Bob looked at me. 'If it's only the Boomtown Rats and Ultravox,' he said, 'it's going to be a fucking dull record.'

CHAPTER 15
BAND AID

Of course, they came. In ones and twos and gaggles, no limos, no entourage, no huge security blokes. The record companies didn't pay for anybody; there was no budget to get people there, so they arrived under their own steam. Many of the musicians looked like they had just got of bed, or hadn't even seen one. Paul Young chatted affably to the cameras outside; Weller bounced in as wide awake as the Duracell bunny; Sting strolled up with the Sunday papers under his arm as if he was searching for a nice café to have breakfast in. Bono had flown in from Dublin accompanied by U2's bass player Adam Clayton, who was still half asleep and looking not quite sure why he'd come. Spandau and Duran both turned up after a very heavy night in Germany; they had been on a TV special together, stayed up drinking all night but were still there at ten o'clock in the morning with Duran's Andy Taylor boasting he had drunk his London rivals under the table.

The important thing was to get the top names and faces of the day. And we did, the stars that Bob and I really wanted had all turned up. Within an hour the studio reception was packed with the biggest artists that the UK had to offer in 1984: Paul Young, Spandau Ballet, Wham!, Duran Duran and Bananarama – they were the biggest girl band at the time. Aside from Jody Watley there weren't any other women there, but that wasn't for want of trying. Sade and the Thompson Twins hadn't been able to make it and Eurythmics' Annie Lennox had promised to send us a message for the B-side. Her name was on Peter Blake's cover but the message never arrived in time.

There were a few strange ones: hot American funk band Kool and the Gang, who happened both to be in town and signed to Phonogram, and Francis Rossi and Rick Parfitt from Status Quo. The Quo were a big band at the time with a lot of hits, and if they put their name to a record they had the whole Quo army to back it up. Marilyn turned up, but nobody knew why. I hadn't asked him and neither had Bob. He was there, and that was what mattered.

Culture Club arrived around eleven – without Boy George. Bob went nuts and yelled at Jon Moss, 'Where the fuck's George?'

'I don't know, I haven't seen him for a couple of days. Maybe he never left New York.'

'Where's he staying?'

Bob grabbed the phone and dialled New York, where it was six in the morning. This sleepy voice answered to hear Geldof screaming at him, 'What the fuck are you still doing in New York. Get up and get here.'

George mumbled something along the lines of 'who's there?'

'Every cunt except you,' shouted Bob, reeling off the names. 'Everybody is here . . . except you. There is a Concorde at 9.30, get on it. This is fucking important, so get here.'

I was a bit worried about being able to keep control. In an interview shortly beforehand I had – how should I put it – been less than kind about my new colleagues. I'd slagged off Duran, Spandau, Wham!, Culture Club *and* Paul Weller . . . and now they were all in the room. I shouldn't have given it a moment's thought as everybody in the studio had criticised everybody else the day before yesterday, but instead of acting like a bunch of prima donnas everybody got on really well. Their egos had been well and truly left at home or locked outside the studio door.

The first couple of hours were chaos. We had to get the school photo – the group shot – done by Brian Aris in time for the *Daily Mirror*'s print deadline. The studio seemed to be crawling with TV news crews – apparently there were only four, but I felt as if they outnumbered the musicians.

Whatever emotion I might have shown to the cameras when we played 'Do They Know It's Christmas?' for the first time, underneath was sheer panic. I couldn't get rid of this unnerving feeling that I was flying by the seat of my pants. I was in a room with Britain's biggest artists, nominally in control of making this record, and in my heart of hearts I wasn't even sure it was a good song. Normally when I made a record I believed in a song 100% and anything done on the production was just going to add to it. Starting with something you have mild doubts about and building it up from there is a whole different ball game. Aside from the handful who'd been down to Chiswick, nobody had heard it. It was a brand-new song and they had no idea what they were coming in to sing.

I shouldn't have worried. They were all there because of Bob's commitment, because they had seen the pictures on the television, because they wanted to do something. It could have been a really crap nursery rhyme but nobody cared: the day wasn't about musical snobbery, it was about being there to do something that needed doing . . . though I do think everybody was relieved the song wasn't too bad.

To keep everybody occupied we recorded the chorus first. Everyone was herded into the studio and lined up with copies of the lyrics. First 'Feed the world' then 'Let them know it's Christmas time again'. Everybody sang it over and over again, then I double-tracked it so it sounded as if there were thousands of voices singing. Then it was time to start on the verses and to record the individual lines.

That was the hard part, trying to decide who was singing what, where the edits were going to be, where one person took over halfway through a line from another. There weren't enough lines in the song to dedicate a line to each of the featured vocalists. It wasn't like a linear mathematical process, so Bob and I were sitting there with little bits of paper, graphs, working out who was going to do what, and with people turning up all the time we had to keep changing the order. Initially I got each person to sing two or three lines which I'd edit later. Start the line with one artist and finish it with another, because to begin with I had no idea how to chop this thing up. Bob and I only sang in the chorus – there was never any question of either of us taking a line. It was more important that we left them for bigger artists. Although I wasn't too sure, Bob never doubted Boy George would get there, so we kept a couple of lines back for him.

Nobody was keen to volunteer to be the first guy up to sing. I had sung in my own little studio where I didn't have the eyes of the pop world following me. Eventually I asked Tony Hadley and he stepped up first. It was a brave thing to stand up there in the firing line, with every nose pressed against the control-room window, staring at him. He did very well, so well in fact that everybody clapped. That broke the ice. Paul Young has got more of the song than anybody else because he was a huge star at the time and because Bowie couldn't make it. He opens up with the first two lines – 'It's Christmas time . . .' – and he comes in again in the middle. Paul nailed it very quickly.

When Bono came to sing he was really concerned about the meaning of his line: 'Well tonight, thank God it's them instead of you.' At the time U2 were a middling successful band, certainly not superstars, but he was not scared to query Bob. 'Why,' he said, 'would I want somebody else to go through this?'

Bob was a real stickler for his words and what they meant and he had a very different angle on what that line meant. He told Bono, 'I'm not saying I want somebody else to suffer, I'm saying I'm glad it's not you.'

I had sung the guide vocal on the demo so everyone could hear the melody. Until Bono the singers had listened to my guide, put on the headphones and sung it parrot-fashion. I'd sung his line an octave lower but Bono decided to change it. He sang 'Thank God . . .' and just leaped an octave, and this huge voice erupted out of this little guy. I was standing next to Bono and I jumped. It felt as if I was standing next to an opera singer, he had the same massive power. That was it, one take. He just ripped it.

There was no one who went up to the mike and had one of those *Pop Idol* moments, where they think they can do it but they can't and everybody around cringes and fails to make eye contact. The singers were all big artists in their own right; they had all been there, done it, established themselves. Simon le Bon had already done his lines but, caught up in the moment, insisted on re-recording them. They were better second time around.

Boy George arrived in the late afternoon. He waltzed in, fresh off Concorde, and went straight into the studio. Before he opened his mouth to sing he had a request. 'Can somebody get me some brandy?'

'No,' I said. George looked surprised. Nobody said no to George. 'You'll have to get it yourself . . . and you can't. There isn't time.'

'Get on with it, you fucking old queen,' shouted Bob helpfully from the back of the studio.

'Ooh shut up, you Irish tart,' retorted George. He sang his lines perfectly then swanned out into the studio to spread mayhem and gossip.

Phil Collins arrived with his whole drum kit. 'It will take me half an hour to set up while you go and get a sandwich,' he insisted. 'You have got to have some real drums on the record. I'll do fills between the electronics.' Bob always claims I was really annoyed about having to record Phil. Certainly I was worried that I'd run out of time, and recording drums can take forever. It was inconvenient so I *was* a bit pissed off . . . but hell, this was Phil Collins. I couldn't say no. He was another huge superstar.

Phil soon had his kit all set up with the high, overly compressed mikes behind the drums to give it his trademark big, ambient, drum sound. He did his sound check, said, 'Let me know when you want me,' then sat at the back of the room and waited. He was in the middle of one of his solo albums and Sunday was his one day off. He didn't have to be there but he sat there nice as pie waiting for his turn. As he knew more about producing records than Bob he understood the process he had to go through. If I'd said, 'Phil, we don't have the time,' he'd have gone, 'Fine', packed up and left because that is the kind of character he is.

After sitting around for six hours, he got the nod. Phil went out and played the first run-through brilliantly. He came back into the control room and listened to it once. To my ears there was nothing wrong with it but Phil wasn't happy. 'No,' he said, 'I've overplayed. I need one more take.' He went back out and played it again, but simpler. That was it, two takes, job done in eight minutes. Then he went home. To have someone of the stature of Phil Collins sit there like a session player, waiting to be told when his chance was, happy to do a few mock run-throughs for the cameras, set a fantastic example. It was the same with Sting: he went home thinking he'd finished but when the film crew wanted to reshoot him he drove straight back bringing his girlfriend, Trude, and their baby.

As the day went on I got more and more stressed. I had to eject Trevor Horn from his own studio and I told Bob to fuck off. Several times.

Trevor had turned up to see what was going on and got caught up in the atmosphere of it all. He suggested doing a madrigal, 'Feed the world . . . feed the world' sung as a delayed, overlayered round, like the French kids' song 'Frere Jacques'. Soon he had Bono, Paul Young and everyone available in the studio trying to do this idea Trevor heard in his head, but we couldn't get it to work – certainly not in the time available. As it was we spent an hour of the time he gave us, of my precious time, faffing about on an idea that went nowhere. It was a vocal mess. Eventually I had to pull the plug. 'Trevor, you're the man, but no, it's not going anywhere, let's stop now, we have to leave it. We are running out of time.'

Bob says I bollocked him all day so that by the end he didn't dare go in the control room. I should have started earlier. Standing in the recording room with your headphones on you are always very vulnerable . . . it's magnified a thousand times when you've got thirty of the UK's biggest artists all watching you. I knew the singers were feeling intimidated, like rabbits in headlights, standing there behind the microphone, with all of their peers sitting the other side looking through the aquarium window, watching them squirm. Can he do it or not? Let's hear how good he really is? Those were the thoughts going on inside my head and I knew I was not alone.

There's a point on the video where I'm sitting at the desk. It's obvious I know how the stuff works, and Bob equally obviously doesn't. Fortunately you can't hear what I was saying to Bob. Prior to recording a line I pressed the talkback button on the desk so I could talk the vocalist through the song, sing him the melody, then cue him on the line. Just as Paul Young was getting ready to sing Bob leaned across me, pressed the intercom button, said, 'This is what you have to do,' and sang a completely different melody. I started off trying to be very delicate but eventually I snapped at him, 'For fuck's sake, Bob, that isn't even the tune. You're confusing people. Just leave them alone, stop!'

He didn't. George Michael, Simon le Bon, Glenn Gregory, no matter who, he kept doing it. They were up there on the mike with Bob giving them his off-key Bob Dylan version. That was not the melody: I'd done the melody, the melody was playing on the damn tape. But the TV cameras were pointing at Paul and I could see he was thinking, I don't know what I'm supposed to be singing. This doesn't sound right . . . but Bob's the man.

Finally I lost my rag and screamed, 'Listen to me, Bob. We've got twenty-four hours to finish this, we've used up ten of them so far. What we don't need is someone who can't really sing, pressing the intercom button and singing a different melody to somebody who can. Because they're just getting confused. Bob, one singer, one song . . . now back off.'

He sat down and didn't touch the button any more. Soon he was off talking to people, or he was back on the phone . . . in my control room. It's funny now, but at the time I could see it all crumbling. Bob telling them how to sing was potentially a major disaster. It was too confusing: there were too many inputs, too many cooks.

Bob also came up with the brilliant idea that the mid-section should be done using those trademark Status Quo harmonies. I had Francis Rossi and Rick Parfitt on the mike for an hour. Francis sang his bit fine but we watched Rick squawk trying to hit the high notes. Finally I despaired and told them, 'That's great, thanks,' knowing we were not going to use any of it, that maybe I could get someone else to do it. I was organising the next line-up when Rossi came up and whispered in my ear, 'Next time you want us to do a harmony part, ask who does the harmony. Live Rick may sing along, but in the studio I do all the vocals.' He'd let Parfitt try and do the high part, because Geldof thought that was a great idea, and they didn't dare tell him it would never work.

The atmosphere was wonderful, maybe because it was all artists. Only Quo and Spandau had managers there and they were part of the party. The TV crews had gone leaving only Brian Aris and one *Mirror* journalist. We didn't have any catering – though the studio did rustle up some curry and chips – or any gofers to go out and get food. The party line was: 'You want a sandwich? There's an Indian shop around the corner. Go and buy your own.'

Stuck in the control room I missed a lot of the fun. On one break I did get to chat with Paula, play with Fifi and snatch a few words with Annabel, and I saw odd sights like Bananarama engrossed in conversation with Bono, or Weller arguing with Marilyn and Jon Moss. On another day he wouldn't have given either of them the time of day.

Nigel Planer turned up dressed as Neil from *The Young Ones* carrying his guitar. He stumbled about determined to add his bit to the record. It was great for the TV cameras, and for me as well because it meant I switched off for fifteen minutes, laughing as I watched this guy doing stupid silly stuff. That single moment, when an actor turned up pretending to be a hippy musician, was the spark that led towards Comic Relief. Eventually he was told firmly where to go, ejected and sent on his miserable way.

The hardest part was not getting people there but getting them to leave. By the evening everybody was in party mood. Guys were popping down the offy to buy a few drinks – George got his brandy eventually – and they were having a ball. Status Quo locked Duran Duran in the toilet. They were all celebrating: they'd done their job. Meanwhile I was trying to get into mix mode. I tried to kick them out, but they wouldn't leave. It was coming on midnight before we managed to chuck everybody out.

Mixing a record can be a long process, something best not done under pressure. Because it was a vinyl single we had to produce a B-side as well. I took the backing track and the 'Feed the world' chorus and overlaid Christmas messages from the stars. Throughout the day we had recorded messages in the studio, though not everybody understood what was going on. Steve Norman, Spandau's sax player and percussionist, made a telling contribution as he obviously thought it was for a radio station ID. 'Steve from Spandau Ballet here,' he said. 'I'd like to say hi to all our friends in Ethiopia. Sorry we can't make it down there, but maybe we'll get to tour there next year!' We didn't use that one.

Bob phoned Holly Johnson, who was in Detroit touring with Frankie Goes to Hollywood, and taped his message over the phone. Holly kept saying, 'I can't get the last line, Bob.' We used that twice. There were messages from Paul McCartney, Big Country and David

Bowie. We had been hoping that Bowie would make the recording but his message was spot on. 'It's Christmas 1984 and there are more starving folk on the planet than ever before . . .'

At three in the morning I was busy mixing when Robert Maxwell, the owner of the *Daily Mirror*, called. Originally Maxwell hadn't wanted to give us the front page of the *Mirror*, but he had put the picture of Bob with Sting, George Michael and Simon le Bon under the headline 'BILLION DOLLAR BAND' on it. Now he wanted exclusive rights to use the Band Aid photograph for a poster. Bob started effing and blinding down the phone, then he started screaming at one of the most powerful newspaper magnates in the world, yelling at him as if he was some roadie who hadn't plugged his guitar in properly.

Bob shouted, 'Fuck off, either the poster money goes to us or we'll pull it, take it to the *Sun*.'

I was trying to balance the mix through the stream of abuse. 'Bob,' I yelled during a lull in the tirade, 'shut up, will you. I'm trying to listen and you are driving me nuts.' Eventually they settled on splitting the poster profits fifty–fifty. I was just glad I had some peace and quiet to finish off the record.

The record had to be finished by eight o'clock, Monday morning, to deliver to the pressing plant who had promised to deliver finished records within four days. The sleeve was already being printed. By 6 a.m. Bob was bored and took to yelling at me, 'Finish, finish.' I was too tired to shout back, so Rik and I just kept on going.

The very last thing we did before we signed off was record Bob saying, 'This record was recorded on the 25th of November 1984. It is now eight a.m. on the 26th. We've been here twenty-four hours and I think it's time we went home.'

I might have finished the record, but the Band Aid story had only just begun.

CHAPTER 16
IN ETHIOPIA

All day I felt I was suffocating, as if every breath I took was first sucked through a giant pillow; my throat was parched dry. It was baking hot but not the humid heat of a beach holiday. In Ethiopia the ground was completely devoid of liquid, a dust bowl where the sun had sucked up every last drop of moisture and drunk it dry. The earth was that distinctive orange-red colour, dry and dusty. Passing trucks kicked up the fine dust particles which drifted through the air like a swarm of desiccated insects until they settled on people, covering their bodies like a shroud.

I'd seen the pictures but the reality of the aid camp was very different from television. None of us can imagine the stench of famine and the taste of death until we have been there. I could smell the fear. It was probably mine. I was petrified. The whole experience was hideous, because of my fear.

I only went to Ethiopia that one time, for one day, 9 March 1985. It was the very first Band Aid shipment and for some reason Bob couldn't go. If Bob couldn't go; I had to go. In the West the famine was already old news. The politics of 'If you don't go, the cameras don't go' defied all logic. 'What do you mean? Is it boring now?' There were millions of people dying but the TV companies would not go any further unless I, some minor pop figure, led them. I had to play the game: if I didn't go the cameras didn't go, if the cameras didn't go more people died.

It was a full plane load, ten tons of high-protein biscuits, Land Rovers, water tanks, one and half tons of hospital tents, twenty tons of milk, one ton of medical supplies and a ton of SMA Gold Top milk. Enough to fill up a Nigerian Airlines 707 cargo plane, but hardly enough to dent the problem. The transporter plane was a normal jet except it had no seats and no windows, so I sat amongst the boxes and the cartons full of equipment for the eight hours it took to fly from Gatwick to Addis Ababa.

I was given leftover beans to eat – excess from flights that had already taken off. About six hours into the flight my stomach cramped and the further south we flew the worse I felt. Just before the plane landed I discovered that the British ambassador and the film crew were waiting to meet us. I rushed into the aeroplane toilet and heaved my head off, threw up everything everywhere. I washed my face and my mouth, cleaned my teeth as best I could, then I walked down the stairs, said hello to the ambassador, pretended to oversee all this stuff being unloaded and posed for the telly dressed in my smart Indiana Jones African safari kit.

The moment I stepped off this transporter plane was the moment I realised none of it made any sense. I was driven to the Hilton Hotel in Addis Ababa to freshen up. Addis was like any major cosmopolitan city, except being a communist country there were statues and posters of black men with their fists in the air, waving red flags, working in the fields, acting out the whole dignity-of-labour thing. It could have been Stalinist Russia except for the colour of their skin. I stood there in my air-conditioned hotel room, preparing myself for the horrors I'd seen on television, but what I actually saw was a swimming pool surrounded by people drinking Vodka cocktails and sunbathing, a holiday resort with its own burger bar.

I wasn't expecting that normality. I could have been visiting Riga or Krakow oblivious to the fact that half an hour's drive away the concentration camps were busy in full vile flow. The inhabitants of Addis seemed to not give a shit about what was happening to those living outside the city. Hopping so quickly between two different worlds was absolutely bizarre. Half an hour later – that was like driving from my home in Chiswick to central London – I was sitting at the entrance to an aid camp. The road started off Tarmac and got increasingly bumpy the further we drove from Addis before becoming a track. We drove through a gate into a fenced-off area. The fence was over ten feet high, topped with barbed wire. The barbed wire was to keep people out. The camp was a haven for 6,000 people. If there were 10,000 people in the camp it wouldn't, couldn't, work.

From the moment I got off the plane I had felt a complete prune wearing my army fatigue trousers, and a safari shirt with pockets and lapels – that's what tourists wear in Africa. By now I was saturated by layers of blood-orange dust. When I got out of the Land Rover dozens of kids, as orange as they were black, ran up to me. I was the new face, a novelty, that day's sport and I had a film crew with me. Kids don't need a lot of teaching when they see a film crew, they go 'hey, hey' and jump up and down, anything to be on the camera, the focus of attention.

Once I reached the camp, like it or not, I was involved. The kids were running round me, holding my hands and it was like being in the nursery or visiting school. They were all hanging on to me. I didn't want to see stuff that I'd seen on television. I was dreading seeing a mother nursing her dying baby, watching bodies wrapped in cloth, with their big wide-open eyes surrounded by wailing mothers. Who needs to see such things? I certainly didn't. But I had to be there because, if the cameras weren't there, the whole thing would go on and on and nothing would change.

It wasn't as bad as I had imagined, as I was in a good camp. Families were being fed: they were being given some sustenance, so the camp wasn't full of the pot-bellied, emaciated, big-ribbed, big-eyed, hollow-cheeked kids who haunted the TV screens. That day three people died, three out of six thousand, so it was a good day. We see the TV and we don't see the really bad bits. We don't taste it; it's not there rattling at the bottom of our lungs; it's not in our nose, stinging our eyes. We get the cold, arms'-length version filtered through the screen. For most people that is disturbing enough.

I was expecting everybody to be dressed in nice bright Masai colours rather than old T-shirts, grubby shorts and faded wraps, but this wasn't a travel programme it was an aid camp. What did strike me was how very beautiful the people were. Both girls and boys had these amazing faces with great bone structure. All the kids who weren't emaciated looked fantastic with their huge chocolate eyes framed by wonderful cheekbones, sparkling white teeth in permanent smiles. They laughed all the time, though I did wonder what they had to laugh about.

I walked around accompanied by the kids, who were very much alive, knowing that in a tent over there were three dead bodies, knowing the kids were surviving on a tenth of my daily food intake, a bowl of rice, whatever was available, barely enough to keep themselves alive. The kids stuck their hands out demanding I give them something. I had some chocolate in my bag but I couldn't break it out – how could I give twenty kids a slither of chocolate each.

There was one face among the six thousand that I cannot ever forget, a boy of about sixteen or seventeen. He spoke really good English, and he was on a different intellectual level from everyone else, educated, but floundering in this sea of displaced humanity. He explained to me that he shouldn't be there, how he was a Grade A student about to start at university but he'd got this illness that made him slow. He pleaded with me to get him out of there. I couldn't do that; I couldn't get him out of the camp, make him any different from anybody else. But here was this kid saying, 'I've got a brain, I can communicate.' He could help: he could speak to his own people . . . but there was nothing I could do about helping him.

It didn't make much sense to me then, even less now. The whole thing was a complete mess. Nobody asked to be there, and nobody should have been there. It was a frustrating, bizarre feeling. I hadn't wanted to go but there I was and someone was communicating with me directly, face to face, begging me with his words and his eyes. He believed I could be his lifeline back to normality and I knew there was nothing I could do. That was as bad as knowing that three kids had died that day.

The aid workers who deal with that for years are seriously special, they have to steel themselves against the horrors they see every day. There was an Irish priest who was brilliant. After we had spent a few hours at the camp we drove back as dusk fell. I don't remember the drive back into town, just the spectacular sunset, blood-red amongst the dust, and thinking, What a beautiful country this could be.

In Addis the priest took us to dinner before the flight home. Thank God they didn't ask us to eat in the camp: that would have felt obscene. Going to a restaurant didn't equate with my Western upbringing. Naïvely I thought if there was no food in the camp there should be no food all across the country. Of course, it doesn't work like that – there are always those who have and those who haven't.

The film crew and I all came up with a litany of excuses to avoid food: 'We can't go to dinner . . . we're not hungry.' The priest told us firmly as we sat and played about with this Ethiopian dish you scoop out of a bowl and wrap in flat bread, 'No, you have to eat. If you don't survive, nobody can help.' He got angry with us, because to him it was a waste of food while because we were only there for a few hours we didn't feel we should have any food. He had been there for months, for years, doing this on a daily basis, dealing with the families of the dead, seeing children die in front of his eyes. In order to help he had to be in a fit state to do it; he knew he had to eat while to me all I could taste was ashes. He was a religious man trying to justify how this could be a greater being's decision, that this child should die at this time. That's a choice I don't ever want to have to make.

I was in Ethiopia for all of fourteen hours. After not eating dinner we got back on the plane for Gatwick. I didn't sleep on the way back, nobody did: how could we after such a bizarre experience. We arrived back at Gatwick at some hideously early time in the morning and had to hang about in the lounge for hours because we couldn't get through customs.

Bono made his own trips to Africa later. Nobody knew about them because he wanted to see what it was all about for himself. I wish I could have had the courage to go there and confront it all again, but I couldn't. It's a basic element in my make-up – it probably comes from my dad – I'd rather hide my head in the sand than confront the horror, or my fear of the unknown. I'm still very surprised that I ever got involved in Band Aid. I'm the kind of guy who says, 'Sorry, Bob, I'm busy on Thursday,' rather than get wrapped up in something that I didn't feel comfortable with. I probably said yes because it was Bob, and got involved because I was embarrassed not to.

I know it sounds selfish, but once Band Aid and Live Aid had calmed down and weren't on the news every day, I was so pleased that I'd actually seen it through and not walked away from such an emotionally draining experience. To this day, when people talk about it I can hold my hand up. I'm happy to have ridden the roller coaster of Band Aid, because it was an amazing experience. Yet there is still this part of me that thinks I just hung on for the ride. In the end I was there and I did my job. I had a task to fulfil, and I fulfilled it. I think I did it well. If I had walked away from it, then, yes, I would have let everyone down including myself.

When I came back home I made a decision not to go back out to Africa. Why would I? You stick your neck in a guillotine, have your head chopped off, you don't do it a second time. It was horrific, it was horrible, and I knew I hadn't seen the worst of it. I probably did more by not going there. I saw the job through and I'm still doing so. It may not be as much work as it used to be, but I'm still there.

I'm one of the Band Aid trustees and my job is to oversee how the money is spent. There is no creative role in it at all except for the odd suggestions. I am hoping that the archive will be sent to the Rock and Roll Hall of Fame in Cleveland. I was doing one of my acoustic shows and I went to see them and have a look round. They were about to do a punk display with the original Sex Pistols posters and they were really keen on displaying as much of the Band Aid/Live Aid stuff as they could get their hands on. The archive comprises two handmade bass guitars used in the video that were donated by the manufacturers, lyrics and a whole pile of art, posters and general memorabilia. The plan is to auction it all at some point in the future.

Recently I have decided I'd like to go out to Africa again if I could see a difference Band Aid actually made. I have always imagined from what little I saw of Ethiopia that it is fabulously beautiful and I'd like to taste its flavour, learn how it smells without the stench of famine and death and to see the sun set there again.

But unfortunately Ethiopia won't go away. Nor will famine. It never has and it never will. I've tried to explain what it was like to my kids but, when I tell them the story, they say, 'Why didn't they go to the shop and buy some food?' I tell them that there were no shops, there was no money and there was no food. No nothing. The crops had failed, the rains didn't come, the crops failed again. There was no food and when there is no food people die. It is beyond their comprehension.

'Do They Know It's Christmas?' stands apart from the rest of my career. It was both a purely selfless act and the most cold, calculated thing I've ever done in my life. It is a song that has nothing to do with music. It was all about generating money – get the artists there, make this event happen, get the cameras there, it will sell. That was the mantra. The names were much more important than the song. The song didn't matter: the song was secondary, almost irrelevant.

Yet over the past twenty years that song has earned some seventy million pounds. Neither Bob nor I have seen a penny of it. It doesn't earn as much as it did, as we haven't actively tried to generate money for the past fifteen years, but because it's a Christmas record it will be stuck on compilation albums from here to eternity. Every single time it is played on the radio it earns money. It's always going to earn money.

Bob believes that since 1984 Africa has never been less than second on the international aid agenda. He gets consulted by Tony Blair and sits on steering committees with a view to trying to sort out the mess in Africa. Without that phone call to *The Tube* one dark November Friday it wouldn't have happened. Our record put Africa on the world agenda.

That's Bob's gig, because he gets the big picture. For me it's always been much more personal. I know that our song saved lives. How many songwriters can say that?

Above left My dad and his brother George in Glasgow in the late 40s – very Ultravox!

Above right Me with my elder brother Bobby

Left Me and Bobby with my gran – Scottish through and through

Below Me, Linda and Bobby. I'm holding my first guitar, bought for £3.00

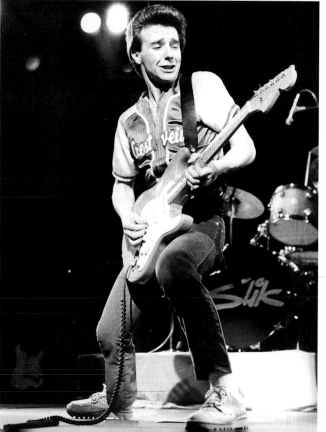

Above Salvation – very cool

Left Performing with Sl⃨k in 1976

ove   Slik – one of the few bands that played live!

ow left   23 March 1978

ow right   The Rich Kids – from left to right, Glen Matlock, me and Steve New

Right The Rich Kids on tour with the Slits

Below With Phil Lynott at Phil's house in Camberwell

Right Make my day!

Right Outside my parents'
house in Buckingham
Drive, with the Christmas
present I bought them

Below The video shoot for
'Reap the Wild Wind'

ht and below Doing
e real work for a
nge in Ethiopia

Left Portrait taken by the classic Hollywood studio photographer George Hurrell

Below My wedding to Sheri

CHAPTER 17
TRYING TO FEED THE WORLD

After we finished the session I went home exhausted, where I listened to Bob introduce Band Aid on Simon Bates's Radio One breakfast show. He was truly eloquent, explaining, 'This is the most important record ever made, the most important moment in British pop history.' As the last 'Feed the world' died away, Bates was left speechless. Bob leaped in again with the sales pitch.

'Virtually one hundred per cent of the money from this record, apart from the VAT, goes straight to Band Aid. I swear every penny will get to Ethiopia. I want everyone listening to buy it. We've only got three weeks. Let's make it the biggest-selling record of all time. Paul McCartney's "Mull Of Kintyre" sold about two and half million and that's the biggest so far. But there's fifty-six million people in this country. So we can easily beat that. Even if you've never bought a record in your life before, get it. It's only £1.30. That's how cheap it is to give someone the ultimate Christmas gift – their life. It's pathetic, but the price of a life this year is a piece of plastic with a hole in the middle.'

I went to bed and grabbed a couple of hours' sleep, and when I woke up everything had gone ballistic. The *Mirror* was out on the streets; the TV reports were being repeated every ten minutes; the record had been played on Radio One again and again. Everyone knew about it. We knew it would be big, but not how big.

At that point the industry hadn't absolutely and definitely agreed to waive their cut. The single was still going to be sold; the record company and the retailers would take their profits, and the pressing plant would recoup their costs. None of that stuff had been properly resolved. It wasn't until it was huge news that everyone fell into line: that's when the industry announced it would not take its profits; the retailers followed suit and the pound the record cost went straight to Africa. The disc we would have been happy to have sold 100,000 of sold three million copies in three weeks.

Radio One started playing it on the hour, which is unheard of, a record on the A list got six or seven plays a day. This was getting 24 plays a day. It rapidly turned into a game with DJs asking who was singing which line? 'Who opens it? Paul Young, right who sings the next line?' So people would hear it on the radio, turn it up and go, 'It's Bono! Right, I've got that bit, that's Sting in the background . . .'

After the video was shot and edited together, David Bowie presented the film on BBC1, five minutes before *Top of the Pops*. The rules that governed *Top of the Pops* at the time wouldn't let them show the song, as it wasn't a hit. Bob was livid. He went straight to the top, phoned Michael Grade, the controller of BBC1, and waited in the lobby until he had seen the video. To make room Grade shifted every programme on that Thursday night back five minutes.

On the Tuesday night Bob, Chris Morrison and I had invited Bowie to dinner at the Belfrey, an exclusive dining club in Belgravia, to discuss Band Aid. We were all sat at the table really early, fidgeting nervously, waiting for Bowie and his assistant, Coco Schwab, to arrive. 'Mr Bowie,' the maitre d' announced, 'is in the building.' At which we all jumped to our feet like naughty schoolboys spotting the headmaster in the distance. Bowie was over from Switzerland to do his Christmas shopping, and he had grown a little goatee beard so he could disappear into the crowds. (Not that Bowie ever could disappear into a crowd.) He was very open to presenting the video, because he thought the whole project was fantastic, but he was miffed because if he went on television he'd have to shave off his goatee. We had a great evening, though Morrison was so overwhelmed he didn't open his mouth. Bob made up for his silence. When the bill arrived I didn't see Bob's hand twitch, let alone move, for his credit card, so I picked up the tab. But I knew Bob was still broke and all his friends joke that he's always been slow to buy a round!

We couldn't have had a better launch – an advert on the BBC was unheard of. There was David Bowie virtually giving a party political broadcast. He sold the whole Band Aid concept in five minutes: 'Pay a pound, you get a record, they get the pound.'

The only thing that never fell into place was the VAT. The government couldn't be seen to let us off, and Mrs Thatcher insisted on taking VAT from the record. We fought it, took it all the way down the line but they took their VAT . . . and then miraculously donated the exact same amount back to Band Aid.

After recording Band Aid my life changed again. Bob and I were responsible for it, and we'd created it, but it wasn't our record. The usual accolades that come with a hit record weren't there; it wasn't like 'Vienna', and we were recognised in a completely different way.

Band Aid was all over the media: it was not just a bit of pop music, but something else, something real and tangible.

However, on the minus side Bob and I were responsible for an avalanche of the world's worst charity records. For which, we both apologise. A flood of tripe descended on the world's radio stations and they had to play it. The Norwegian one, the French one, the Canadian song, USA for Africa ... need I go on? Everyone had to make one of these records and they were dire to a man. In that genre of record Band Aid was the first and the best.

'Do They Know It's Christmas?' eventually sold nearly four million copies in Britain and another eight million round the world. It sold a million in the USA but because of their bizarre chart system never got into the Top Ten – despite outselling the official Number One four-to-one. America still likes to believe that 'We Are The World' came first, even though it wasn't written and recorded until two months after Band Aid and not released until March. That's how America sees itself: the centre of the world. If you watch the six o'clock news in America, reports about anything happening outside the US borders last 35 seconds, if you're lucky. Everything that happens inside America is important and what happens outside – the outbreak of World War Three or half the planet's fallen off – that comes later.

As with Band Aid, the USA For Africa recording session would never have happened at all but for two people – in their case Ken Kragen, Lionel Richie's manager, and Harry Belafonte. Harry had seen Bob on TV in New York talking about the famine and what we'd done in the UK. He told the press that he was 'ashamed and embarrassed at seeing a bunch of white English kids doing what black Americans ought to have been doing'. He called Kragen and the pair of them set about setting up the recording session. They invited Bob, who was the public face of Band Aid in America.

'We Are The World' was written by Lionel Richie and Michael Jackson in two hours – which made Lionel me to Bob's Michael Jackson – and produced by Quincy Jones. There was an amazing turnout of stars at A&M, Charlie Chaplin's old studio, but it was all the Hollywood shit that upset Bob. Everyone was queuing up in their limos while inside was this excess of ridiculous catering – a giant fish carved out of ice, spouting caviar and champagne, as if it were some Oscar party. The place was crawling with hangers-on, stuffing their faces while pretending to save famine victims. Geldof told me the whole thing was absolutely obscene. To sing a song for a country that's starving, while all this food was draining away and going off because nobody ate it. Outside, the limo drivers started fighting each other over who should be next to drive in and pick up their artist. All this mayhem had nothing to do with starving kids in Africa, and everything to do with ego massaging.

'It was nonsense,' he told me when he came home, still shuddering. 'Fucking pitiful, nothing like the atmosphere we created.' The artists, to be fair, took it seriously and it made a lot of money for famine relief and, if they hadn't done it, it would have been even harder to get acts for Live Aid.

The whole analogy of Band Aid – it was Bob's idea to call it that – was that it was a sticking plaster to cover a cut. We soon realised that if you've got a limb hanging off then a plaster's going to do no good at all. The first seven million pounds we raised from the record was a drop in the ocean, scarcely enough to feed the starving of Africa for two weeks. Africa's harvest always hangs on a knife edge. If the rains fail to come, the crops don't grow, and people starve. Within a few weeks we realised that Band Aid could not be a quick fix and it had to develop both short-term and long-term solutions.

One of our first bits of advice came from George Harrison, who warned Bob, 'Don't let this be another Concert for Bangladesh. When you collect the money, make sure it's all above board; make sure nobody dodgy can get their hands on it, and above all make sure it ends up going where it is meant to go.' George had raised hundreds of thousands of pounds only to discover that most of the money never reached the flood victims it was intended for. George told us to make sure that we had great lawyers and proper bona fide accountants, as that way we would not be directly responsible and nobody could point the finger.

We formed the Band Aid Trust. Bob was the chairman, which was logical. I was a working musician, still active with Ultravox, while Bob was perceived as a musician who didn't make music any more. Lord Gowrie, the Tory Minister for Arts, was the figurehead sponsor and there were two heavyweights from telly – Michael Grade and Lord Harlech, the head of Harlech TV – while the music business was represented by Chris Morrison, John Kennedy, a well-respected industry lawyer, and Maurice Oberstein, the chairman of the BPI (British Phonographic Institute). The accountants were Stoy Hayward, who Morrison recommended.

For the first six months of 1985 I was swept along, embroiled in four-hour meetings every day. We had discussions about ships, jeeps, high-protein biscuits, medication, trucks, sorghum. All the time I was thinking, What is sorghum? I don't know what we are talking about.

How come I'm responsible for all this money, and I can't walk away from it? Bob was thinking the same thing but we were all enveloped and overcome by the whole scenario.

Some of the chaos was because we were a bunch of rock-and-rollers, amateurs in the charity business. However, we weren't amateurs in the moving and shaking business. We had this gung-ho attitude which meant we suggested a lot of stuff that regular charities couldn't – or wouldn't – do. 'Let's charter a ship, fill it full of trucks and sorghum and high-protein biscuits and medication and Land Rovers. Let's get it out there now. Why should we wait a month? We saw what is happening on our televisions today.'

Bob's big thing was cutting through the red tape. Or ignoring it. That is something we were used to in the rock business. 'What do you mean you can't get the truck to Newcastle for tonight's show? Of course you can.' There is always a way around such a problem. If you had to drive an extra three hours to get to the venue that was what you did. You always did the show. I don't think that pure rock-and-roll attitude impressed the aid agencies, and some of the charities didn't like what we were doing. There was an accusation that their intake was down because we were taking all the money. I could see their point, but I believe Band Aid tapped into an entire generation who had never donated to charity. Charity was something that old people did and we were appealing to the young.

Without Band Aid there wouldn't have been Comic Relief, which has now been going for fifteen years. It does huge amounts of good, raises huge amounts of money, and is hugely entertaining. I love it and I watch it every year. I knew Rik Mayall and Ade Edmondson, all of that crowd, and they wanted to do something from their world. In 1986 when Rowan Atkinson was doing a three-week run in London he gave up three nights to Comic Relief. Frank Bruno was there, French and Saunders, the Young Ones, all doing a series of sketches.

Bob and I did the classic John Cleese bank manager's sketch where we tried to get the bank manger to understand the concept of charity. 'You give us a pound and we give you a little flag.' Stephen Fry played the bank manager. It ended up with Bob and I walking away scratching our heads saying, 'Why don't we do a concert instead?'

We had seen the original on *Monty Python* but we did a wee bit of rehearsal in the afternoon. It was chaos backstage, full of people rehearsing on stairwells, but great fun. Trying to do comedy in front of comedians is tough, but it wasn't about the comedy, it was that Bob and I were there. Later in the evening we sang 'Do They Know

It's Christmas?' – the only time we have ever performed it together. That was an interesting experience, with me playing in time and Bob pulling the speed and going all over the shop.

That's one of Band Aid's legacies. Most of the money went into long-term development, where it has made a difference. Another ongoing resource is a huge library, documentation on every project that it supported with all the reasons why it worked, and all the reasons why it didn't, which has been sent out to universities all over the world. Anyone who has an idea can go and look it up and maybe discover that Band Aid tried it back in 1990 and why it didn't work. The real legacy beyond that is that young kids don't think that charity is such a fuddy-duddy thing to do. My kids and their schools do it all the time, and they don't feel embarrassed or that it is out of place or uncool to care. I believe that Band Aid is directly responsible for that.

When I wasn't worrying about the price of sorghum, I was, in part, allowed to slip back into my life, to go into my studio and record some songs. Bob wasn't. Even when he did a tour with the Rats people wanted him to talk about Ethiopia. He had this precious ability to cut through the crap, like when he told the United Nations, 'You need an enema,' or his confrontation with Margaret Thatcher at the *Daily Star* Awards. He told the Prime Minister in front of the TV cameras how it was ridiculous that her government was spending £10 million to dispose of surplus EEC butter when part of the world was dying of starvation. He really got Maggie riled and somehow managed to get in the final blow – 'nothing is as simple as dying' – before she was dragged away. I couldn't have done that, it's not in my make up. I'd have shuffled and looked at my feet. My job was to be alongside Bob – or perhaps three feet behind him.

At the 1985 Brit Awards Ceremony we were both presented with a special award. Bob launched into a speech, laying into the industry, while I stood there with my hands together grinning like an idiot. The following year the Brits asked me to present an award so when I went on stage the first thing I said was, 'I'd like to thank you, eventually, for the award you gave me last year. I didn't get a chance to speak with Bob standing up here next to me.' That got a laugh.

I sat in dozens of Trust meetings where Bob was so passionate about everything but he always listened to what others were saying. He respected everyone round the table and, if we said, 'Bob, you've lost it, this idea doesn't make any sense,' he'd be big enough to admit it.

After three months we discovered there was a serious problem. We got the aid to the port, where initially they tried to charge us import duties to take stuff that had been given to them. Bob had jumped on a plane and seriously bollocked the government until they rescinded the threat. The biggest problem was that there was a major truck cartel operating out of Djibouti. We couldn't get our aid up country without using the trucks and they wanted half a million pounds to move it. It was a vicious circle. The only way we could solve the problem was to break the cartel. If we had another four million pounds we could buy our own fleet of trucks, our own spares, own tyres, and put it in situ. If every aid agency used our fleet, the money that was spent to hire the trucks could go back into the system. It made perfect sense . . . but we didn't have enough money.

Just after I returned from Ethiopia, Bob came into a meeting and announced, 'I've got this idea on how to raise the money we need. We will have a huge concert in London at Wembley; there will be another concert on the same day in America and we will link the two by satellite. I want to call it Live Aid.' Bob had this concept in his head and he announced it. Whether he knew it was practical or realistic I have no idea. I just stared at him in disbelief. Again.

CHAPTER 18
LIVE AID

Terror. That was my overriding emotion, sheer toe-curling fear. It was a boiling hot Saturday in July and I faced a sea of faces and bodies stretching far and away into the Wembley stands. This was uncharted territory. Nobody, not Bowie, not Queen, certainly not me, had ever done anything like this before. This was the biggest show I was ever going to do.

I hadn't slept much the night before with all the usual worries raging through my brain. We'd only had a fifteen-minute sound check. What if the drum machine didn't work? What if we overran our allotted eighteen minutes and Harvey Goldsmith pulled the plug? As usual, none of this fazed Warren. He was fast asleep in the dressing room and had to be wakened before we went on stage.

My face was hidden behind mirrored sunglasses and I wore the long, grey, silk coat I'd bought in Los Angeles two days earlier. My mouth was dust-dry. I must have said something but I have no idea what; the drum pattern clicked in, then Billy's synthesizer, then my cue. As I sang 'Reap The Wild Wind' the fear cascaded away to be replaced by this huge wave of excitement. By the time I got to 'take my hand, take my hand' the cheers were deafening.

The atmosphere in Wembley Stadium was electric, buzzing. I could have walked on stage, coughed and people would have applauded. It was the same buzz as I had when I'd had my first hit, the first time I went out in front of an audience who had paid money to see me, who were gagging for me, ready for me. Live Aid was that moment magnified a million times. The crowd were so ready, so up for it I didn't have to tickle them at all.

We followed with 'Dancing With Tears In My Eyes' then 'One Small Day', but when we started the intro to 'Vienna' the crowd went ballistic. This roar just grew and grew until it engulfed us inside a tidal wave of cheering. It was a perfect moment. I had never experienced anything like that before, felt 80,000 people lapping it up, having a ball. When we finished I felt this huge sense of elation: I was completely and utterly high. On the front page of the *Sunday Times* the next day was a head shot of me, the crowd clearly reflected in my sunglasses.

Passing terror aside, it was a fabulous concert. In the morning we were flown in by Noel Edmonds in a helicopter. It was the only way to get in there. When I looked down there was Wembley Stadium, completely empty, with thousands and thousands of people milling around outside.

Backstage in the Green Room we were all thrown in together: Ultravox and the Rats, the Style Council, Nik Kershaw, Adam Ant, Spandau, Sting, Sade and Phil Collins, an ill-matched, mixed-up collection of pop and rock stars. But once Status Quo kicked off the show with 'Rocking All Over the World', irrespective of what genre of music you were tied in with, it was fabulous. Everybody had stupid grins on their faces. Even Paul Weller. Live Aid was real, tangible: it was happening. We all knew that we were part of history in the making. It didn't matter how long our careers had been, how many hits we had had before or might have in the future, none of us had ever done anything like this.

I hadn't had so much to do with organising the nuts and bolts of the concert. Bob came into Trust meetings every day and updated us on the saga. How he had convinced Pete Townshend to put the Who together, that he'd seen Freddie Mercury in a restaurant and marched straight up to his table. 'Right, Freddie. Live Aid. July 13th. You're doing it.'

'Oh, darling,' said Freddie, 'I'm not so sure.'

'No, you are doing it . . . or I will tell the world how you, not Queen, turned it down.'

It was a charity event so it should have been easy to convince people to take part, but it doesn't work that way. When an artist gets a phone call about doing a show their standard response is 'Who else is doing it?' It's not about the charity, it's about the profile. With Live Aid we were trying to do concerts simultaneously in London and Philadelphia. Geldof was behind it . . . except Bob Geldof wasn't a name in the States. The reality, which Bob happily admits, was that he was a washed-up pop star in England and a never-was in America, which made what he did an even more incredible feat.

Bob has this amazing talent to cut through the social formalities. It was like watching this Tasmanian Devil hack its way through a jungle: he just went through trees, whatever was in his way. It was Geldof's terrier attitude that got most of the British artists, plus Harvey Goldsmith and Maurice Jones. Bob got Harvey onto the Trust and then Maurice came on board to help organise the show. Maurice never got as much credit as Harvey, but he was equally responsible for its success. When the two biggest promoters in Britain knocked on doors, people listened; when they phoned the Stones, the Stones answered . . . even if only to say they couldn't do it.

Harvey phoned up artists with advice. 'If you don't do this, you're going to be hung up and quartered, so get your arse over here and do it.' There were no great refusals and in Britain we had the biggest and best that the country had to offer. Eurythmics should have done it, especially given their track record of supporting causes. Dave Stewart just didn't want to know. I wonder if he regrets that now.

We wanted the best from every generation. We asked the Stones but they were five people managed by five different managers, living in different parts of the world. (In the end Mick sang duets with Tina Turner and David Bowie while Keith and Ronnie backed Bob Dylan in a deeply shambolic performance.) Dealing with any of those megastars is hard work. You get the secretary, you get the PA, maybe the management, but seldom the star. Live Aid was a logistical and legal nightmare, which is why there was no official video (the DVD finally came out in 2004). It was hard enough trying to get people to commit to being there, let alone clearing the rights to all the artists and songs through a multitude of record companies and lawyers.

Backstage the Hard Rock did the catering. It was all free, except that when you went up to get your burger or your chilli there was a great big bucket on either side for donations. We all ended up paying fifty quid for a burger. Everybody else around was watching to see who would eat it and walk away leaving nothing. Nobody did. Watching all these £20 notes being dropped in the buckets I thought it was a stroke of genius. Your food was free but you had to make a donation.

After Ultravox performed I was sitting backstage chatting with Parfitt and Rossi when I saw Freddie Mercury. I'd met all the rest of Queen but Freddie was the invisible man: I'd never got near him. I went over and said, 'Hi, how are you doing?' and shook hands with him. He wouldn't let go of my hand.

After he'd been holding my hand for two minutes, he said, 'Tell me, you're that lovely boy from Boomtown Rats, aren't you?'

'No,' I gasped, 'I'm the lovely boy from Ultravox.' Annabel was staring at me with her mouth open; Rossi and Parfitt were pissing themselves and I was breaking out in a cold sweat. This flamboyant gay rock god was hanging onto my hand and not letting it go, while

I stuttered, 'I've just got to go and talk to my girlfriend. Ooh look. She's right over there.'

Sting had originally planned to do his set with his full band. His musicians – who were all black – demanded payment before they went on stage. Sting told them to fuck off and walked on with just an acoustic guitar, where he did an impromptu set opening with 'Message In A Bottle'. Yet after the concert we were lambasted for not having enough black artists on the bill. It became this anticolonial diatribe, 'You whities, telling us poor black guys what to do.' It was unfair but it happened. We couldn't get any black superstar to perform at either concert and it wasn't for lack of trying. We asked Prince, Stevie Wonder, Diana Ross and Michael Jackson, who were all otherwise engaged or not interested in doing it. As a result a wealth of American artists missed out on being part of Live Aid.

Cat Stevens turned up at Wembley with no warning and a huge entourage. Maurice Jones went to see him. 'Cat, how are you doing?'

'It's not Cat. It's Yusuf Islam. I've come to play for the world.'

'No, it's not possible. Say "Hi" to Cat when you see him.'

Mind you, if it had been Bruce Springsteen it might have been different.

David Bailey was set up in a makeshift studio, photographing odd combinations of people – Bob and I, Freddie Mercury and whoever – for the book. Everybody in the audience had a programme so I signed loads of autographs. I saw Bob a few times over the day, running about backstage, totally manic; he didn't relax at all. I felt I had done my bit and I didn't want to shout down phone lines at people.

There was also something niggling away inside me. In the weeks leading up to Live Aid I had felt increasingly sidelined. For the six months since Band Aid it had been the two of us – Bob Geldof and Midge Ure. All of a sudden it was Bob everywhere while I had been relegated to the same stature as every other artist. I wasn't doing Live Aid to get patted on the back but I did feel increasingly edged out; the ranks had closed and I was nowhere to be seen. The machine that had built up around Bob had decided that my job was done, which pissed me off. I had been working at it just as hard as everybody else.

When Live Aid was first announced I wasn't on the platform. I was standing backstage with Gary Kemp, Adam Ant and Elton John, chatting away, having a drink, when I heard Bob next door, thumping on his chest, announcing Live Aid. That hurt, but I let it pass until I noticed that I wasn't being invited to a lot of the public stuff while Bob was being pushed into the forefront. He became the face of Live

Aid while I was just another guy at the Trust meetings. I did get miffed, primarily I guess because I knew that our partnership wasn't there any more. I did try to keep my feelings private, but poison had taken root.

At Live Aid Ultravox were originally scheduled to go on before the Boomtown Rats. On the day someone from Harvey's office came to me and said, 'Look, do you mind if we move Ultravox's spot. It's a technical problem to do with Adam Ant's equipment.' We moved down the list and Bob went on early. I didn't think anything of it, as neither Bob nor I were going out on the worldwide global broadcast; we were both on in the first hour which meant that most of the world never saw us.

After I came off stage I went up to the press bar where one of the journalists asked me, 'How does it feel to be dumped for Bob?'

'What do you mean?' I asked.

He explained, 'Your slots were swapped round because they wanted Bob to perform for Charles and Di. The royals had to go back to the palace after an hour.'

'Don't be ridiculous,' I snapped, 'that's stupid'. I denied it absolutely. I knew the journalist could see a headline but I wasn't going to sit there and sully such a day with a tantrum. Anyway it was unbelievable that anything like that could happen to me. But it had.

It didn't spoil the day for me. Nothing could have done that. But it did start to hurt much more in the months afterwards: the more I thought about it, the more it ate into me, burned away at my insides. All my misgivings about my role had crystallised into a moment of personal embarassment when I'd been put on the spot by a journalist sniffing a scoop. I was never going to spill the beans to the press but I did feel dreadfully let down, as if I had been stabbed in the back by people around me. We were all supposed to be working for the same aim.

It might sound like an overreaction nearly twenty years later but it was so unnecessary. It was being lied to that upset me. All of us had built this organisation to fight against huge, big conglomerates, to cut through the red tape. Now we were doing the exact same thing, becoming what we vowed never to be. Somebody, somewhere, in the inner sanctum had moved the goal posts. They were subversive about the whole thing, which was what upset me. If I'd been told the truth on the day I wouldn't have had a problem. Bob was the front person, the one sitting with Charles and Di, the one going on television, saying, 'Give us your fucking money.'

My negative feelings passed long, long ago. I never mentioned it to Bob; I'm not even sure he'd believe it could have happened the way

I know it did. He'd be aghast at the thought because Bob, more than anyone, has always known what I contributed. He was at a Capital Awards Ceremony for Band Aid last year when I was up in Scotland singing for my supper. Bob stood up and said, 'I will start straight off by saying this would never have happened without Midge Ure.' The entire audience stood up. I got a standing ovation and I wasn't even there.

On the day of Live Aid I refused to believe what the press were telling me, dismissed it completely from my head and sat out the front in the artists' enclosure and watched the concert like everybody else. My memories are all pretty vague. I just remember sitting watching and thinking how good they all were, even the Who who weren't up to their usual standards. I've always loved watching Townshend. I'm not an Elton John fan but I remember thinking, God, he's good. There was nothing not to enjoy except sometimes when the TV kept cutting in and out to America. Some of the bands from round the world were a little odd and it got a bit Eurovision at times, but that was the world's contribution and the music didn't matter.

Each artist had exactly eighteen minutes on stage, which meant you could do four four-minute songs if you were brilliantly tight, or three five-minute songs and get off early. There was a traffic-light system at the side of the stage. The stage manager warned us, 'If you see the lights go from green to amber, you've got one minute left. You won't see it turn red because that is when the power goes.' The fear of being stranded in front of millions of people, while the power went off, was enough to keep everybody absolutely on time.

U2 only managed two songs. Bono pulled a girl up from the audience to dance during 'Bad' while the Edge gave it his guitar thing, playing the riff over and over and over. Commercially it seemed they blew it, because they didn't play their new single, but instead they won the hearts of the world. The week after Live Aid, all four U2 albums were back in the charts. They had proved themselves to be this brilliant band who were real and not contrived. Within two years they were the biggest band in the world.

Queen did the opposite. They rehearsed a mini-set for a week and delivered a segued medley of all their greatest hits, exactly eighteen minutes long. The sight of the whole stadium clapping along while Freddie conducted the audience during 'Radio Gaga' was remarkable.

There was only one major technical failure in the whole day. It just happened to be Paul McCartney's microphone when he was singing 'Let It Be' – his first live appearance in eight years. It didn't matter. The audience knew all the words.

The finale was planned to be everybody singing 'Do They Know It's Christmas?', which was the one song that nobody had rehearsed. Everyone was hastily assembled in the Hard Rock and hurriedly photocopied sheets of the lyrics were passed out. Nobody even had an acoustic guitar and Bob tried to dole out lines. Bowie was due to take the first two because Paul Young had left early – ironic, as they had been specially earmarked for Bowie at the original recording session.

Then there was a power cut. We sang it through in the dark, a total mess. Bob, Bowie, Alison Moyet and Pete Townshend were summoned on stage to sing the chorus of 'Let It Be'. We tried another run-through. It was still a shambles. Then there was no time left, and we gave up trying to assign particular lines, just got on stage and sang it.

The Boomtown Rats played the tune and did it well. Everybody sang the whole thing – even Harvey Goldsmith – no one took solos. There were seven mikes that people gathered around. I stood at the back.

My natural tendency has always been to back away from seizing the moment. I didn't want to grab the microphone so that all of a sudden it could be me up the front. I didn't want to hog the limelight. There are guys who will push you away, shove their granny in the back and trample over her just to grab that mike, but that is not in my nature. I'd rather be the guy who was there than the twat who grabbed a mike away from Bryan Ferry.

The bottom line was that it was more important that the cameras focused on Bob, George Michael, Bono, Macca and Bowie – that was the hierarchy of the whole show. The shot that people were going to see all around the world was this mass gathering, the best musicians that Britain had to offer all on stage, all singing the same song.

I was there. That is good enough for me. After all, they were singing my song.

After we finished the final 'Feed the world' we were ferried off stage. The backstage area was Wembley Arena and, when we came out, we were all pushed into vans and mini-buses and the door was slammed shut behind us. I had no idea who I was crammed in with, until I turned and saw I was sitting next to Bowie. It went quiet as we were driving across the parking lot.

Not for long. The Parfitt and Rossi double act were behind me on the backseat. One turns to the other and says deadpan, 'I don't get it.'

'What?'

'Why were we singing "Feed the Welsh"?'

The outstanding moment of the whole day for me was not musical. I was stuck in the traffic going home where my plan was to watch the rest of the concert on TV. I wasn't going to the party at Legends. I was knackered, as I'd just flown in from LA and I was too jet-lagged to think straight.

Out of the car window I saw scenes that I have only ever seen in Scotland at Hogmanay when families throw their doors open. The streets were full of people with huge grins on their face, singing songs, going into strangers' houses, having a party while watching Live Aid on television. It was unheard of in London, a place where nobody knows their neighbours, where people keep themselves to themselves. Maybe at the end of the war people had felt like that, so elated that there was this fantastic camaraderie. And there it was happening in front of me, all because a bunch of pop stars had thrown a concert for the starving of Africa.

CHAPTER 19
GOING SOLO

My career was unscathed by Live Aid. I didn't have to play Saint Midge because that burden was spread across Bob's shoulders. I was allowed to slip out of the back door into my day job and be a pop star again. Bob was far beyond that: he had become something else entirely, a spokesman for unruly youth, a pseudo-politician, a living conscience. He didn't like it. I finished my solo album, put it out and went on tour. 'If I Was' became a Number One hit and at Christmas I was back headlining at Wembley Arena. Bob sent me this massive bunch of flowers with the cryptic message 'Congratulations. I wish to fuck I was you.'

My first solo single was the result of a bartering deal I did with John Hudson at Mayfair Studios in the early 80s. He was bogged down with a band and needed help. I didn't want any points but I agreed to do it for some studio time. I went in, recorded and mixed 'No Regret' in two days.

I'd loved the song (which was originally written by Tom Rush) and wanted to sing it ever since I heard the Walker Brothers' version. It stuck in my mind as a ballad which started very quietly and built to this huge crescendo. I recorded what I remembered. When I actually listened to the Walker Brothers again I discovered that their version started and finished at the same level. I didn't know what to do with this monster track, all bombast and crescendo, so I took it to Chris Morrison. After I played it to him he was silent, for what seemed like hours.

'I was just messing about,' I said. 'What do you think?'

He grabbed the tape off me, rushed out of the office into the street, jumped into a cab and shot up to Chrysalis in the West End where he barged into Roy Eldridge's office and played it to him. Roy, who was head of A&R, looked at him and said, 'How much do you want for it?'

Chris replied, '£5,000.'

Roy agreed. Chris got back in the cab, came back to the office and told me the good news. It was a Top Ten hit in the summer of 1982.

'No Regrets' was a one-off because I was far too busy to fit anything else in. A year later I did another single, 'After A Fashion', with Mick Karn, the bass player for Japan – the best part of that was doing the video in Cairo. At the end of 1984 we decided to have a six-month sabbatical from Ultravox, but my idea of relaxation was a busman's holiday . . . recording at the bottom of my garden.

When I turned the Grosvenor Road annex in the garden into my own recording studio, I had floating rooms built inside the existing structures so the vibrations couldn't carry the sound from one room to another. The studio was my major extravagance. It was like watching a baby being born before my eyes. I bought all the equipment brand new: a 24-track machine, a Harrison desk and a two-track machine. The day it was finished I rushed inside and realised I didn't have a clue how any of the machines worked. I had never operated alone before and all I had to help was a deep pile of manuals. The answer was to get myself an engineer, so whenever I bought a new bit of equipment I gave him the manual and went to play with my new toy. Once he'd read the manual he told me how it worked. Even to this day, when I buy a new bit of kit, I play around with it first and then I go back to the manual and find out how it actually works.

I never had an entourage or a bodyguard or a gofer. I never asked someone to run around for me. I had Rik Walton. He was my luxury, an engineer who knew what he was doing. Rik worked for me for nine years and he was in there every day. I used to let other people use the studio as well, and Rik worked for them. Recording equipment needs looking after, maintaining, if it's not been used for a while it has to be stripped and cleaned, so he did everything like that.

The Gift was a secret record: nobody knew I was doing it. I'm not sure I did really; I was messing about putting a batch of very simplistic songs and instrumentals together. It was a reaction to Ultravox because I thought we'd been getting too heavy and precious and I wanted to do something light and fun. *The Gift* was a very 'up' record. It had its miserable moments – the dark instrumentals – but most of it was up.

'If I Was' was an outstanding track that Danny Mitchell sent me as a demo. I had known Danny since I produced the *Modern Man* album. (His synth duo the Messengers were signed to MusicFest, a label Morrison and I had started through Chrysalis. I wanted to start a label as an outlet for productions I was doing. Chrysalis gave me the label identity and covered the cost of production but they didn't give me any advances. It ended up costing us money.) I thought it was great, instantly catchy and I needed some up-beat numbers. I called Danny and said, 'Let's do a Lennon–McCartney on this album. Irrespective of who wrote what let's go fifty–fifty on it.' The bones of the song were already there so I rewrote parts of it and recorded it. Danny and I ended up doing four songs together.

'If I Was' was one of those magic songs. It came out and instantly appealed. It was ageless. Kids loved it, and so did their parents. When I went on Saturday morning kids' TV to sing it, the doorman, who was in his sixties, gave me a thumbs up and said, 'Killer song. I love that.' 'If I Was' is the most commercially successful of my solo records.

Originally I didn't have an avenue planned for *The Gift* and it got delayed when Band Aid took over my life. Eventually I played it to Chris Morrison and we sat around wondering, 'Yes, it's interesting, but what are we going to do with it?' Chrysalis knew; they were thrilled as they hadn't seen it coming at all. There was some dealing with the business-affairs boys as they had to temporarily cut me out of the Ultravox deal and then cut me back in again. These things tend to be a lot easier if you are successful.

I decided I wanted to do a solo tour. That autumn I did my own version of *Around the World in 80 Days*, playing 1,200-seat theatres in America, Canada, Australia, Japan and Europe, culminating with the show at Wembley Arena.

I put a good band together. My old mate Kenny Hyslop was the drummer, with Kevin Powell on bass. Danny Mitchell was on one set of keyboards and he recommended Craig Armstrong, from a Glasgow outfit called Hipsway, on the other. I hired Mick Ronson to play guitar. The idea of playing with Mick in my band was incredibly exciting as he was one of my all-time heroes.

Every day Mick came in and he'd forgotten the song we'd rehearsed the day before. I'd told him I wanted his trademark, big, driven, distorted guitar sound and he'd play his Stratocaster, a roll-up ciga- rette hanging out of his mouth, and out came this horrible clean, twangy, country sound. Or he'd play slide guitar on a number which didn't need it. It was very weird because at the end of rehearsals these dodgy, unsavoury-looking characters turned up and hung around waiting for Mick to finish, then he'd drive off with them. After what I'd seen with Steve New I was sure that they were dealing him drugs. Drugs would help to explain the crap playing.

A week before the tour Danny, who is the most placid man in the world and who idolised Mick as much as I did, phoned me up. 'Midge, you are going to have to kick Mick out of the band. It sounds fucking awful.'

I knew he was right, but I'd been putting it off. I phoned Mick and woke him up. It was one of the hardest things I'd had to do in my life, to tell my hero he couldn't do the tour because he wasn't good enough. I was gutted.

Chris O'Donnell phoned the next morning to remark in his usual witty way, 'I hear you are a Ronson lighter.' I felt dreadful until the day Mick died in 1993. Maybe he was already suffering from the cancer that killed him and nobody knew. Instead I chose to believe the worst about him. Sometimes leaving the loose ends to tour managers isn't the right thing to do, because the worst thing was that he never got paid and he was too much of a gentleman to call me and tell me. I'd have paid him no question; he'd blocked out his time for me and it was my decision to fire him.

Fortunately Kevin Powell, who had been touring with Elkie Brooks, knew Zal Cleminson. I'd known Zal years before when Tear Gas were hot on the Scottish scene and then watched his success with the Sensational Alex Harvey Band. After Alex died he'd struggled to get regular work and he was driving a taxi in London. I phoned him, and he turned up the next day and learned the entire set in a week.

I hadn't seen Kenny much since Slik folded, though whenever I swung by Glasgow we'd hang out and drink far too much. To begin with he found me a hard taskmaster. I recorded 'If I Was' with a drum machine and Kenny hadn't been playing much since his Simple Minds stint so when I told him, 'I want it exactly like the record,' it meant his right leg was pumping away for five minutes nonstop. A lot of the new tunes had that rhythmic thing so he was knackered. When we took a lunch break he stayed in there trying to get it absolutely right, learning to play like a machine.

On the day of my Melbourne show Danny Mitchell, Chris Morrison and I decided we wanted to go horse riding. Danny and I had seen horses in Glasgow but that was our total association with man's four-legged friends. We went to a stables which boasted of having ten acres of bush to ride in; the guy saddled our horses, heaved us on top, opened the gate and left us to it. Chris was on some nag that appeared to be on valium; it ambled along at half a mile an hour and, as it knew how to open the gate, spent all its time trying to get back into the yard. My horse was a lot more lively. Like a kid I yelled, 'Look at me, I'm a cowboy,' and charged off into the bush. Danny and I were racing over fields full of dips, potholes and tree stumps. Suddenly my horse stopped. I didn't. I flew right over its ears and landed head first with this almighty crunch. I thought I had broken my neck. I just lay there, a heap in the dirt, moaning until I realised I could feel my legs.

Away in the distance Chris thought I was dead. By the time his horse had plodded over I had dragged myself to my feet and was wandering around in a daze. I was a bit wobbly and by show time my neck was as stiff as a board. I was so immobilised that to turn my head I had to move my shoulders first. I had also cracked my front teeth so I sang through gritted teeth like a ventriloquist's dummy. According to Morrison out front, the whole show looked very robotic, very Kraftwerk.

Otherwise most of my adventures on the solo tour were in restaurants. I love Japanese food and in Australia the record company took Morrison and me to a Japanese restaurant. We were talking about Kobe beef, which is unbelievable to eat but almost impossible to buy outside Japan. It costs $100 for a small quantity because the farmer's wife feeds the cow rice wine and milk and massages its stomach with her feet. Not to be outdone by the Japanese, the promo guy told us, 'If you like beef you have got to go to the best beef restaurant in Oz.'

The next night we went to this tiny place and were sat in a booth. There was a glass butcher's counter in the corner packed full of raw meat. Every so often a bloke in a bloodstained apron hacked chunks off with a cleaver. The wallpaper consisted of pictures of grazing cows looking soulfully down on us. There were only two types of hors d'oeuvre, so we had both: the kebab was made of solid meat and offal, the sausage from brain. The only vegetable – they didn't even do potatoes – was coleslaw, so Laurie, our solitary vegetarian, didn't get much of a meal. The steak was so huge it hung over the edge of the plate. I could only eat a tiny bit of it with those cows looking down on me.

After Australia we went to Japan where Chris and I decided we wanted to go to a working-man's café. We sat up at this L-shaped bar on high stools. We didn't speak Japanese so Chris asked, 'Sushi? Sashimi?'

The cook trotted over to a fish tank in the corner, scooped out this big fish, brought it back, showed it to us and asked, 'Sashimi?'

Chris nodded. 'Hai.' The fish was flapping about so the guy picked up his knife, flipped it up into the air, caught it by the blade, whacked the fish's head and stunned it. He grabbed the knife again, sliced off a whole side of flesh, turned it over and pointed his knife at me. I shook my head. He chopped up the flesh, added the garnish, placed it in front of Chris, picked up the fish and lobbed it back in the tank.

The fish woke up, lay on its good side, still very much alive, and glared at Chris while he tried to eat.

To top it off, when the only other guy in the bar put his order in, the cook went to another tank with a net. He disappeared into the kitchen and we just heard this hissing sound until he came back out with a plateful of tiny crabs.

Another night Morrison and I went to a hotplate restaurant – where they cook everything in front of you – with a couple of English models, very pretty girls. We ordered lobster, prawns and steak. The cook brought out the lobster, very much alive, which got the girls squealing. He took a cleaver, chopped the lobster right down the middle and banged it on the hotplate. Then he tossed the prawns on with them. As they were still alive, they started jumping off – one landed on my plate – until he held them down with a spatula. They were grey on one side, pink on the other and wriggling like mad. I politely asked the girls, 'Would you like some?' but they looked at me as if I was mad.

The girls were just company, and both of us were good as gold. At the time I was with Annabel. As we sat on the plane going home, I turned to Chris and asked him, 'Do you feel any better for behaving?'

'No!' he grumbled.

On tour I'd been with a bunch of guys who knew I was the boss, so there were no arguments. It wasn't a democratic scenario any more, and, if I said, 'No more drinking before you go on,' they stopped. In Ultravox there were no slapped wrists. I didn't dare criticise in case it set Billy off. My solo tour was great fun. Coming off that and going back to Ultravox was bound to be a letdown. Especially when I heard the material they had been working on in my absence.

CHAPTER 20
THE END OF ULTRAVOX

It must have irked Ultravox having to hang about waiting for me to finish my little solo outing. Billy had built a home studio and they'd been closeted away working on a few bits and pieces. I was really excited about the idea of working with them again so I bounced in with fresh ears. What I heard were slabs of music that sounded very dated and random. Some of the ideas were off the wall, incredibly poppy and Billy was well into working with some really cold sequencers which sounded old-fashioned. After two years away the musical climate had changed. Where Ultravox had once been cutting edge, synthesizers and electronic drums were now everywhere. The solo stuff I'd been doing was simple, but everything in Ultravox seemed so complicated.

We had a joke in the band. Q: 'If Ultravox want to scratch their nose, how do they do it?' A: 'Use their elbows.' In other words, the most awkward way possible. It had got so complex, touring was a nightmare; we'd had 24 keyboards on stage, plus drum pads and triggers. We refused to use tapes or pre-programmed sequences and because everything was played live all the equipment had to be customised. This was before Midi (an interface that lets a drum machine talk to a synthesizer). Nowadays it's easy, you buy whatever equipment you want, and it all understands each other. Back then everything had to be altered and changed, which meant we had to have two of everything.

On the *Vienna* album Warren had written a good chunk of the lyrics, but on subsequent albums I didn't want him to. I wanted to sing my own lyrics, so he must have felt pushed out even though we split it all four ways. In some ways having an equal split is good as it means everybody has an equal say, but there were times when I knew that I was agreeing with something that was wrong and all we ended up with was a watered-down idea. There was no room in Ultravox for a dictator.

There are always tensions within a group. One of the facts of life is that the lead singer will always garner more attention than the drummer. Whoever sings gets the most attention and nobody wants to interview the drummer. Warren played the drums and he had a great deal of difficulty with that. Billy, too, sometimes resented my role as frontman.

By 1986 Ultravox was heading off on four separate paths. Something had to change, so we had a big meeting to discuss getting back on the same track. My idea was to go back to the way we wrote *Vienna*. I was to have a guitar and a keyboard, Billy three keyboards and his viola, Chris his bass and one synthesizer, and Warren just one drum machine and his drum kit. We all agreed to try it, except that at the first rehearsal Warren turned up with the Iron Lung: the massive metal frame which sat behind him and held all his electronics, his drum machines, his mixing desk, his clap traps, his triggers and all sorts of sequencers. During our period apart Warren hadn't played his drumkit once.

He wouldn't pick up his sticks, as he was more interested in drum machines than hitting his skins. He'd rather spend hours programming, laboriously hitting buttons. We could all programme drum machines but we didn't want to. Machines can't make mistakes, which means they do it too well most of the time. We needed the looseness, the flexibility of a human drummer.

As a band we were floundering, so we ganged up against Warren. He was a nice guy but by that stage personality didn't count. It wasn't a coup planned out in our heads. Individually Billy, Chris and I all thought, This is the element that's not working properly. Rather than fix it, let's change it.

We called another meeting and I did the dirty work. I couldn't look at him, only down at the carpet as I said, 'Sorry, Warren, you're not in the band any more.'

Warren was shell-shocked, as he hadn't seen it coming at all. When he got the news he didn't say anything. He just got up and walked out. It was a very dignified exit but I could tell from his face that he thought it was disgusting. He was one of the founding members, and he'd been playing with Chris and Billy for twelve years and me for seven.

He walked out of the office and I haven't seen or spoken to him since. He decided he wanted to be an actor and he lives in Los Angeles now. I've sent messages on to him, sent him my regards, but I'm sure there's a very deep hurt and some serious bad feelings there, which is perfectly understandable.

The band was already finished but we didn't realise it. We needed a scapegoat, so we took it out on Warren. We excised the weakest link and believed we could survive without a drummer. We thought it was a whole new start, that it would make the three of us stronger, would give us a new interesting edge. It didn't, of course, as the foundations were gone. Sacking Warren was the beginning of the end.

We decided to go back to recording with Conny Plank, back to when it was fresh and exciting. Conny liked his own desk but we couldn't face going out to Cologne again. So we compromised and recorded the album in Billy's studio, my studio and Germany, and then went out to Montserrat to mix it. Conny hated Montserrat: the studio had a big SSL mixing desk he detested and he couldn't stand the automation. Suffice to say when we came back the mixes sounded dead and flat. We ended up remixing most of it with John Hudson and Rik Walton.

Soon afterwards Conny went off to do a tour of South America playing avant-garde trumpet – although he wasn't really a trumpet player – with a couple of German musician friends of his. He came back with some dreadful chest illness and died from it. He was much too young.

The last Ultravox album was called *U-Vox*. We should have called it U-bend because it should have gone down the drain. It deserved to. It was an album that should never have been. During the recording of the album we were headless chickens, and our song ideas were splintered. Billy was writing his big George Martin orchestrations – 'All In One Day' came out of that. The one track that I am still proud of today was 'All Fall Down', which had more to do with the Chieftains and me than Ultravox. I wrote the whole thing, start to finish, and the Chieftains played it and Mark Brzezicki played drums. It was my baby, where my head was at the time. I felt it was exactly what I did when I joined Ultravox. By using different instrumentation I had got the mix back, the balance right. Ultravox were not a synthesizer band, they were a band who used everything: synthesizers, electric guitars, acoustic drums and acoustic piano. All I was doing was looking sideways, mixing the electronic and the organic once again.

Ultravox were still a successful band: the album went into the Top Ten, and both 'Same Old Story' and 'All Fall Down' were Top Forty hits. A big tour was lined up but just prior to the rehearsals I realised I'd had enough. I called a meeting and said, 'Look, I'm not happy. I'll do this tour but once it's over I'm leaving. There was an Ultravox before me, there's no reason why there can't be an Ultravox after me.'

Chris was feeling the same way so when I announced I was quitting he said, 'I'm leaving as well.'

Billy took it very badly. I took him out to dinner and suggested a couple of options: he could go to Los Angeles where there was still a big buzz about the band, write film music, or find a female singer and some new musicians and change the concept of Ultravox completely. It had happened with Fleetwood Mac; they started off as a blues band then ended up as a Californian hippy-pop band. He wasn't listening: he was really sad.

For the final European tour we went down to Taranto, right in the heel of Italy, a couple of days early to get the band up to scratch. Billy was still so devastated that the band was finished that he got smashed, so off-his-face by midday he was playing a beat and a half behind the rest of us. There was no point in rehearsing. He took it really personally, whereas for me it was just something that didn't work any more. As a band we'd lost it and I'd lost interest.

Chris Morrison had always been wary of our playing more than a couple of one-off dates in Italy. It had this gangster reputation that bands never got paid. Gerry Bron, Uriah Heep's manager, had refused to let the band go on stage – until the promoter shot the tyres off the truck. After that Gerry changed his mind and told Heep, 'On you go, boys.'

Chris had been talked into doing an Italian tour to support the *U-Vox* album and when he arrived for the first show in Modena he was crapping himself. We were playing 5,000-seaters and hadn't sold a single ticket in advance. As we were going on stage Alfredo, the guy from the record company, told us to lock the dressing-room door after us but insisted we take our wallets with us. 'Everybody in Italy,' he explained piously, 'ees a thief.' The place was packed – though we discovered that they always let in the first 1,500 for free, otherwise there was a riot. Apparently any excuse was good for a riot, or a riot was the excuse for everything. We went out on stage and the first thing to greet us was this sea of tape recorders being waved at us. One bloke had even set up a recorder the size of a table with two directional mikes right next to the mixing desk.

The last thing I glimpsed before I sang 'Same Old Story' was Morrison going mental screaming at the promoter in the wings. Apparently he told Chris, 'The first person who arrive in the queue he has a tape recorder. I say to him, "You no bring it in." He argue. Five thousand people behind in the queue they riot. I have no venue. The people with recorders, they get in. This ees Italy.' Chris gave up.

At the end of the show we were leaving to go to dinner, which was something Alfredo did very well, as he knew the best restaurant in every town and they would always stay open. The gig was at a sports hall and in the corner of the dressing room was a medicine ball. Alfredo picked it up, put it into his bag and shrugged. 'It ees for my kids.'

I looked at him and said, 'You are right, Alfredo, everybody in Italy is a thief.'

'Ees Italy' became a stock phrase for everything we had to put up with, though the food and the scenery helped a lot. A lot of our gigs were in static circus tents. Out of season they were used as venues. We turned up at one, did the sound check then asked the promoter for the dressing room. He beckoned us to follow him outside and pointed at a great big elephant trailer, with the back door open and a ramp dropped down into the mud. Inside there was straw on the floor with the odd bit of dung still nestled in it. It stank. He went, 'That is where you change.'

I said, 'I don't think so.'

For the tour we had expanded the band so I ended up doing very little playing, concentrating on my singing instead. Mark Brzezicki was busy touring with Big Country so we got in Pat Ahern. There was another guitar player, Max Abbey, and two guys from my solo band, Danny Mitchell on keyboards, loops and samples, and vocals, and Craig Armstrong playing violin and keyboards. Craig was very talented but I do remember shouting him down in rehearsals; he was faffing about and I yelled at him, 'Fucking hell, Craig, it's not that difficult!' Who would have guessed he'd go on to be string arranger to the stars, working with Massive Attack and Kate Bush, as well as composing some wonderful soundtracks. Craig had been listening a lot to Ry Cooder's *Paris, Texas* soundtrack. During the tour he told me about his plan to put this band together using a slide guitar. He had the name, Texas, and a wee girl he knew called Sharlene Spiteri who worked in a hairdressers wanted to be a singer. Craig set it all up, did the first album, co-wrote their first hit 'I Don't Want A Lover' then left them to get on with it.

When we finally finished that tour, no one absolutely called it a day. I simply walked away saying, 'See you, guys.' Six months later, the day before I was about to embark on a solo tour, I got a phone call from Billy asking, 'What's happening?'

'What do you mean, "what's happening"?'

'What's happening with the band?'

'Billy, you were in the room when I said I was leaving.'

'I'm not hanging about for you,' he snapped. Then he put the phone down. It was a really weird conversation, but I never did know what was going on in Billy's head.

In actual fact we never announced we'd broken up, as we left it so it could reopen if we wanted to. Billy cut a couple of solo albums that didn't do particularly well, and he wanted the name back. I had no rights to it at all, so I agreed. That closed all the doors. He put a new Ultravox together, recorded an album and did some things in Europe, but it was very different. It would have been nice to have been able to leave it for five or ten years and then maybe get back together, without any big fuss about it. Find out what we had learned as individuals, see if we could do something interesting as a collective. I couldn't do that now.

Why did Ultravox end? A lot of it was my fault. It wasn't about my ambition. I simply felt I was hitting my head on a brick wall, and it wasn't fun any more. I had to move on. I certainly didn't see the effect my leaving would have on the others' lives. I know that Billy, and probably Warren, believe that Chris Morrison and I teamed up to screw up their futures.

There is the other side. They could also think, The day Midge walked into the band everything changed. We were lucky enough to forge something very special together, and make fantastic sounds. It became successful, which gave everyone a great income. It was weird towards the end, but brilliant at the beginning. It was the best thing I ever did, to spend seven years in a great band with a bunch of mates and travel all round the world.

CHAPTER 21
NO ANSWERS

Even though it came out three years after I'd been there, *Answers To Nothing* was my post-Ethiopia album. My trip to the aid camp had a profound effect on me. It wasn't immediate but over the next couple of years I had a clean-out of my life belongings, and cleared out the excesses of my life. I was living in an eight-bedroomed house on the river with a garage full of classic sports cars. I had always vowed when I was a kid growing up in Glasgow that if I ever was in a position to live like that I never would. I'd always said I'd buy a nice little house, pay it all off and stick the rest in the bank. It didn't quite work out that way. Coming back from Africa, where they had absolutely nothing, reminded me of where I really came from, of what I had forgotten.

Annabel and I got married at the registry office in Plymouth, Montserrat, on 30 December 1985. A bunch of us had rented a villa so it was a small wedding party – Billy Currie and his then wife Judy, Yvonne and Malcolm Kelly who ran AIR studio, Lexi Godfrey and Spandau's John Keeble and his wife, who were holidaying nearby and came over for the wedding.

We moved home in April 1986. I had a hankering to move to the country and she didn't. Our compromise was Zachary House, a fabulous old house right on the River Thames in Chiswick. It was a brilliant setting, the river in front of us and a huge garden behind it. It was a rollicking big house with two garages. There was a double garage over in one corner that had belonged to the house next door and a massive building on the other side. That was a six-car garage and underneath it was a massive open workshop, which I converted into the studio.

I loved the house: it had a great atmosphere, and it suited it having company and there were many great nights there. The kitchen and sitting room were on the first floor and looked out onto the river through these beautiful tall Georgian windows. The kitchen table was the centre of Zachary House. It comfortably seated fourteen people and many a night was spent righting the wrongs of the world. Annabel

did a regular make-up and beauty slot on the Saturday morning kids'
show *Going Live* and we became good friends with the presenters
Philip Schofield and Sarah Greene, who was married to the Radio
One DJ Mike Smith. They were all regular visitors to the house along
with other people like Janet Kay, the hand model, Mick Karn, the
bass player from Japan who is also a brilliant sculptor, Glenn and
Lindsey Gregory and Andy and Nicky Hill, the songwriters behind
Bucks Fizz.

The Thames did have its drawbacks early on a Sunday morning,
with coxes screaming and shouting at their crews and the ducks and
geese and swans making a racket. The one main disadvantage was
that the house sat right on the towpath between three pubs. On a nice
sunny summer's evening people would come along to the pubs, wander
up and down the towpath and sit and dangle their feet over the edge
– it was the closest thing they could get to the seaside in London.

It was tranquil and beautiful except at half-eleven at night. After
kicking-out time at the pubs there was always some wag who thought
it would be hysterically funny to press my intercom and sing 'Vienna'
at me. It would have been funny had they had the brain cells to realise
that this had maybe happened once or twice before. It was dull to say
the least, but then at 11.30 when you are smashed out of your brains
a lot of things seem to be funny. The bonus was that I was never short
of glasses. People lined up their pint glasses and wine glasses along
the wall running along the front of my house, so I'd organise raids to
stock up on glasses when I had a bunch of lads coming round the next
day for a barbecue. When I left I had enough to stock a small pub –
in fact, I still have.

I liked classic design and collecting classic objects, a Halliburton
suitcase, a Harley Davidson, or a Burberry raincoat, it didn't matter.
So all the stuff I had bought were classics whether it be the sofas, the
chairs or the Willis Jeep. That was another one. Chris Cross and I
found this place in Battersea that sold these 1950s ragtop Willis Jeeps
– left-hand drive ex-US Army Jeeps like they used in *M*A*S*H* – for
£1,500 each. The whole top came off, the windscreen went forward,
and it had canvas seats so we didn't care if it got dirty. We thought
they were fantastic – though we used to get real catcalls driving around
in them, as people thought we were real dicks. Mind you, I could have
gone out and bought a brand-new Porsche and been a dick in a Porsche
but I never did.

I had a thing about cars. Boys toys, that's what they all were. The
stupid thing was, any time I wanted to use them, either the tax or the

MOT had run out, the insurance hadn't been kept up or the battery was flat. So in effect they were redundant objects. I slowly unloaded them. The Porsches ended up in this classic-car showroom in Battersea. The Mercedes G Wagon was shipped out to Monserrat where Malcolm Kelly and I christened it 'the car that saved the island'. After the hurricane swept over, American aid arrived on the island in the form of huge tarpaulins to cover roofs. After a hurricane passes it stays rainy for weeks which, when none of the houses have roofs left, can be dangerous. Malcolm and I drove round with a car load of tarpaulins throwing them over what was left of the roofs – including my own. Sometimes the only way to get them over the house was to stand on the roof of the car. The roads had trees lying all over them but the G Wagon could drive on beaches and across rough land so it was really useful – and, unlike many of my cars, it actually worked when it was needed. I spent two weeks helping out and getting my own house watertight before I went back to LA.

When I went out to Montserrat my modern car was a flash Mercedes estate. I gave it to my dad for the year but I think he was too petrified of it to drive it. It was very fast and he'd never seen anything so expensive. When I came back I had this real hankering for a dark-green Mini, but at the time you couldn't really find them. I went to this Mini garage outside of London where they had one in orange. I told them I'd have it as long as they painted it green and put on a wooden dashboard. I used it as my London run-around for ages.

Seeing all that horror in Ethiopia also changed what I wrote about. It was obvious first with 'All Fall Down' but, when I started working on my first solo project after leaving Ultravox, I felt it was time to sit down and right the world's wrongs. Finally I was master of my own destiny. It should have been a relief, but instead I recorded *Answers To Nothing*. I didn't have any answers, so I was just pointing things out, making my opinions clear. I had no solutions and I offered none. It was the beginning of my bleak period.

After the success of *Vienna* Chrysalis pretty much left Ultravox to our own devices, to do whatever we wanted and to make our own mistakes . . . and we made loads. When it came to my solo stuff, which initially was very successful, there was no A&R guy working with me. I didn't want anyone telling me what to do, advising me as to who I should work with. I did what I wanted to do and of course I made mistakes. With hindsight, *Answers To Nothing* was probably a bit of a mistake.

There is both security and frustration about being in a band. You speak as an entity, everything you say, everything you do, everything you write is part of this collective. So you feel empowered to do whatever you want. Once you step outside and you have to start speaking for yourself, as an individual, as a person, it can get very confusing as to exactly what you should be doing. *The Gift* was easy because I still had the security of Ultravox around me.

With *The Gift* I was dabbling, but when it came to the first chapter of my new career I was too solemn. I tried to prove to the world that I could write serious songs about serious subjects, show a high level of musicianship. I worked with Mark Brzezicki and bass players Mark King and Mick Karn, using great musicians to show just what I was capable of. The outcome was just too over the top, too po-faced, too serious. I had gone too far, and actually become everything people had criticised Ultravox for.

I didn't realise because I was producing the record myself, writing the songs and playing a lot of the instruments. Embroiled in my own little world, in the studio, it was very difficult to step back and tell myself, 'Don't go there.' I couldn't see the wood for the trees because I was standing right in the middle covered in leaves. There are moments that still stand up today but generally the production is too busy, and there's too much going on, too many countermelodies. 'Sister And Brother' was a duet with Kate Bush which was fantastic. But in addition to Kate I had the Campbell brothers from UB40 on backing vocals. I was making a huge stew that spilled out over the top because there was too much in it. I'd chucked in two kitchen sinks for good measure. Mine and Kate Bush's.

I'd first met Kate back in 1978 when *The Kick Inside* first came out. Both she and the Rich Kids were signed to EMI and we ended up doing loads of TV shows together. Everybody in the band fancied Kate and wanted to get to know her better but nobody ever did. We were both at the Prince's Trust party at Kensington Palace so I asked Kate if she'd do a duet with me. She asked me to send over the multitracks because she was in the middle of recording her own album. I did, but I didn't really expect to hear back for months because I knew she was under pressure.

She called up a couple of days later and said, 'I've done something, do you want to come over and hear it?' I drove out to her house and she put on this tape and said in her little-girl voice, 'I really hope you like it, Midge.' I sat there listening with a tear in my eye. It was fantastic. She had taken hours multitracking and overdubbing lead and harmony vocals. I was really touched that she'd spent so long on something I'd done and asked for nothing in return.

We have stayed friends ever since. Two years ago I presented her with her Classic Songwriter award at the Q Awards. It was the least I could do.

I woke up one morning with 'Dear God' in my head. That doesn't happen very often – like never. Usually when I hear things in my dreams, I hear completely orchestrated, full-blown songs. I wake up at four o'clock in the morning and – I've tried this umpteen times – sing the melody into the Dictaphone I keep by the side of the bed. Usually when I play it back the next day it sounds as if I was drunk, because I've got no recollection of what the hell it was. I sang the melody I dreamed OK, but the arrangement's not there and I've forgotten it all.

'Dear God' is a very childlike naïve song, which is why I remembered it all. Lyrically it appears to be a child's prayer: 'Dear God, is there somebody out there, is there someone to hear my prayer.' But it's also saying, 'Dear God, what a bloody mess we're in.'

Chris Wright and whoever was the head of the American record company at the time came out to Montserrat when I was mixing the album. It was ten o'clock at night and I was supposed to play them my first proper solo album, that I had been working on for the last year. At dinner Chris Wright sat there asking the locals who were serving us, 'Do you know the radio station here? Can you get them to play Eddie Grant's "Hope Joanna", it's a great song.' It was not a good omen. I was waiting to play my album and they were rabbiting on about somebody else's tracks.

They came in and listened to the album and went, 'Hmm, very good.' Very noncommittal, so I said, ' "Dear God's" obviously a single.'

'Yeah,' grunted the American. 'Brilliant song, but it'll never be a single in America.'

'Why not?'

'It's got God in the title.'

'Well, the song's called "Dear God". It's got God in the title, so what?'

'Well, you know, we're so intermixed, it's not just God, Jews . . . it might upset people.'

It turned out to be a Top Three Indy single, and KROQ in LA played it all the time. These guys got it completely wrong, but that was par for the course with America. Maybe I should have changed the title to 'Dear Dog'! Or reminded them that George Harrison had a big hit called 'My Sweet Lord'.

I believe in what I do, so naturally I thought it was the best thing I'd ever done. But nobody else did, and they thought it was crap or, worst of all, boring. I was Midge Ure and I should be singing three-minute pop songs, not trying to right the world's wrongs. Commercially *Answers* died a horrible death. It was the first time in eight years I'd had a serious failure. I felt awful. It was like having a kid that turns out wrong: you take great care raising it and then it goes out and robs a bank. As any artist will tell you the first thing that happens is you blame yourself and start thinking, I've lost it completely: I don't know what I'm doing; I can't write songs any more.

I heard 'Answers To Nothing', the single, when it was played on Radio One's *Round Table*. I sat there listening and some American who was reviewing said, 'It's not got much of a tune, has it?' I thought, You bastard, of course it's got a tune, but I do have to admit it is a bit of a repetitive one. I still like the song on a certain level, but it just didn't work for the rest of the world.

Even the video shoot for 'Answers' was a complete disaster. The original concept was brilliant, this long line of people high up on a hillside, and the entire clip was to be one long tracking shot. It started off with me singing high up on a hillside. The camera was to pan through various people that I'm talking about in the song, cut from faces to a little scenario going on in the background, a Russian and an American shaking hands over a bomb, then back to the next face singing the lyrics. Everyone knew the lyric and was singing the song and we had a couple of hundred people standing in this field waiting all day. We never got past the tenth person because the camera kept going out of sync. I had to redo it a week later in the studio.

The only place I toured the album was in America. Part of my plan during my tax-year out was to live in Montserrat and break America. I did a six-week club tour. Then I got a call from Howard Jones, who was really big in the States at that time, asking me to open for him, playing sheds (open-air arenas). I'd never done that before, so soon I was out with him, coast to coast and back again.

For that tour I did something that technically had never been done before. I premixed the band (two keyboards, a percussionist playing guitar and vocals, an electronic drum kit with live cymbals bass and my guitar). That was something technically I had wanted to do with Ultravox, so then we could have opened for other artists. The technology had changed now so that machines were talking to other machines.

At rehearsals I had everybody around me in a circle (like we used to do in Ultravox), then I'd get the keyboard player to play flute on the right hand, cello on the left. I'd balance it up so it all sounded right to me. Every song had its own memory. This saved us when we came to do the shows with Howard. A lot of times Howard was sound-checking all the way through and we would only have five minutes left until curfew. (In America, roadies have a union and they have to have silence at six o'clock.) The premixing enabled us to do it. The sound engineer only had to stick all sixteen faders up on his desk and I knew the mix was going to sound really good up front.

The opening night of Howard's tour was in Boston. It was a good place for me to start because Ultravox had been big in Boston. The next day the *Boston Globe* ran a review asking 'Why is the king of electronics opening for the wimp of electronics?' We had to hide the paper from Howard, as he would not have been amused and it is not a good way to start a tour by pissing off the headliner.

It was a great tour. Howard was still incredibly popular so we were playing to between three and twenty thousand people a night. It was the middle of summer and the weather was glorious. We played a 45-minute set and were allowed an encore, which again was very generous of Howard (many headliners find ways of pulling the plug and claiming technical problems if the support is doing too well). We got really good reviews, though I didn't know about them until 2003 when we put out a recording of the shows through my website. I read the cuttings which said things like, 'If this doesn't elevate Ure into the same status as Peter Gabriel and Sting nothing will.' Nothing did.

The second age-old thing that happens after a commercial failure is that you blame the record company. I couldn't entirely blame Chrysalis, because they had actually done everything that they promised to do for *Answers*. They made the videos, took out the adverts, put up the posters, and we toured the radio stations. They did their job and I can't blame them at all. For that.

However good Chrysalis were in Europe I was desperate to get off the American label. I was so tired of having huge hits in Europe then going to America and being treated like some piece of trash, virtually asked what the hell I was doing over there, or being greeted at the airport with the news that the last single was already dead when it had been out a whole two weeks.

The American arm of Chrysalis had an amazing ability to find any drive I had, suck it out of me and throw it away. The corridors in their offices were lined with pictures of Pat Benatar, Billy Idol and Debbie Harry, all big in the States. I was a multimillion-selling artist too, but I literally had to spell my name at reception. 'Midge who? Will he know what it's about?' Between 1980 and 1985 there were nine presidents of Chrysalis in America . . . and only one president of the USA.

At the bottom of it all it was my ego. The pinnacle of any artist's career is to break America, as it is the biggest market in the world and the hardest. If an act makes it big in America it doesn't matter what happens overseas, so there is no real incentive for an American company to break a foreign act. A British artist has either to do what U2 and the Police did – go out there and tour constantly – or get lucky, have a hit and capitalise on it . . . by touring constantly.

Ultravox never cracked America. We should have done, but maybe we were a bit too arty and serious, although our music certainly appealed. After *Vienna* came out Ultravox had a foothold, and the tour dates were all sellouts. We sold 60,000 copies of the album yet Chrysalis admitted to Chris Morrison that they didn't know where these sales were coming from. He pointed out that the first person through the dressing-room door at the end of the show was the local college radio programme director. College radio played Ultravox all the time. Chrysalis told us, 'College radio doesn't sell records.' Two years later Mike Bone (who later became a president at Chrysalis) broke A Flock of Seagulls and the Thompson Twins through college radio – and then MTV.

Chrysalis America failed to capitalise on both college radio and our videos. At home we were allowed to make our own decisions, to take risks, make outlandish videos and have high-art album covers. It worked. In the States we had to play by their rules.

We played so many nights at the Whiskey in LA we were virtually the house band. Chris O'Donnell tried to convince Terry Ellis, when he was the big boss in America, to stick a wall of TVs showing our videos in the window of Tower Records just down on Sunset Strip. People would walk past and do a double take. He told us, 'No, it's all about radio in America: if radio won't play it, it isn't going to happen.' Two years later along came MTV, which ate up our stuff. Ultravox were leaders in the video field, and we won awards (not surprisingly, as nobody else was making classy videos). Only the Brits.

'If I Was' was a hit just over the border in Canada and a Top Ten hit all over the world, but it could not get a play on American radio. I was told helpfully, 'The problem is you are using dance beats and right now radio is playing R&B beats. You should record an R&B record next time.' Sure, and when I do they'll be playing rock beats on the radio. It was crap, and we got fobbed off with excuse after corporate excuse.

It drove Morrison crazy. His particular *bête noire* was a president called Jack Craigo. Over a breakfast meeting in LA he asked Craigo, 'Why can't we get radio, Jack?'

Out came the party line: 'Ultravox will get played on the radio when they start writing music for American radio.'

Chris was incensed. 'If we all thought like that, Jack, we'd still be listening to Glen Miller.'

Craigo exploded.

This all sounds like sour grapes. Maybe it is. But we felt that we weren't getting a fair crack at America as long as we were on Chrysalis. Morrison tried everything to get us off the label. He told Craigo that to his face. The answer he got still appals and astonishes me. 'I won't let Ultravox off the label . . . in case they're successful.'

Getting out of the deal was a long, slow war of attrition. We never wanted to go into head-on warfare, direct confrontation – like George Michael did later with Sony – because that would have put my career on ice for years. After I left Ultravox I saw Chris Wright and told him I had to get off the label in America. When Wrighty said I was still a jewel in his crown Morrison came in all heavy and said, 'OK then, we'll have to audit.' That made them throw their hands up in shock horror.

The other leverage we had was to do with Max Headroom, the computer-generated talk-show host. Chris Cross and I wrote the soundtrack to the original Max Headroom movie, then Chrysalis remade the original movie as a series for MTV and redid the music using ours as a template, with a couple of notes slightly different. A court case would have been interesting. Max was huge in America, he was selling loads of 'M-M-M-M-M-Max' T-shirts, mugs and videos. There was a moot point in my contract where it could be argued that I was due a percentage of any merchandising royalties.

It was a very grey area but that was the leverage that got me off in December 1990 . . . plus the fact that we were going to audit. Record companies hate to be audited. It's expensive but can show up serious underpayments. When an American country artist threatened an audit once the company promptly offered a six-million-dollar settlement. That makes you think.

It was important for me to make the break because I still thought I had a crack at breaking America. The longer it dragged on the less chance there was of doing it. By the time I got off the contract in 1990 even that chance was dead and gone.

CHAPTER 22
JAMMING WITH LEGENDS

I've always done a lot of charity gigs. It's not just because I'm a good guy and that I believe in doing charity work; it's because first and foremost I'm a musician. Would you turn down the chance of being on stage with Paul McCartney or George Harrison? We're all fans of each other – Clapton is a fan of BB King and Bob Marley – that's why I first learned to play, why I wanted to get into the industry. We never cease to be fans and that love doesn't go away. If it ever does I shan't be there any more.

It's not a matter of ego: it's about being a musician. It's not a hardship to go on stage and play a couple of songs to raise money for a good cause, and if there are people there who I respect and admire – some of whom are the reason that I'm a musician in the first place – I want the chance to be in their company. At charity gigs I've swapped guitar licks with Eric Clapton and Pete Townshend, done things I dreamed of as a schoolboy, stuff a kid from Cambuslang never does. I've been the lucky one.

I did the first Prince's Trust Rock Gala in 1982 after George Martin stroked my ego by telling me Pete Townshend thought I was a great player. If Pete Townshend was saying he wanted me to be his lead guitarist, I wasn't going to turn that down. The band met up in AIR Studios with the artists who were going to perform. Robert Plant came in with one of his solo hits, and Garry Brooker was singing 'A Whiter Shade of Pale'.

It was going fine until Kate Bush produced her choice: 'Wedding List'. As we were trying to gauge each other's abilities everyone was being very cool and we listened to the song in absolute silence. It was so difficult none of us knew whether we could actually play it or not. When it finished, Kate said, 'That's it easy, we won't bother to rehearse it until next week,' and waltzed out of the room.

'Well,' went Townshend to break the ice, 'that'll be a piece of piss, won't it?'

On the night it was Kate who had the problems. She wore a halter top and halfway through the halter bit broke and there were just a couple of pins stopping it from falling off. Kate had to sing on while holding up her top to stop her boobs falling out, which amused us all.

In 1986 the Prince's Trust was celebrating its tenth anniversary with a star-studded concert at Wembley Arena. Chris Poole approached me to become musical director, but first he told me the band line-up: Elton John on piano, Clapton and Mark Knopfler on guitars, and Phil Collins on drums. Rod Stewart, Tina Turner, George Michael and Paul McCartney were confirmed to sing.

'No way,' I said. 'This is obviously the job that everybody's turned down.' It didn't take long to talk me into it. It might be a daunting prospect to be in charge of a band with all those luminaries in it, but how could I refuse? My job was to break the songs down, figure out how they all fitted together and oversee cups of tea, or something stronger, every ten minutes. I knew Clapton was not interested in learning all the chord sequences, and he would just play on to the top of what everyone else was playing. I was scared to death the first day of rehearsal. My main rule was: don't bring your own trash – leave your management behind because that just screws things up. I'd said all that to them all, but secretly I was just waiting for the Ego to land.

It did in the shape of Rod Stewart. We were rehearsing at the Wimbledon Theatre when the doors flew open and a couple of heavies in suits and sunglasses came in first, casing the theatre for God knows what – popcorn assassins, maybe. In strutted Rod, all attitude, he came up to me and demanded, 'Is my song ready?' He ran through 'Sailing' a couple of times and stormed straight out again without even a thank you. It was totally unnecessary, especially in front of Clapton and Elton, mates he'd known for twenty years. I know him and Elton have got this camp game, calling each other Elsie and Doris or whatever, maybe it was that, and he was doing it to wind up Elton, but I just thought, What a prat, he's been in America too long. Tina Turner had been sitting in the audience, watching what was going on for five hours. She didn't say a dickie bird, just sat there waiting on her turn, the total professional. Was Rod's entrance a wind-up? I don't know.

Entourages fuck things up. The Bee Gees were experts at that with their two managers who loved to play good cop, bad cop. In 1988 they came over to England to do Nelson Mandela's Birthday Tribute and then were added to the Prince's Trust bill at the Albert Hall. They only came over in the first place because they were appearing at an all-expenses-paid Pro-Am golf tournament. At the Mandela show they brought a sound engineer and monitor guy, which was fine, except they took for ever to get the balance right for their harmonies. They kept complaining the monitors were crap and feeding back, but as they were standing two feet away from the microphones it was no wonder they couldn't hear.

On the night of the Prince's Trust concert I was backstage in the communal dressing room chatting to Phil Collins and Mark Brzezicki when this woman came storming in. 'Who's the musical director?' she demanded, and then started laying into me about how she had been told the Bee Gees were going to top the bill.

'There is no top of the bill,' I said, 'and I decide who's going to close the show.'

'We're the Bee Gees; we're top of the bill and we're going on last.' Although there were ten of us crammed in the dressing room a deathly hush descended. This woman was screaming, virtually spitting in my face. 'If we don't top the bill, I will pull them out of the concert. Then you'll be sorry.'

'Fine,' I said, when she paused for breath. I looked her straight in the eyes. 'We've got a great bill tonight. I don't give a fuck whether the Bee Gees play or not. I know why they're here; I know how they're here, and I know what else they're doing. You want to pull out now, fine. Goodbye. The Bee Gees' last hit was three years ago, and Peter Gabriel has just had a huge Number One. "Sledgehammer" is an infinitely better last song than anything your guys have got. It is a finishing tune. Peter Gabriel is going to close the show. Now take your band and fuck off.'

The entire room cheered. She stormed out. Five minutes later the Bee Gees wandered in, one by one, very nonchalant, looking as happy as pigs in shit, saying, 'We don't care when we play; we're just happy to be here.' The other manager was nodding his head like a donkey on the back shelf of a Cortina, agreeing with everything and anything. It was all just a try-on. If you can eliminate that stuff, dealing with the artists is easy and it has always been an absolute pleasure doing it. As soon as management turns up stamping its little foot, ego becomes an issue.

Because I wasn't being paid to do it, and an artist in my own right, I could tell her where to shove her band. Anyway, it had taken me a lot of persuading to get Peter Gabriel to do the show. Peter doesn't like doing one-offs, and I had to really talk him into it promising, 'It will be fine; we'll take David Rhodes on guitar, use your brass samples. Believe me I'll have it a hundred per cent right. We've got Phil and Mark doing drums; it will be great.' He got very nervous but he loved it and had a ball.

The Bee Gees manager might not have known who I was but that same night I was given a Grammy Award and a standing ovation. I'm not sure I should have got that Grammy. It dated back to the first Trust concert I md'd at Wembley. That whole day had been real seats-of-the-pants stuff. Jagger and Bowie had rolled up on the night and decided to recreate a very impromptu version of 'Dancing In The Street'. Howard Jones was the only person on the bill who knew what the chords were so we jammed it in the dressing room for fifteen minutes and then went out and did it. Musically it was chaotic, but that didn't matter because it was all about Mick and David trying to out-queen each other.

We were filming the show, but as we couldn't book a mobile recording studio we hired a van and built our own. Rik Walton was in there overseeing it right up to the wire. Curiosity Killed The Cat were on stage and for the first minute they had no bass drum sound because he was still plugging up the cables. We fixed it later and I mixed the sound for the video.

Eighteen months later I was hanging about in the dressing room at the Albert Hall when Harvey Goldsmith ran in yelling, 'Midge, quick, quick!' He shoved me out onto the stage and, while I was still blinking in the spotlights, awarded me this Grammy. I looked out at the Albert Hall and there were Charles and Diana standing up and applauding. Bloody hell, I thought, I don't know why I've got this in my hand but they are giving it big for Midge. I'm not sure if I actually warranted winning anything at all, as it was the Prince's Trust who won the Grammy for Best Music Video – but it's mine now.

After the Wembley show Charles and Diana hosted a party for all the artists at AIR studios. I had the dubious honour of showing Prince Charles around the control room. He pointed at the big Neve mixing desk and said, 'I suppose this is Japanese.' Neve are a British company based in Burnley, so I just coughed and suggested he try out a microphone to see how it all worked. The engineer had plugged a microphone into a harmoniser and as Charles spoke into the mike I altered the pitch so he sounded like a member of the Goons. As his voice went all wobbly he gave a very non-royal giggle.

The party was in the main studio. Diana was in her element, mixing and mingling with everyone. Unlike her husband, who was always a bit formal, she was completely at her ease and loved chatting to pop stars. When I was talking to her she was bemoaning the fact that she had asked the Trust 'if we could have the party back at our place' – and they'd said no.

'That sounds like a great idea,' I said. 'You should do that next year.' I never expected anything to come of it.

The next year everyone who'd ever performed at a Prince's Trust concert was invited to 'our place' – Kensington Palace. The atmosphere was very stiff to begin with until, to loosen things up a bit, HRH asked Jools Holland to play the piano. Jools launched into his regular boogie-woogie make-it-up-as-you-go-along routine. Soon the lights had dimmed, champagne flowed, faces glowed and everyone had a ball – especially Diana.

By 1988 I had a track record as a musical director who could be trusted to put the band together, and make sure everyone was happy, which is why I got the call for Nelson Mandela's 70th Birthday Tribute at Wembley Stadium. There was this gaggle of loose artists – Fish and Joan Armatrading, Curt Smith from Tears for Fears, Paul Carrack, Paul Young, the Bee Gees – who didn't have a backing band. I called up some of the guys who had worked with me on Prince's Trust concerts and soon had a pretty good band. Mark Kelly from Marillion and Paul Carrack played keyboards, Mick Karn was on bass, Phil Collins and Mark Brzezicki on drums, the Phantom Horns were the brass section and I played guitar. We rehearsed some specials like Paul Young and Carrack duetting on 'Don't Dream It's Over'.

On the day of the show I was standing backstage, when I got a tap on the shoulder. I turned around and I'm staring straight into this beautiful blonde's breasts. It was Daryl Hannah, the Hollywood superstar who was going to introduce us on stage. Nobody had warned me and there I was drooling out of the side of my mouth, mumbling, 'Oh my God.' She was Jackson Browne's girlfriend at the time and he's a very politically conscious, right-on character. Daryl went on stage and did the whole 'Ladies and gentlemen, please welcome Midge Ure's All Star band' thing. There was huge applause. Unfortunately she announced it ten minutes before I was meant to be on, so I was still floating around backstage. Nobody had given us any warning and there was something of a gap before we all toddled on.

The Prince's Trust Albert Hall gig was a few weeks after the Mandela show and after that I decided it was enough. I told Prince Charles that in order to keep it bright and fresh he should ask someone else. I'd done three years in a row and that was plenty. After I walked away the balance changed; it turned into Cliff and Kylie and then into Party In The Park.

If I'd never done those shows I wouldn't have stayed up all night playing the guitar with one of my all-time heroes. I was out in

Montserrat having a break with Annabel. Eric Clapton was up at AIR studios playing on Sting's album *Nothing Like The Sun*. Sting wasn't even there; he had booked the studio, flown Eric out for a week and told him, 'Bring a bunch of guitars, play on whatever you fancy and I'll keep the bits I want.' Eric went into the studio and played on everything the first day – he's all over the album, too. The rest of the time he lay out in the sun.

Eric doesn't like to hang around and he hates doing videos. Lol Creme told me about a Clapton video he had done. They had ten cameras in the studio to shoot him. He did one run-through, sang the song once and left.

One afternoon we were basking in the sun out by the pool when Eric said to me, 'I've got some Vaughan Williams with me, want to hear it?' As I had no idea who Vaughan Williams was I thought he meant Sarah Vaughan, and mumbled something about how I liked 'Passing Strangers'.

'No, no, Vaughan Williams.' Eric was laughing so much that he had a hard time playing me the piece. It wasn't the music I expected Eric to like, but he was full of surprises. We'd certainly consumed a few that stage. In those days Eric was getting up in the morning and drinking champagne to get him going, then he just carried on drinking through-out the day. He'd have wine for lunch and then drink all afternoon by the pool before he moved onto the heavy stuff – he liked vodka in the evening when we sat around playing games. God, I was a rank amateur compared to Eric. I couldn't keep up with him in those days. Eric was always ahead of me – he quit the booze long before I dreamed I had a problem. I remember throwing up violently in the flower beds while he stood there laughing his head off. Most of the top guys did that – when Ian Gillan and Roger Glover were out recording a solo album I couldn't keep up with them either. Elton went through the drugs and the drink cycle, too. It was the lifestyle, what those guys did: you can afford to do it, so you do it. They didn't live by anyone else's rules.

We sat up drinking into the wee small hours, Eric, Annabel, Yvonne, who ran the studio, and me. He knew I could play guitar from the Prince's Trust gigs, but in his eyes I was probably still the guy with the sideburns standing behind a synthesizer. We were talking about music and I mentioned John Mayall's *A Hard Road* album.

'How come you know that?'

'I was brought up on that and the Bluesbreakers album. I cut my teeth on those tunes. I was fourteen, and I wanted to play guitar like you so much I wore the damn record out.'

I had a million questions, questions I'd had for twenty years, technical stuff I wanted to ask Eric. How do you make those notes sustain? How did you get that sound? Instead he kept talking about cricketers, about Ian Botham, how they were real men who could stay up drinking all night, fall into bed at five o'clock in the morning, get up the next day and wander out into hundred-degree temperatures in Australia, then stand out there and play a game, match, cricket – whatever you call it – for the next seven hours. Eric thought that was the ultimate, that these guys were modern gladiators. He promised to buy me a set of cricket whites.

'I don't know anything about cricket,' I kept telling him. 'I don't play it. I don't understand it. It's an English game.'

Eric wasn't to be deflected. 'I'll get you the whites, then you'll love it.'

I didn't want any damn whites. I was sitting thinking, What I'd really love is one of your old SGs, one of your Les Pauls, imagine me owning one of your guitars.

At some point I pulled out my guitars. We sat and played the original bluesy version of 'Crossroads', the way Robert Johnson did it, not Cream. He played acoustic and I played lead on my electric. Then we swapped guitars and played another old blues number. We played for at least three hours. I was in musical heaven and I still dream of it today.

Moments like that don't often happen. I've been lucky. Other than Rod the Sod I've not been on the receiving end of any rockstar tantrums. Everyone says, 'Don't meet your heroes.' Well, I've met most of mine, and I've not been disillusioned. They've all been good guys, and I haven't seen the bad side at all. Be it Bowie, Eric, Townshend, Phil Collins, whoever, they've all been good, salt-of-the-earth people.

Probably it's because most of them are from serious working-class backgrounds. They all come from a Cambuslang of their own.

CHAPTER 23
IN THE TAR PIT

Since the first day I made money I have ploughed it back into studio equipment. All the time we were trying to get out of Chrysalis I was self-sufficient. I could record and I didn't have to think about the mortgage next month. By the time BMG came courting *Pure* was 95% finished.

Heinz Henn and his wife Caroline were both big fans, and they came down to my studio in Zachary House. Heinz was already hooked on my songs but he hadn't heard the big hit single, and all record-company guys need to hear a hit single. I played him a backing track which had a real African feel, all slidey fretless bass and Burundi drumming. I cranked the speakers up, stood next to him and sang the melody and rough lyrics in his ear. He signed me on the strength of 'Cold, Cold Heart', right then and there. On the surface it was a nice little pop song, but underneath it was really nasty, an emotional-failure song wrapped up in this lovely bubble-gum package.

I signed to the man, not the company. In contrast to Chrysalis, BMG were a major record company. BMG itself was a German multi-national that had swallowed up two major US labels: RCA, who had once had Elvis and Bowie, and Arista. Heinz had the serious title of 'Senior Vice President, BMG Entertainment International A&R and Marketing'. I knew dealing with Heinz would be tricky because of his very German kick-it-up-the-backside attitude, but his passion for my music overrode that. He desperately wanted me to be part of his record company. I didn't see that from anybody else. Although BMG International were based in New York I didn't foresee any major problem. I was promised that the label in the UK, or indeed anywhere in the world, could be changed to suit what I needed, even if we had to go outside the BMG group. I signed on that promise.

It never worked like that. In America I should have been on Arista, but I couldn't stand the thought of having Arista boss Clive Davis putting me through his mincing machine and coming out as a meat patty. He had done it with all his artists – Curtis Stigers, Whitney Houston – and they all came out sounding the same. I knew that Annie

Lennox had had a hard time with Arista so I ended up on RCA, which wasn't such a great label in America. In the UK I was on Arista, which was a 90% black label. The only other white artist on the label was Lisa Stansfield, who is an R&B singer. I was a fish out of water.

'Cold, Cold Heart' charted here, but not very high. Believe it or not, it was one of my most successful records in America, another Top Three independent radio hit. I got rave reviews but didn't follow through. I thought 'I See Hope In The Morning Light' was another hit but it wasn't delivered. That was when BMG started doubting their own tastes and decided to re-A&R me. My career was in danger of slipping away which was incredibly frustrating. Writing songs has peaks and troughs, and hopefully gets better and more interesting the more you do it. Maybe *Answers To Nothing* was my fault, but *Pure* was well thought out, palatable, interesting, and there's no reason in the world why I couldn't have done a Sting or a Peter Gabriel. Like them I'd come out of a successful band, and the industry talked me up as having similar talent to those guys, but they were selling millions of records, and I was missing the target.

This is going to sound like more sour grapes, that old cracked record of an artist not selling any more so it has to be the record company's fault. BMG International were a label for dinosaurs. It was a place where once-successful musicians went to die. Everyone they had on the label had been signed before – Deep Purple, Joan Armatrading. They also signed Al Green, but he would only make gospel albums. It was a roster of talented dinosaurs, but dinosaurs nonetheless – myself included.

Music industry personnel can change at a rapid rate, especially if a company isn't doing very well. In the early years of my new deal there were a few key people in the UK who gave me respect – when it was due – and tried to work on my behalf. But within two years I hadn't a clue who my contacts were. I stopped having meetings after it became glaringly obvious that, no matter what I came up with, nobody was interested. The first thing any new record-company boss does is bring in his own team of people. He sweeps the board clean, which includes dumping a lot of artists. They couldn't drop me because I had a watertight contract, but I was somebody else's hand-me-down so they did the next best thing, which was sign their own acts and ignore me.

It's customary for record companies to send their artists a Christmas present. In ten years with Arista I got one Christmas present, a bottle of champagne with a typed label with my name on it: 'To Mitch Ure'.

Is it too much to expect them to spell my name right? That summarised my standing as the red-headed stepson. When I rang up to make an appointment with the head of A&R the girl would ask, 'What is your name again? How do you spell Midge?' Fans ringing up to find out about release dates were told there wasn't any Midge Ure on the label.

There was a constant bickering between two record companies – the Germans running BMG International in New York and the UK – owned by the same corporation. They were at loggerheads, two arguing parents where I was the kid who lost out. Chris thought I was being paranoid, but eventually he saw it too. Everything came to a head at a big corporate event at Capistrano, in California. All the managing directors from round the world flew in and showcased their new acts. I went out to say hello, have a few drinks with the powers, the usual back-slapping stuff. I noticed Heinz in the corner looking really despondent, talking to someone from the English company. He said, 'We'll give you a hand doing that,' and this English exec just exploded. 'You're not giving me a bloody hand. Don't tell me what to do. I'll run my company the way I want . . .'

As this whole drama unfolded before my eyes I realised what had been bubbling under for years. The UK office couldn't stand Heinz forcing stuff down their throat, while Heinz couldn't stand this guy not doing what he supposed to be his job. Different countries, completely different mentalities. I was signed to one lot, so the others weren't interested in anything I did. Here's me thinking, Oh, they're all BMG, surely they all get on together. Wrong. There was a hate campaign going on and the UK didn't give a toss about anyone who was signed to the American label. It was a no-win situation and it spiralled from there. I realised that, no matter what we did, it was never going to happen in the UK for me again. I was a pawn – another age-old artist's gripe – but I didn't have the power to change it unless I came up with a big hit. That wouldn't happen for seven years.

Heinz had signed me as an artist who could produce, direct videos and write songs. Then, when *Pure* came out and didn't do what they expected, he wanted to change everything. Suddenly they were convinced that I was this megalomaniac who didn't want anybody else elected into Midge world. They wanted me to work with a producer who could shake me up a bit.

Chris O'Donnell came down to my studio and heard this instrumental track I was working on. He said, 'It reminds me of silence; all you can hear is somebody breathing in and breathing out.' Then, being Chris, he cracked some joke and talked about something else. That was the trigger which started me thinking about breathing. I finished 'Breathe' in 1991 and sent it to New York as a finished master. BMG dismissed it as too electronic; they were thinking, He's done it in his own studio and he's produced it himself; we want him to do something different.' That original recording isn't much different from the huge hit – it's the same vocal.

I played Heinz, and whoever his puppy dog was that day, the demos they had insisted I made. From their mouths I heard the classic line: 'This is the best batch of songs I have ever heard in my life, every song is a killer. All you need is the right producer.' A record exec's idea of finding the right producer is to look at the Billboard Top 100 and think, Mutt Lange must be really good because he's sold fifty million albums. Let's stick him in the studio with Midge. They never think, Will he be compatible, and will he make Midge write better, stronger songs? That is who they should have been looking for – the people who don't know the rules are the ones who come up with interesting stuff. Two years later there was still no producer.

It should not take five years to A&R a record. Heinz focused on me for five minutes, kicked everything into touch and then walked off for six months. I couldn't get hold of him and the UK company didn't return my calls. I felt as if I was running up a down escalator. Eventually I went out and found a producer myself. Richard Beck, who was my publicist at the time, gave me a tape of Milla Jovovich's *The Divine Comedy*. I was a bit dubious as she's a model turned actress turned singer, but I loved it. The production was exactly what I was looking for: organic, jangly, sparky but with a real power behind it. Richard gave me a listening tape, so there was no information on it at all, but eventually we tracked down the producer – Richard Feldman, a guitar player/songwriter from Texas, who lived in Los Angeles. I thought he was just the guy.

Feldman was told by BMG to 'poke me like a caged tiger'. He was a good producer, I'll give him his due, but his brief must have been to deflate me. 'Yeah, Ultravox, not sure about them. You sing high, don't you. It's no good writing something you're singing high in.' It was his way of saying, 'You've really got to come up with the goods now,' but I didn't enjoy it. The whole recording process was a love–hate relationship. In 1994 I had left London so I brought him over to my new home studio outside Bath because I didn't want to pay all the money in his studio while mine was gathering cobwebs. He resented it when I suggested we did a couple of weeks' work there before going off to Ireland to use all the Celtic musicians.

Creatively it proved a difficult album for me to make, because a lot of the time I just sat at the back of the control room. Why buy a dog and bark yourself? He was paid to be there and oversee bringing in the hurdy-gurdy player. I had no real job except to say, 'Yes, it sounds fine.' We had niggles about how it should be done and where it should go, and there were a few heated debates along the lines of 'That's no good' and me snapping back, 'Who are you to judge me?'

The album was full of different sounds and instruments – fiddle, Celtic harp and uilleann pipes. I used musicians like Robert Fripp, Paddy Moloney of the Chieftains, the singer Eleanor McEvoy, the Hothouse Flowers, Ofra Harnoy, who played cello on 'Fallen Angel', and Shankar on double violin. On *Pure* I had only used half a dozen musicians, but on *Breathe* it was closer to twenty and I hardly played a thing. After I'd written the songs and done the vocals, I kind of lost interest, until I brought in my friend Brian Tench to engineer it. It was an interesting process, but not one I'd choose to go back and do again. In the end BMG achieved what they set out to achieve. They got an album that wasn't just another Midge Ure album. They still managed to lose it.

After I delivered the album to New York I got a message back saying, 'We're not going to put it out right now because the head of RCA in America has just left, and we're looking for somebody else to head the company up. There's no point in putting it out because we want to have the full machine working.' Fair enough. Six months later Chris and I flew out to find out what the hell was going on. During the meeting Heinz got a phone call to say that the head of Arista in the UK had just been dumped. We flew back with our tails between our legs, deflated, knowing nothing was going to happen until two new guys were in place. Eventually they got themselves sorted and *Breathe* came out in 1996. Heinz was very excited about it, so the spend on promotions was pretty good. They spent £70,000 making the video and the EPK (Electronic Press Kit) using a director that I found. We played some special one-off gigs for the media and the record companies, including a brilliant show in Latvia, and got a good response everywhere except the UK.

That Riga gig was amazing. The club was stuffed with all these tall long-legged women in miniskirts and legs up to my head. The album reached No. 3 and was outselling Oasis and Blur. I got mobbed in the streets, which hadn't happened since Slik, and radio journalists told me that the president was a big fan. Yeah, right. Two months later, when we were invited back to play at the Baltic States Music Festival, I got a personal call from the president, Guntis Ulmanis, inviting me to tea. I had a motorbike escort, sirens going, the whole works all the way to his palace. I sat there having tea (which I don't drink) with the president and his mate, the drummer, who was also part of the government, chatting away through an interpreter. The president, who was young, funky and pretty laid-back, told me I was a national hero in Latvia because 'If I Was' had been one of the songs that inspired Latvia's struggle for independence from the Soviet Union. It's funny the way things work out.

Ultravox were big behind the Iron Curtain, bigger than we knew. We toured Poland long before most bands, playing in big circular auditoriums that were built for Hitler to give his speeches in. Very fascist interiors they were, with tall columns and a high domed roof, while behind the festooned curtains a massive swastika was still painted on the wall. A few years before the buzzer had gone in Zachary House and there was Billy Bragg standing at the door. 'I've got some presents for you,' he said. He'd come back from three weeks in Russia doing his right-on bit and singing some songs. Twice he had been stopped on the street by people asking him, 'Do you know Midge Ure?'

'No,' he said, 'but I know where he lives.'

A cosmonaut took his peaked hat off and said, 'Please give this to Midge,' while somebody else handed him a giant poster. I've still got them both.

Unfortunately Latvia was the highlight of the *Breathe* promotion. The record had taken two years to put together, a year to make and it had sat on the record company shelves for eighteen months. Five years is a long time in music, an eternity in a career. Britain had gone through a whole new musical movement – Britpop. *Breathe* fell out rather than came out – nobody paid much attention to it. Except *Q*, who reviewed it twice. They gave it a bad review the first time, then came back and kicked its head in.

I sat there with a record which I believed was as good an album as I'd ever made, and it was about to be my worst-performing record since Slik. Quite possibly ever. I felt as if I had been thrown in the river with my hands and feet tied. I felt helpless and hopeless. I'd been put through the mill by my record company, treated like a pawn, as if I hadn't already sold millions of records. That is the sort of shit that happens to an artist at the beginning of their career before they have proved themselves. I no longer wonder why some of them don't survive, because it nearly finished me.

I couldn't even bear to drag myself into my studio. I preferred to sit up all night drinking a bottle of Jack and chatting to a mate than write a new album. I was in no fit state to start writing. What would I write about? Depression?

Added to which, I was almost broke.

CHAPTER 24
GOING BROKE

Sometime in 1988 Chris Morrison and I went for a drink in Andy's Rum Shack in Montserrat. We sat on top of wooden barrels around an old Formica table, drinking rum and orange, eating deep-fried chicken and chips. 'Hey, Chris,' I said, my face and hands covered in chicken grease, 'I guess I'm a millionaire now.'

'Yeah,' he replied, 'I suppose you are.'

Four years later we were sitting in the Plaza Hotel in New York eating breakfast, all linen tablecloths and hot-and-cold running waiters. We were on our way to meet Heinz at BMG. 'I suppose,' I said, 'I'm not a millionaire now.'

'Unfortunately, Midge,' he replied, 'you are absolutely right.'

I was a single, divorced father, living in Zachary House, an eight-bedroomed house overlooking the River Thames. I also owed half a million pounds to the bank and the taxman.

After 'Vienna' was a hit I never signed a publishing deal. My songs remained 'copyright control', which meant CMO collected the money due to me from all the different territories. I didn't sign a publishing deal until 1988, with Warner Chappell. I arrived at their office when they were still fine-tuning the contract. I hung around for an hour until the lawyers finished bickering with each other, then I signed the contract. Warners gave me a million pounds and I never heard from them again.

They just gave me this money and I was left on my own. Not once did they try and put one of my tracks on a movie or ask me to write for another artist. I'm not sure if I can do that, but it would have been nice to be offered. Write a hit song for Kylie and she goes off and recoups a quarter of the money for the publisher. Midge Ure was the only vehicle to recoup that money, so I had to sell a lot of Midge Ure records to pay that advance back. It took a long time.

That night Annabel and I went out to dinner to celebrate, at the Hiroko, where else, with Phil Collins and his wife Jill. I'd just got a million-pound cheque but I was sat next to someone who had infinitely more. That put me in my place.

After Molly was born on 7 March 1987 Annabel and I were just like any other naïve young couple telling everyone, 'The baby will have to fit into our lifestyle.' Bollocks, it doesn't work that way. I was lucky enough to have a studio at the bottom of the garden, so if the intercom rang and it was Annabel saying, 'Molly's up and she wants you,' I could stop work and deal with her. I balanced my life like a set of scales – once Molly was settled at night I'd go to the studio, and most of the day I was around the house, helping out, being Dad.

It was hard work. Unlike studio equipment, babies don't come with instruction manuals. It was very much suck it and see. Why was she crying? Why was she up all night? I read lots of books but they didn't help. Nobody had warned me of that. Fortunately I didn't have a nine-to-five job, so I could help. I have done that with all my girls – I was always on call. Once Molly learned to walk she'd toddle out into the garden and come into the studio. I was there for 99% of her first two years. I saw her first steps, I heard her first words. Most fathers aren't so lucky.

By 1988 Annabel and I were having problems. Our love died slowly with no blame attached; we each wanted different things. After I signed my publishing deal I needed to spend a year out of the country for tax reasons. I was excited, and I had all these plans for a fresh start. I had American tours lined up; I was going to live in Montserrat with my wife and new baby. It didn't happen. I ended up there alone.

The core of my life was gone, swept away, and I couldn't handle it. My way of dealing with the break-up was to be steely, hiding the turmoil of emotions. I ran away to Montserrat because I thought it was the best place to be. Missing Molly was the biggest wrench of my tax exile. When I was over in LA Molly came out for a month with a nanny. Every weekend the two of us took off like Ryan and Tatum O'Neal in *Paper Moon*. I rented a car, drove to Disneyland, to San Diego Zoo, to Sea World. One night I kept her up late at Disneyland in Anaheim. It was dark, ten o'clock, and we were on a ride when the fireworks went off and Tinkerbell flew past followed by a line of lights. Molly was three years old, sitting in my lap watching this magic unfold – she'd never been up that late before. It is one of those moments I can never replace and she probably doesn't remember it at all.

When I got back to England I was still having family dinners, doing salad and pizza together with Molly. That went on for a while until Annabel and I both found new partners. Only then did we get divorced. As divorces go it was pretty civilised. Since then we've been adult and sensible. Sure, it's been volatile in places, but that's what happens. We've got to deal with each other until such time as Molly decides that she wants to do her own thing. It's the only way to do it. We'd seen too many people break up in similar circumstances so we have both tried to keep it as sane as possible, because fifteen years down the road we are still dealing with each other, only now we have to talk about schools and boyfriends and driving lessons. Responsibilities don't stop just because you don't live together any more.

Montserrat had taken two years to set up, so I had to go. I did the year out. It was the hardest year ever – I spent all that time on the island away from my friends, drinking too much rum with anyone who dropped by. It was hot every day. I was desperately seeking seasons, to see change, some snow. All I had was paradise, but it wasn't paradise, it was hell. Nothing I planned worked. I took out a fax machine in my suitcase, but that wouldn't work out there because the phone lines weren't up to scratch for faxes. I had a computer but nobody had ever heard of the Internet. So much for my high-tech year out. I went back to what I always did best – I worked, submerged myself in the studio and on the house, invited musicians over and started on *Pure*.

While I was in LA I did a production job for Hollywood Records. They had a boy/girl band who hosted a Saturday morning kids' show, and they wanted to do a cover of the Ronettes 'Walking In The Rain'. With the money I bought a new Harley Davidson Heritage Classic Softtail and made myself smile again.

The day after I bought it I jumped on and headed for San Francisco up the Pacific Coast Highway. I thought, LA, great weather, lightweight jacket, no helmet. Unfortunately, PCH was freezing cold because of the mist coming off the sea, so I turned right and drove through the desert, which was lovely, a warm breeze blowing in my face. By the time I got to San Francisco my head was a cinder, burned stupid by the baking-hot desert sun. I stopped off in a hotel for the night, turned round and came back again.

After three months my plan was to sell the bike. Then a friend of a friend said he was desperate to buy a Harley. We struck a deal where he would pay it off in instalments and then when I was in LA I could borrow it whenever I wanted. Of course, the guy got into a smash; I lost contact with him and the bike disappeared. Three years later somebody spotted it in the back of a Harley dealership, still smashed up. The dealer told me I'd have to pay storage on it for the past three years, which came to $5,000.

Another friend knew an English film editor who did some part-time private-detective work. He said he'd sort it out for me. Apparently when I had shot the Bananarama video on the day of the Brixton riots he was the editor. The next day I had dropped by with a bottle of whisky for him, which I still don't remember doing. He went into the store, pointed out to the owner that he was harbouring stolen goods and got my bike back. We found someone to fix it up; it went into his garage, and I sent him the money to pay for the repairs. Lo and behold, he put the bike outside the garage and somebody stole it. I gave up then: there was no point trying to sue anybody. I just kissed another £14,000 goodbye, just as everything else was falling around my ears.

Initially the half-million-pound debt wasn't a huge problem. I wasn't worried because I knew there was a substantial advance due from the record company. I had assets: Zachary House, Montserrat, a flat in Notting Hill. The bank were happy as they were making money and charging me interest. And, of course, my next album was going to do really well; I'd got it right; I was writing good songs. The advances were good money if you are expecting to make an album every two years . . . not so good when it takes five.

All my life I had never dealt with the business side. I'm an artist. I go into the studio where I make music; I give it to the machine; the machine feeds it out; people hear it and buy it. If I had to do my own VAT returns and tax assessments I'd never get anything else done. I can't do the left-brain bit, and I needed a security blanket of managers and accountants and lawyers to protect me. The Catch-22 is that when something went wrong I found the machine I had created was sucking it all up. I thought there was nothing I could do to change it.

Even though I was earning all the way through, money disappeared down this black hole. My business was set up so that 40% of my income went straight to the tax account and 17.5% to the VAT account, but when I got divorced it ate great big chunks out of my cash reserves. The cash that should have been in my little reserve wasn't there for me to live off, so they had to take it from the VAT or tax accounts. And then the taxman wanted to be paid.

I should have been more aware of it, but I preferred the bliss of ignorance. When I found out how much I owed it was a massive shock. I felt as if my head had exploded. I ran up the wall I was in such a state. I couldn't see a way of paying my debts so it started to worry me. A little niggling problem in the day became a massive problem at night. I'd lie awake tossing and turning in bed with all my problems magnified a million times.

It wasn't as if I was living the OTT pop-star life. I had got rid of the six classic cars in the garage, the boys' toys, by the time the early 90s rolled around. I lived a comfortable life but it wasn't Elton John extravagance – you can't take all the Scot out of Midge. I never blew twenty thousand quid on flash birthday bashes. Just before the *Answers* launch I invited most of the Chrysalis staff down to the house for a big barbecue, but that was the most extravagant thing I had ever done and it was business led.

I had bought the place in Montserrat – which maybe I shouldn't have done – but that wasn't a million-pound house. It had cost me 125 grand . . . plus rebuilding and rebuilding again. No one believed it was a bad investment as the bank had it listed as a quarter-million-pound asset. I knew the volcano was coming but when it erupted it ripped a huge chunk out of my portfolio. That was hard to explain to the bank.

What killed me financially was the housing-market crash. I'm not bad at making money in the music industry, but in property I'm dreadful. Don't ask me for advice. I lost a fortune. In order to buy a house for Annabel I took out a bridging loan on the flat. The property market promptly went tits up; nobody was buying anything and I couldn't shift it. It was like watching liquid money dribbling out of a bucket with a huge hole in it.

Bad luck comes in clusters and everything seemed to happen at the same time. I had bought my parents a house in Devon and put them on my payroll. They loved the cottage but it burned down. Twice. Baker's Cottage was a beautiful thatched house that had been abandoned for a long time. I had the builders put in central heating, a new bathroom, a new kitchen, had the floors sanded. My mum went out one day and left my dad with the dog, who started going crazy, barking the place down. Dad went out into the porch to find smoke everywhere. The light fitting had sparked and set fire to the thatch. As thatch burns from the inside out, you see smoke but not flames, so by this time the fire was halfway up the inside of the house. The neighbours, bless them, phoned the fire brigade and formed a chain to pull all the furnishings out into the garden, because anything not damaged by smoke and fire would be destroyed by water. Six months after the house was rebuilt a spark went through a crack in the chimney and set fire to the thatch again. This time the whole top of the house went up. The surveyor looked at the damage and told me that even though the beams were 400 years old they had never seen a fire that hot. After that I moved Mum and Dad into a place with a nice solid slate roof.

The second time it happened I opened the front door of Zachary House to find two coppers standing there saying, 'I have got some bad news for you, Mr Ure. Your parents' house is on fire.' Instead of going, 'Are they OK?' I just groaned, 'Jesus Christ. Not again!' God knows what sort of son they thought I was.

I suppose I didn't give them much choice about moving. I announced, 'I've found this fantastic house for you and you should move south,' and they did. It made sense as all their children lived in England and it was only an hour away from Poole where Bobby lived. Dad, who had finally retired, would have been happy staying in Glasgow, but when they got to Devon it was a different story. They were very proud because it was the first house they had ever owned.

To solve my financial problems I deliberately downsized. When I eventually sold Zachary House – it took two years – I hatched a plan to move into the flat and spend half the year in LA, trying to break into film directing. My only responsibility was Molly. She was sorted: she had a nanny, her mother and her own bedroom in Cambridge Gardens. If I spent four to six weeks at a time over in California I didn't need anything more than the flat. There was a flat directly below owned by the Select model agency and so there was this bevy of beauties constantly flitting in and out of the house. Years later I was musical director for Wicked Women, a breast-cancer charity concert in Hyde Park. Max Beesley was playing percussion in the band and at the time he was going out with the gorgeous Melanie Sykes. I went up to say hello to her and she said to me, 'Midge Ure. When I first came to London we used to get so excited when we saw your mail popping through the door.' Talk about missed sugar-borrowing opportunities.

I naïvely believed I could do something in movies. Back in the Ultravox days, flushed by our video successes, Chris Cross and I had bought the film rights to *No Mean City*, a novel about the Glasgow razor gangs in the 1920s. It was pure delusions of grandeur – making a record is one thing but a movie is different; you have to go out and schmooze, cajole people, knock on doors, get serious about raising the couple of million pounds it would have taken to make a period movie about the Gorbals. It was a pipe dream we were simply too busy to make. Realistically, if you want to be a movie director you have to come up with the story, write the screenplay, then punt it.

In hindsight my dream was a no-hoper. I've got friends who've directed for twenty years, and they've made a couple of movies but have never had the golden script. Russell Mulcahy was infinitely higher up the food chain of directors than I was, and so were Godley and Creme – Lol eventually got to make a film about some women in Jamaica. Russell was brilliant at the five-minute video but not particularly good at directing people. He was a great visualist who put things together brilliantly – shadows, wet cobbles, atmosphere, those were his forte. He was superb in the cutting room but not at telling an actor 'your motivation is . . .' Russell used to run away from that when he was doing videos. During his first feature, *Highlander*, Sean Connery got so exasperated that he pinned him up against the wall and said, 'Tell me what to fucking do.' I was never going to get there, though maybe if I'd gone to Los Angeles I'd have made a few shorts.

Living in LA first seeded in my head after I shot the video for 'I See Hope In The Morning Light' in 1991. That was my first, indeed only, Hollywood moment. I had my own police cordon on Sunset Boulevard on a Saturday night. I had my own walkie-talkie so if I said, 'Stop the traffic,' the police did just that. The cars would wait until I'd done my shot. The storyline started with me, dressed in a tux, driving along in this very expensive car – Lol Creme's Mercedes sports car – having a ruck with my model girlfriend. It ended up with me dressed in old denim swapping the Merc for a 1966 Ford Mustang convertible, driving into the desert where I met and fell in love with a beautiful girl. Like you do.

Intercut with the storyline was the performance. I hired a gospel choir, who had learned all the lyrics, and every take they sang it live. It was the most amazing sound, eighty big black women singing one of my songs, telling me, 'This is what we need to hear on the radio in America.' It was crossover rock, pop, gospel, 'hair on the back of your neck standing up' stuff.

It was a great shoot. At the end of it, the studio owner said, 'You should be here all the time; you've got a great knack of being able to get people to do things they wouldn't normally.'

I had been in and out of LA a lot since Annabel and I had split up. Every time I shot a video the message was the same: 'You are brilliant at this. You should have been here last week because there was a directing job going which would have been perfect for you.' Usual LA bullshit or no, the idea appealed to me.

In the meantime I tried acting. I got a call from my former art teacher Andy Park to see if I was interested in playing Angus McCurdie, a modern-day Glasgow gangster and drug dealer. I even got to shoot for five days in Glasgow in the dead of winter. Talk about an offer I couldn't refuse. Andy is a man of many talents, and after he left Radio Clyde he got into producing TV movies. *The Bogie Man* was based on a cult underground comic, and Robbie Coltrane, who I'd met umpteen times before, played the lead, Francis M Clunie, a fantasist and a bit of a nutter.

My actual acting debut had been way back in 1977 when the BBC put on a series of plays called *Jubilee*. I was in *Our Kid* with ex-Professional Martin Shaw, all about fashion and music in swinging London. We were the Slick who made it big in music. It was a real tough acting job playing a band in the 60s, but at least I got to say my three lines and sing a few 60s hits.

Learning my lines for *The Bogie Man* was hell. I can't remember my own songs, so somebody else's dialogue was a nightmare. The only way I could do it was to record on a cassette the other lines I had to react to, then leave a gap long enough for me to say my line back. I drove around talking to myself on a tape machine. My big scene was standing in a graveyard surrounded by my henchmen. Robbie had stolen something from me and I wanted it back. I stood in front of this guy who is six-foot-six, any which way you measure him, and declared, 'In this town I'm Mr Big.' I kept a straight face because Robbie is very serious about it: he's not the comedian when he is acting.

I got shot eventually, I think dead, but I was never quite sure. I had to be shot quite a few times and lying about a cold graveyard in Glasgow at three in the morning was not my idea of fun. My worst acting moment was when I had to lounge about in the bath trying to have a one-way conversation on a mobile phone. I was crap at that. It didn't help that when they finished the film they had 'Vienna' playing in the background. (There were also a couple of other in-jokes, references to Ultravox and a mysterious 'Mr Ure' in the script.)

However, when I did my rant about the state of Glasgow – how it was not the way it used to be when the razor gangs ran the slums, how it had gone soft and tame – everybody I know in the acting profession thought I did incredibly well. That was good, but my weak bits were rubbish. The show came out at Christmas on BBC2 and disappeared. It was another classic 'pop star tries to turn actor' moment. Every pop singer thinks they can do it. But they can't.

It didn't happen in LA, just like it wasn't happening with BMG. I started seeing an actress called Sheridan Forbes. A year in she fell pregnant and that was the end of my career as Cecil B de Mille.

CHAPTER 25
THE LEAVING

I fancied Sheridan long before I met her . . . and then didn't realise it for months. Soon after I came back from my tax year out I was sitting in Zachary House having a few drinks with Josh Phillips and Mark Brzezicki, watching the telly, when a commercial came on for British Gas. There was this very pretty girl with long beautiful blonde hair watching her boyfriend play football in the rain, sheltering under an umbrella. It cut to them all cosy, sitting in front of a lovely warm gas fire. She was snuggling up to him when he leaned forwards and switched the football on, at which she got really miffed and thumped him.

I turned round to the boys and said, 'That's what I need. I need one of those.' Way after we met I suddenly clicked that it was her in the commercial and that I had been granted my wish.

After I returned home in April 1990 I was determined to have some fun. That's when I started cooking. My perfect evening was getting all my friends together and filling up Zachary House. Jackie B was a regular, and she knew everybody. I had known Jackie Bucknell since the Blitz days. She was a record-company girl who got into acting. (Now she's the girl in the Flash adverts and married to Brian Capron, who played Richard Hillman, the infamous *Coronation Street* killer.)

One night I went to Circa, Rusty's club on Berkeley Square. The usual clique were there: Jackie B, Rusty, his wife Penny, big Glenn, the hand model Janet Kay and her photographer boyfriend Neil Barstow. Generally I don't do clubs very well because I don't do dancing; if we grabbed a table I'd stay there all night. For some reason we went down to the dance area, which was when Sheri offered to buy me a beer.

Sheridan had met Jackie on a commercial and they'd become friends doing a sitcom in Germany. She was a drop-dead gorgeous actress with long gold ringlets and a body to die for. She was 25 and just stunning. Knowing Jackie B, the fairy godmother, she had fixing us up already in mind. Being a mere male I had no idea and Sheridan didn't either. I fancied her like mad – everyone did, you would have to be dead not to fancy Sheridan – but I just didn't think I was ready for it, or that it would be reciprocated. For whatever reason, I just wasn't ready to try it on. For one thing, I was thirteen years older than her and I wondered, 'What would she see in me?' As I didn't think she was interested in me we only ever said hello.

Everyone in my business has – at the very least – a minor ego and we like to think everybody knows who we are. I was giving a dinner party for my thirty-seventh birthday at Zachary House and Sheri got there early and announced, 'I've got you a birthday present'. She gave me this beautiful book, a history of guitars – she did know I was a guitarist. I opened it up and inside she'd written: 'Happy Birthday to (some unreadable squiggle) love Sheridan'. I don't know what it said but it certainly wasn't my name and I still don't know what she thought I was called. It was a pleasant surprise to find out that after knowing me for a couple of months she didn't have a clue who I was . . . and didn't particularly care.

I was still reeling from the previous mess. I had started to find my feet as a single guy again and the last thing on my mind was starting another relationship. Being a very feisty, independent character – I soon learned never to start an argument with Sheri about politics – she wasn't looking for anyone either. Sheridan was floating free as I was, so inevitably over the months that followed we got to know each other. We were always the two spare ones in the crowd. Then one day we weren't spare any more.

I used to get invites to movie premières and Prince's Trust events and, as I had no girlfriend, I'd ask either Sheri or Penny Egan to be my partner for the evening. Sheridan regularly turned up looking stunning in a micro-miniskirt, so the paparazzi thought I was a lucky bastard. A première was a great night out, with limos taking us there before going on to the party, but there was no pressure on either of us. Our relationship wasn't forced or pushed, and it just unfolded over the course of the next year.

Sheri's a good Northern working-class girl. She was very right on, a member of the Labour party and used to campaign for them. Of all the people she ever met in my company, all the musicians, Phil Collins, Eric Clapton, nothing shook her as much as meeting two leaders of the Labour Party.

I'd been asked to go and review a movie for a new TV arts show so we went along to see it at ten in the morning. It wasn't particularly good and it was weird to stagger out of a cinema in daylight, so we jumped in a cab and went back to the production house so I could do my talking head to camera. As I walked in Neil Kinnock was sitting in the corner. I'd met Neil at various functions, backstage at Prince's Trust parties and when he was doing the Red Wedge concerts. As I came in Neil stood up and went, 'Hey, Midge. How are you doing?' and came over to shake my hand.

Sheridan came over all coy, gulped and went, 'He knows you, you know him. How? What is going on?'

The other great moment in Sheridan's life with me was after I had moved into the flat in Cambridge Gardens. It had no bath and the kitchen was a pipe sticking out of the wall, so for the first few weeks I experimented with all the restaurants in Notting Hill. One night we were sitting having dinner in this little Italian restaurant when I noticed John Smith having dinner in the corner with his family.

I mentioned this to Sheri, who turned into a shivering, quaking wreck – she could hardly lift her fork to her mouth. I know how annoying it is to have a chunk of chicken in your mouth with somebody tapping you on the shoulder trying to get you to sign a menu, so I said to her, 'Wait until he's finished eating his dinner, then wander over and introduce yourself. He'll love the fact that this beautiful girl is a party member.' So she did, and he did love it. Sheri came back to the table all happy and ecstatic, and then as he was leaving John swung by our table and, in true politician style, shook hands and started chatting away. He was oblivious to who I was – as if he should know – and said to Sheri, 'Maybe you can bring him into the party as well.' While he said that I could see his daughter – who I later found out worked for *Top of the Pops* – cringing dreadfully. I can imagine her giving him an ear-bashing on the way home – 'Dad, how could you? Don't you know who you were talking to?'

He died the next year and Sheri was really upset. A few years later we were on holiday in Mull in Scotland and went to visit the island of Iona. It has fifty-odd kings buried there and John Smith, who was a major son of Scotland. We went along together to see this grave-stone, a massive oval-cut stone that looked like a whale, and read the inscription: 'An Honest Man's The Noblest Work Of God'. The best epitaph any man can ask for.

For months Sheri and I went to Rusty's clubs on a Saturday night, just hanging out as part of a group. When I did 'Cold, Cold Heart' on *Top of the Pops* – the last one I ever did – a bunch of my friends, including her, came along to the Beeb. On the *Pure* tour I played at the Albert Hall. It's all confusion in the dressing room after a London show because everybody you know is there, and they all want to say hello and to have two minutes of your time. I passed round in a daze then all of a sudden the room had cleared and the only people left were a few stragglers, Sheri and me. I was going to the Halcyon Hotel to meet up with Heinz and Caroline and the two Chrises for a few drinks, so I asked her along and promised I'd drop her home later. We went to the Halcyon, had a chat and a laugh and as we got up to leave we were holding hands. Simple as that. Nothing needed to be said. We got into the taxi and before we knew it we were kissing and locked in a deep embrace which didn't end until we stopped outside Sheridan's place. I got out too. I didn't see it coming. After all, we were pals.

I didn't know if it was going to last, you never do. We spoke the next day and the day after that. I was back out on tour so we both had time and space to think, but when I came back home our first proper date was at Julie's wine bar in Kensington and I walked in to find Chrysalis in the middle of their Christmas party. We were both nervous and drank too much but that didn't matter a jot. The others must have seen it coming long before we did – or perhaps we'd delayed so long they'd written us off. When we arrived, obviously together, at Embargo in Chelsea – another of Rusty's clubs – there was much shrieking.

It had been blatantly obvious to everyone but we couldn't see it. It was similar to when Bob and I were sitting there talking about Ethiopia: 'Doh, we should write a song.' This time it was 'Doh, we should be a couple.' We were mates, pals, but I didn't see what was really happening until it hit me in the face. If it hadn't there'd be none of these lovely little Ures running about. I was in love with Sheri long before she got pregnant. It was always easy, and there was nothing awkward between us. She was my friend first – no, she was my soul mate. That was the best way for it to happen.

Sheri was wary of getting herself involved in a casual relationship. I was very protective of Molly. Even after we were an item it took a long time before I let Sheri stay the night. And vice versa, if I stayed at hers I had to get up at a hideous time in the morning to get home before Molly woke up. It just felt so right. We went down to Chris Morrison's house. He'd seen me with all my previous girlfriends and at the end of the weekend he told me, 'I've never seen you so relaxed and happy with a girl before.'

There was this avalanche of conflicting emotions; we were an item but we didn't live together. Sheridan suggested she have the baby and they'd live in her flat. I said no. 'Move in here with me, you have those drawers and that bit of wardrobe and I'll have those bits.' Not overly romantic, I admit, but we moved in together and set up home in Cambridge Gardens. It wasn't ideal but we got on with it. After the initial shock we got very excited and started nesting furiously. Kitty was born on 30 March 1994. I was at the birth as I have been for all my gorgeous girls – I wouldn't have it any other way.

I didn't do much recording in the flat. It wasn't the right environment; the gear was set up in the gallery landing above the sitting room and once the baby came along I didn't want to make any noise. It was hard bringing up Kitty there. If I did the Tesco run I had to double-park, run in with all the shopping, open the front door, throw it all into the hallway, run back to the car, drive round until I found a parking space, get the baby out of the car, walk back, take the baby up two flights of stairs, put her somewhere safe, go downstairs and grab the shopping.

I needed to try something new and I thought this might be the time to dip a toe in the country water, find a house big enough for us to grow into – little knowing I was going to end up with four daughters.

One lovely Sunday afternoon in 1994 I was doing one of my Out Alone shows – just me, my guitar, my songs and a few stories – at the Theatre Royal in Bath. I started to look in estate agents' windows. Sheridan wasn't too sure, even when we found a lovely old house in Monkton Farleigh. I had sold off a chunk of the Ultravox catalogue, which enabled me to pay off my tax debts and put a deposit down on the house. It was a necessity for me to move financially and selling the Notting Hill maisonette bought a farmhouse outside Bath. We moved when Kitty was six months old, which immediately eased up a lot of problems.

That is the way life works, shifting sands: things change when they need too. Moving from Zachary House to Notting Hill had been traumatic for me, a psychological down move that brought its own baggage. I had had to put a lot of stuff in storage, so moving to Monkton Farleigh was great. I saw my old table again, my chairs, the bits and pieces I love which I have gathered over my life.

Sheridan had always been a city girl, so moving to the country was a really big wrench. It didn't matter to me, as my work environment is a room full of computers and wires. I promised her if it didn't work after a year we'd move back, but with a new baby we soon met like-minded people, other new mums. Nobody speaks to each other in London, but down in Bath everybody was really friendly, and we knew who our neighbours were. Staying for the second year was Sheridan's choice. She was still doing castings, which she hated. After a year of being down in Bath she gave it up – why jump on a train and travel two hours up to London to be dismissed in a second? It is soul-destroying. I couldn't deal with that. Once we moved I realised I didn't have to be in London, that I could drive up and pick up Molly on a Friday afternoon and drive her back on a Sunday.

Living in Bath is like peeling layers off an onion: the more I peel, the more I find. It has a very musical, very creative community. Peter Gabriel's world-class studio Real World is down the road. There is a wealth of great musicians in this area – Van Morrison, Hugh Cornwall, the Tears for Fears guys – as many as Notting Hill but without all the stress the Gate throws at you. There are website designers, graphic artists, video directors and a brilliant engineer who did Peter Gabriel's album can come round and mix my record. I think it is where ex-Londoners go to die; they are all there on my doorstep.

Soon after we moved to Bath Paula left Bob Geldof for Michael Hutchence. I've never asked what happened and as I've no idea what went on behind closed doors it's not my place to speculate on what pushed her to break up the family home. I knew Paula had pictures of Hutchence and Liam Gallagher, or whoever it happened to be, on her fridge, but she had always had pictures of pretty boys. By then there was a whole different generation of pretty boys to hang out with, but that was a part of who she was.

During the whole break-up process I wasn't ever in touch, and I wasn't a friend to her after Michael died, which I feel bad about. I did worry that, had I bumped into Paula, inevitably there'd have been a photographer lurking around, and a chat would be turned into something it wasn't and I'd end up a pawn in the game, forced to take sides. I was down in the country so it was easy to keep my distance. Bob kept this immense dignity throughout the entire process: he remained very controlled, not getting into public slanging matches or screaming and shouting from the rooftops, 'I'm telling my story now.' He just kept control and he kept control, I think, for his girls.

Bob's been deathly straight for years. He's very self-controlled and very focused, and he knows what he wants to do, and he draws himself a clear line. What really shocked me was to see Paula trying to keep up with Hutchence. All of a sudden her days didn't exist any more; she was living a nocturnal life hanging out with him. Like Phil Lynott, Hutchence was very much the rock and roll star; he played that game and it was exciting. In order to keep him happy she had to do what he did, but when he died she found she had lost all her anchors. The drugs and the drink were completely and utterly out of character. I'd never seen Paula drink anything, ever. The idea of her popping down the local offie to buy a bottle of vodka, then going home and drinking it all while taking heroin was just appalling. I didn't think Paula was going to die, so I always thought there would be a time to rebuild the bridges.

I prefer to remember the last time I saw Paula. She was walking down Kings Road, surrounded by her kids, one attached to her front, holding hands with the other two, chattering and giggling with them. By the time I'd found somewhere to park she was gone, lost in the crowd.

Bob wasn't the only person going through a crap time in the mid-90s. Moving to Bath was a great thing for my family but it only masked the black hole of my career for a short while.

About half of *Breathe* was recorded in Monkton Farleigh, the rest in LA. I really believed in it, so when, after all the crap I'd gone through making it, it completely disappeared I hit the depths of despair. My livelihood was evaporating before my eyes and I couldn't do anything about it.

I talked about it with Heinz who admitted, 'I don't know what's happening. I don't know how to fix your career. It's gone.' That is not what I wanted to hear from the same man who had sold me his bag of dreams. I was struck by inertia and indecision. I couldn't drag myself into the studio and start work on another record. I had no motivation. Me, the guy who had to be dragged from behind the mixing desk and sent on holiday. I'd made one of the best records I'd ever made, so why would I want to go and make another one that nobody was ever going to hear. I had the studio all set up yet I didn't step inside it for weeks at a time. It was at the far end of the house and I'd walk past it, pretending it didn't exist. When I did go into the studio I just tinkered about for a couple of hours in the morning or perhaps after lunch, but then I'd always be out by five. As I'd demoed over twenty ideas for Heinz I had loads of thumbnail sketches for songs but they didn't inspire me. Nothing did.

I have blotted out how I spent my time – probably getting in Sheridan's way, or staying up late drinking Jack with a friend round the kitchen table, putting the world to rights. Most nights I started a bottle and sometimes I didn't need a friend to help me finish it. I was sitting about waiting for a record to come out, which had never happened before. I had nothing creative to focus on so I started to slip into bad habits. There was a rot setting in which started to worry Sheri.

I couldn't sit about and do nothing but I couldn't work on a new record either. I did the cooking sometimes. Sheri liked to run, but I certainly did nothing physical until she organised a personal trainer for me. He came three times a week and made me lift heavy things and run up and down country lanes. It certainly worked because after a few weeks I started to see bumps where I had never seen bumps before. But I still didn't like it much.

We did spend a lot of time driving around Bath. When Kitty fell asleep for her afternoon nap we'd put her in the car seat and drive around, exploring all the avenues, seeing where it all connected up. At least Sheridan and I could spend some time together talking as adults.

I was caught between two extremes of emotion. I was ecstatically happy with my girls, doubly so when Sheridan became pregnant with Ruby. Otherwise everything bad had seemed to happen at the same time and it all became a little overwhelming. What else could go wrong in my life? At times it seemed as if the only good things that I had to cling on to were Sheridan, the babies and Molly. I loved living in Bath, and my family was my life. That was wonderful. The family kept me sane. The rest of it was hell.

Music, the one thing I was passionate about, the one thing I was good at, wasn't working. Everything that I had ever bought into had gone wrong, and my self-belief was shot, magnified by the memory that from 1980 to 1988 I had been Midas, when everything I did turned to gold. Now I was Minas, in the wrong business at the wrong time. I had bought property when I shouldn't have bought property. I had to hold onto it through all the bad years and was forced to get rid of it when it started to turn good. Everything had turned to shit or was covered in volcanic ash.

Not only was my music out of sync with what was going on but my entire life seemed to be out of sync. Every step I took felt like the wrong step. Maybe I am being over-melodramatic, but to me it felt like my entire world was crumbling, caving in on top of me. I got increasingly depressed, walking on some very thin ice heading God knows where. Fortunately I never found out.

In the late autumn of 1997, I got a phone call from Heinz Henn. 'Something's happening in Italy,' he said. 'There's a real buzz going on.'

A few days later he called again: 'We're sniffing a hit.'

CHAPTER 26
A NEW BREATH

Two days after Valentine's Day, 1998 and expectation was running hot through the Rolling Stone in Milan, as the cheers of the crowd rattled the dressing room. The theatre was packed to the rafters and buzzing: 1,200 people, average age 18, all come to see me. Six months earlier I'd have been lucky to draw 300.

I wasn't nervous, for once. Not a butterfly, no sweaty palms, I felt relaxed and ready. My band sounded stonkingly good. I walked out on stage to rapturous applause. The kind that starts at the back and rolls forwards gathering momentum and volume until the wave crashes over the stage soaking me in pure adrenaline. Live Aid all over again.

Yes, I thought, savouring the moment. I'm back! Back on the map again.

I opened with 'I See Hope In The Morning Light' with its uillean pipes and rousing gospel-choir chorus. Then I launched straight into four songs from the *Breathe* album – 'Fields Of Fire', 'Free', 'Fallen Angel' and 'Sinnerman'. The band were hot, the music full of light and shade, with lovely atmospherics and subtle textures laid over by Troy with his whistles and pipes. The kids at the front went crazy. The hard-core fans standing at the back, the ones who'd been there since the early days, seemed as bemused as I felt.

Then I played 'Vienna'. The old stagers cheered and the front half of the audience went 'Huh? I know that song. But why is he singing Ultravox covers?' They had come to hear this faceless guy sing 'Breathe', and they knew 'Hymn' and 'Dancing With Tears In My Eyes' because they are on the radio all the time in Europe, but they hadn't made the connection. Then realisation dawned across their faces.

When the minidisc kicked in with Kate Stephenson's breathy 'huh, huh, huh' there was this nanosecond of absolute silence. It lasted through the slow panting intro as the drums walked in and then the vocal . . . 'With every waking breath I breathe / I see what life has dealt to me . . .' Except the roar from the audience drowned out the words. It was a fabulous moment.

Normally on stage I kind of blank out, and I focus on a fixed spot at the back of the hall, a light, a sign. I never look at the people down the front, never: I look way up and beyond that. Most of the time I'm on stage I am thinking, Remember the next bloody line. Not this time. The whole *Breathe* tour was ecstasy. I was riding a double whammy – a whole new audience, and some of my old audience back again. A Number One in Italy, a hit across Europe. I was the magic, golden man of the moment again . . . but, above all, I was right. I hadn't written a piece of crap.

None of it would have happened without Roberta Baldi, Luca Toccaceli and Piero Sessa. When 'Breathe' was first released in Italy the CD sold less than 600 copies. One of them was bought by Decam, a company in Milan who specialise in putting contemporary music together with TV commercials. They loved the song and thought it was a complete travesty that nobody was ever going to hear it. For over a year they waited to find the right vehicle. In early 1997 Decam presented 'Breathe' in a batch of six songs to the agency who did the Swatch commercials. They had an new advert: 'How long is a Swatch minute?' and 'Breathe' fitted the imagery they had – babies being born, people winning races – perfectly. They took the ad to Nicolas Hayek, who owns Swatch, and he fell in love with the music and decreed, 'I want to use this.'

Decam then approached BMG and my publishing company for permission to use the song in a TV-ad campaign in Europe. While Warner Chapell were delighted as it would pay back a huge chunk of my advance, Heinz initially told them where to go. Decam wanted a piece of any sales that might happen after the commercial, which was understandable as they'd made the breakthrough. Heinz, however, was not going to take anyone telling him what to do, so he stomped about being obstructive. Eventually Chris got on the phone, told him he was missing the plot and made it happen.

Ten years earlier I might not have given my permission, but that was when the system had worked for me. In 1997 radio didn't play my records so I had to look at other avenues. This is an ever-evolving industry: it morphs and changes all the time. If commercials are the way to do it that's what you do. 'Breathe' wasn't written for a commercial: it was a piece of music that already existed, so as far as I was concerned I hadn't compromised my position or sold myself down the river. I saw the ad, which was very tastefully done, so I shrugged my shoulders and gave the OK. Nobody had heard 'Breathe' so why not go ahead; perhaps someone might hear it and take the time to go and find out what it was. I didn't expect anything to happen; getting a track on a movie doesn't mean it will be a worldwide hit – even if it is *Spiderman* – it's usually the bit that is tagged on to the very end of the last credits, if you hang about the cinema long enough. Then I forgot about it.

What I didn't know is that Swatch is a big fashion item in Italy, where they are really passionate about such things. The 30-second TV advert only featured a bit of a verse and the chunk of the chorus, but after the commercial launched on 1 September the key radio stations in Rome and Milan got 600 telephone calls in a day asking what it was. Although all the radio stations had had a copy of the album sitting in their library for two years, because they had never played it they had no idea who sang it. Fortunately, enough people phoned up Swatch head office who, being Swiss, told the callers what they needed to know. The song was called 'Breathe' by Midge Ure, and the album was on BMG.

BMG in Italy were smart, and they didn't release 'Breathe' as a single. They re-released the album and it sold 350,000 copies, so people knew every song on that CD. Just before Christmas I got a call from my agent asking if I could put a band together and tour. Sheridan was pregnant but very understanding. These things go cold very, very quickly – wait too long and you're last week's thing.

I had a month and because I was playing *Breathe* material I needed a very different band. Josh Phillips, who had been my keyboard player for a while, got the musicians together with Berenice Hardman, my tour manager. Berenice knew Troy Donockley who played uilleann pipes, whistles, mandolin and electric guitar – you don't get many like him. Josh used to play in Diamond Head, a heavy-metal band, with Dave Williamson on bass. Russell Field was a funky little drummer in the Dharmas. They started rehearsing without me and I'd never met Dave, Russ or Troy when I first walked into Real World.

'We've done "Fields Of Fire",' said Josh. I picked up my acoustic guitar and went 'three, four' . . . and this fantastic sound came out. They had really done their homework, and Troy's pipes sounded vibrant. Within two hours we were all like blood brothers. That doesn't happen often, walking into a room full of strangers and all of a sudden you're best mates.

That entire European tour was an absolute hoot, and I loved every second of it. It was like being on holiday with four of your best friends, the way I remembered it being with Ultravox. I didn't have to struggle to sell tickets; we loved the music and were obviously having a ball, which was reflected in the audiences. The record had a long shelf life, and it stayed Number One in Italy for ages, and as the advert rolled out across Europe the other territories caught on, so as the hit spread there was time to book another tour in Germany.

Swatch tied themselves in with a double campaign. They pressed up special watch-shaped CDs for club members who could get tickets in a special cordoned-off area, so they started to think they were controlling the whole thing. We'd turn up at the venues and it looked like I was working for Swatch, as there were foyer displays, huge watches and banners everywhere. Every day I told them, 'You're not sponsoring this. Thank you very much for helping us get the hit, but I'm not Mr Swatch, take it all down.' They didn't get the message. Next venue, same problem. Every single day I told them to take it down. As we used to say in Ultravox, 'Ees Italy.'

We ate better than I have eaten in my entire life. Our bus driver, Max, couldn't get us out of the city in the morning, because he never knew where he was, but somehow he knew every good working-man's restaurant in Italy. He'd drive up side streets or up dirt roads and deliver us to a boat. We'd walk on and somebody would come round with a big bag of monkey nuts and throw them on the table. We'd eat those while they brought out course after course. I lost my rag one morning. Yet again Max was driving round and round in circles and I just screamed, 'Buy a fucking map!'

The tour promoter picked up all the hotel costs and his rep Franco was travelling with us. The hotel in Rome was so dingy that, when I switched on the light, it had an amazing bulb that could suck all the remaining light out of the room. I'd had a couple of drinks so I announced, 'We'll go to the bar.'

'Ees no bar.'

'What about a room we can sit in and chill, have a few drinks?'

'Ees no room.'

I went off on one. 'Shite, this is fucking shite,' was the gist of it.

The next morning Franco asked Berenice, 'What is this word Midge says all the time – Shite?' I felt like I was in a Larson cartoon talking to the dog where the only word he understands is 'fucking . . . fucking . . . fucking'. I apologised, and he laughed but I had made the point. We had a really nice hotel in Florence because our families were flying out and Claudio took us to a fabulous, family-owned restaurant run by an Italian called Dennis.

As Russell and Troy were both magicians, constantly trying to outdo each other, we were more like a touring carnival. On a plane to

Singapore going to do a Womad show in September 1999, the two of them sat on either side of the aisle doing their tricks. It ended up with this cluster of people, including all the stewardesses and stewards, hanging round, watching them perform. One favourite trick was to put a coin on top of a plastic membrane over a glass and hit it. The coin disappears and pops down into the bottom of the glass. But the membrane isn't broken.

They walked through the airport going, 'Here we go' and throwing lightbeams at each other while passers-by ducked out of the way. That was a simple trick that even I worked out. Both of them had bought illuminating false thumbs. It slips over the top of the thumb and when you put pressure on it lights up. Russ pressed his thumb and feinted throwing to Troy who also pressed his thumb. Two lights, and the brain fills in the gap. People swore they could see the light flashing from one hand to the other.

Troy's best trick was in Tokyo, the final surreal moment in a very bizarre trip. I was offered a substantial amount of money to do a week's residency in Sweet Basil 139, a club in Tokyo. Ultravox used to be a draw in Japan and it gave me a chance to put the band together again, and get paid loads of money. Everything in the club was absolutely brand new, the best PA, the best mixing desk, Vari-lites, the best backline equipment money could buy. The night before we were due to start we popped down to see the Average White Band. There were only about 150 people there so I thought, They can't be very popular here.

We arrived the next day to play the first show at six o'clock in the evening. There were maybe fifteen businessmen there. At the second show there were fifty people, including the original fifteen. After three days of this I was so pissed off I went to the owner and told him, 'I can't do this, no matter how much you are paying. This is soul-destroying. Can I do one two-hour concert, or play two and a half hours but do it at nine o'clock.' No, he said, I couldn't. I didn't understand what was going on, and I still don't. The club was spending money hand over fist to get international artists from all over the world to play to a handful of drunken punters. My record company didn't know I was there, and there was no advertising, no publicity, nothing. We couldn't get to the bottom of it. It was hideous. After a week I had completely had it.

At least Ryoichi Yuki, a Japanese artist that I produced a couple of years prior, came to some of the shows. On our last night he took us to this beautiful vegetarian restaurant, up the back streets in Tokyo, and we had this traditional Japanese meal sitting on the tatami mats where we drank our own weight in sake. I picked up the tab (despite Berenice kicking me repeatedly), which was so hideously expensive it ate up huge amounts of my fee. Fortunately the Buddhist owner took Amex.

We went back to the hotel. No one, except the chambermaid, had been in my 7th-floor hotel room since I left at four o'clock in the afternoon to go to the sound check. Troy came up for a final drink to say our fond farewells. 'One last trick,' he said, and produced his deck of cards. 'Take a card.' I pulled out the six of clubs. 'Remember the card.' He put it back, shuffled again, then suddenly he stumbled forwards and threw the whole pack against the huge glass window looking out over Tokyo. 'Is that your card?' He pointed to a card on the window. I went over to try and pick the six of clubs off the glass. It was on the outside of the window, seven floors up, no veranda, no ledge, nothing. I know it's a set-up, but I've still got no idea how he did it.

Breathe was huge all over Europe. Except for one place. The TV campaign was only on satellite TV in Britain, so there was not the same demand for radio to play it. In the trade press the Number One European record was *Breathe*. The UK could see what was happening but they did nothing. Record companies waste so much on nonsense, but it wouldn't have cost them a penny to re-release it. They already had the tools, and we had spent £70,000 making this fantastic video up on the Westbury White Horse. Yet rather than cash in on a guaranteed smash, because of the UK versus America, because of the anti-anything to do with BMG International, they chose to ignore it. That's called shooting yourself in the foot. It beats me how some of those executives ever got into their position of power.

On the tour I recorded a live album, *Glorious Noise*, mixed it all and paid for the whole thing. Then I gave it to the record company and suggested putting it out as a cheap album. It was free, as it wasn't in my contract so I didn't want any extra money. Rudi Gassner, the big boss of BMG International, turned it down. 'I don't want the next Midge Ure album to be a live record.'

Because I had had to go out and repromote *Breathe* it was another year and a half before I had time to go back in the studio. BMG were willing to take the chance on not having an album for two years. I wasn't. I pleaded with them, 'You've got to put this out somewhere, sell it for a fiver, pretend it's a bootleg . . . that works for the Dave Matthews Band in the States.' I'd clawed back some of my career and

I was giving them the tools to keep the momentum going until I was ready to go out with the next proper album.

By the time I'd finished and delivered *Move Me* there was nowhere to put it out. Rudi Gassner died out jogging with his wife just before Christmas 1999. That was a real shock as he was a fit man, who looked after himself properly. BMG International had spent a lot of money and not generated much in return, so with Rudi gone the plug was pulled; the walls closed in and Heinz soon departed. There was only one person left at BMG International that I had a relationship with: Gaby Sappington, an Austrian girl (from Vienna ironically) who still believed in what I was doing. She fought tooth and nail for months to find me a label. After a lot of hard searching, she found BMG Entertainment, which sounds like a cabaret label.

The Italians had been dead keen but by then I'd missed the boat yet again. Another classic missed-the-target moment. By the time the record came out there was no momentum behind it, and I was just another guy with a one-off freak hit. BMG Entertainment only existed in Germany and didn't have an international department. I did a bit of promotion for the record and got the best reviews I've ever had. Nothing happened.

I told them, 'I'm going to give you a video for this.'

'We can't afford a video,' came the reply.

'No,' I said, 'I'm going to shoot a video and *give* it you.'

'You can't do that.'

I went out in my car with my camera, and shot the video with my old photographer/director friend Neil Barstow and Lee Curran, a cameraman. I put it into Final Cut Pro on my Macintosh and sat there for five days editing it. It was a simple idea: life happening inside the car. I gave them the video. They played it, gulped and asked, 'How much do you want for that?'

'I don't want anything for it: I'm giving you the tools you need. I understand how the business works these days.' It was frightening the way they just kept turning things down. Now I wish I'd charged them five grand.

The album reverted back to me when the UK turned it down – at last they had the opportunity to dump me. I found a very small label to put it out on, Curb, which meant we got it into the shops. But there was only a small print run and without the BMG corporate muscle we couldn't put it out at £13. It cost £17, which was much too expensive. The record disappeared but this time, while it still mattered, I didn't take it personally.

I had loved every minute of *Breathe*'s success. It was my perfect moment, exactly what I'm in the game for. I got the clap on the back, the kiss on the cheek, all wrapped in one, coming at the end of six years of shit. But the ultimate kickback was: I was right.

That makes me sound like a megalomaniac or very arrogant. Yet before the Swatch ad broke I was a workaholic who couldn't drag himself into his own studio. I had started to doubt myself. I was lost. What mattered most was that my sensibilities had been proved right. I was correct all the way along. I was writing good songs.

At the same time I left Ultravox to go solo I appeared to acquire the uncanny knack of being in the wrong place at the wrong time. It's as if I am constantly swimming upstream, forever striving for something that nobody else wants. I am naturally out of sync, and my music doesn't fit in with what everybody else seems to be doing. I'm fine with that, but I have to be prepared to take the pitfalls, the crap reviews, that come with my choice. Striving for individualism is what makes music interesting.

Every so often I do synchronise with the moment. It happened with 'Vienna', with 'If I Was' and then I had to wait another thirteen years. 'Breathe' wasn't a throwback from Band Aid or Ultravox. I was an invisible man who had written a song that people loved.

Which is why it didn't matter so much what came next, or that there was no follow-up hit. There is another 'Breathe' in me somewhere. I know it will come out maybe next year, or the year after, or ten years' time, whenever. But I know it's there.

However, before I could find it I had a major problem to overcome. I had to stop drinking.

CHAPTER 27
MY BROTHER JACK

I can remember exactly where and when I had my first serious drink. Backstage with Ultravox at the Whiskey a Go-Go on New Year's Eve 1979. Somebody handed me a Jack Daniels and Coke. 'Try it,' he said, 'I think you'll like it.' Small beginnings.

For years it was all about having a drink or two after a show, having a laugh with the lads because that is what being in a band is all about. I drank because I could. I had a job where nobody told me what to do. The rock and roll lifestyle is synonymous with excess, and it is all part of the bravado. I'd walk into my local offy and, before I had even closed the door behind me, the guy had put a bottle of Jack and one of diet Coke onto the counter. There was nothing to be ashamed of, nothing to hide. That's how it started.

It went on like that until Sheridan told me I was going to kill myself. She told me I should stop drinking. Ten years ago, in 1994, I was drinking a bottle of Jack a day – or a night I should say. Usually I shared it with someone else but I did get to moments on a run when I could polish off a bottle on my own and not feel completely and utterly smashed. Drinking Jack was a regular nightly occurrence which should have sent alarm signals going off. After Sheridan asked me to, I stopped the Jack. It was easy to stop and I only drank it occasionally. Parties, New Year, high days and holidays; after *This Is Your Life*, I thought I might as well have a couple. For three years I just drank a beer or a cider at night.

Then I started sneaking the vodka.

There was no major spark. No earth-shattering moment that kick started my drinking in secret. It was everything, every career disappointment I'd been through in the last ten years, and nothing. One day I thought, I fancy a drink, and I bought a bottle of vodka. I kept on doing it because I thought I could get away with it – that's a key thing, a classic symptom of somebody who does things to excess. I could get away with it, so I did. I chose vodka because nobody could smell it. It was strange behaviour for me as I am not a sneaky person, but I didn't want Sheridan to know. She never did.

There was a trigger, a kick-in point at eight o'clock every evening. It didn't matter whether it was prior to going on stage, or at home making a stir-fry but a little bell went off in my head and I'd think this would all be a bit nicer if I had some of that soft-focus on. I needed what I call 'the Miss Ellie filter'. When they were filming *Dallas* she always had this lovely soft, Doris Day glow in all her close-ups. I couldn't handle seeing the world without that glow on, without feeling a little fuzzy. By the end I was drinking a bottle of vodka a day, straight, no mixers.

For eighteen months from the summer of 2001 I never took a sip before eight at night. It was all over and done by midnight. I'd fall asleep on the sofa while Sheri went upstairs to read a book. What I didn't see was that it was causing a whole lifestyle change, causing huge rifts between us. I was waking up at two in the morning in a drunken stupor and climbing into bed, passing out then reviving, getting up at 6.30 to see to the kids.

My songs knew I had a problem long before I did. God, yes. Take 'Let Me Go' on the *Move Me* album – 'Sipping comfort from my writer's cup, the one that is constantly filled up, the one that doubles as a crutch, the one I cling to oh so much.' I wrote that six years ago but it's one thing knowing it and a different thing doing something about it. Any alcoholic and drug addict can justify the next hit, not giving up until the next day. There was this voice in the back of my head telling me that I wasn't drinking any more than I had been two years ago, ten years ago. I didn't know that the effects were stacking up, and it was getting easier and easier to achieve oblivion.

I kept it under control for a long, long time. I didn't realise I was an alcoholic until I tried to stop and then went, 'Hang on a sec, why do I want to stop?' I didn't admit it for a lot longer. Up until that point drinking was great fun. I've had years of great fun. After all, I wasn't drinking in the morning. I'd say, 'I'll stop tomorrow,' and that's when the excuses came tumbling out. Tomorrow happened to be Friday and then it was the weekend so I'd put it off until Monday. Then it was windy on Monday and raining on Tuesday: there was always a reason, a justification. The bottom line was that it was easier not to. That was my comfort zone.

I was sneaking off, lying and cheating to get my little fix. I couldn't keep going to the same shop every day so I drove around Bath to different little offies and corner shops. That was incredibly tacky, one step up from sleeping on park benches, and just as cheap, dirty and nasty as disappearing down back alleys to score smack. I'd do the school run, drop the kids off, then on the way back stop off, pick up a bottle and then hide it somewhere in the house. After that I was fine because I knew where my evening tipple was.

Justifying my drinking to myself was the easy part. 'If I drink alone, I am in danger of becoming an alcoholic.' Then I drank alone and thought, That's not bad, that's fun. I did that for ten years. Then I decided, If I drink more than a quarter of a bottle I'll get worried. I ended up drinking a bottle and thinking, That's no great shakes. Next I decided that if I started drinking during the day I'd worry about it. I did and I didn't. The last taboo was: 'I must not start drinking in the morning.'

Just before Christmas 2003 I started drinking in the morning. The final trigger was that I had decided to leave my management company, CMO. I had felt redundant in the office for some time. It represents some cool people – Blur, Gorillaz, Morcheeba, Turin Brakes and then this guy Midge Ure. I might have more gold records on the wall than they do, but I was not cool any more.

For twenty years CMO had been my parental figure. I'd been allowed to run about and play to make things with my musical plasticine, then they put it out, and it made money. I didn't write cheques, and I didn't know how many bank accounts I had, or what I owed the taxman and the VAT man. Ridiculous, I know, for a guy who has just turned fifty, but that is how it had worked historically. I was a legacy from a bygone age and nobody else at CMO had the same set-up. Protecting the artist from the big bad outside world, dealing with the problems and not bothering him is a great concept, but protecting the artist from the outside world and not dealing with the consequences leads to huge problems.

In the past when I was in the red I always had the next advance coming. In 2003 I had come to the end of my BMG and my music-publishing contracts and there was no great tranche of cash coming along to float the sinking ship. I knew there was some kind of tax implications but in my mind it had all been sorted. When I was presented with a bill for £170,000 in August it was a hell of lot more than I expected. The news was dumped in my lap via a letter, which I thought was not only tactless but also downright cruel. I felt insulted and incredibly let down. I might as well have been a council dustman as an artist who had kept the office alive for a long time.

I can lay blame at the feet of the company for the situation, but not at any individual – Chris Morrison is one of my best and oldest friends. Trying to manage my life, which is what they did, is a complicated enough task for anybody. However, I should have been called into the office, had a financial meeting with the people I have paid a lot of money to manage my affairs and been presented with a creative solution. Instead I was dumped with a problem that I had to solve. That was good in one way because it gave me a boot up the backside, and showed me once and for all that the system didn't work. Finally I realised I didn't need an expensive lumbering machine to run my life.

It was left to me and my accountants to sort it out. I had already sold the house in Monkton Farleigh because it was too big. I was away doing more and more acoustic shows and we wanted something more manageable to help simplify our lives. I wanted to spend the money on the kids and their education to create a nice big financial buffer between me and the outside world, but suddenly that was all sucked up and away. That was depressing to say the least.

I knew things had to change but over the Christmas period the idea of cutting the CMO umbilical cord, of going out into the big wide world on my own, became too much. There were immense pressures on me, family pressures, financial pressures, stuff I'd taken on years before and I couldn't see any light at the end of the tunnel. Ten years ago, when things got bad Sheridan was the one who worried and I was going, 'Don't worry about it.' It was fine saying that knowing I had two large album advances signed up for . . . but without that the roles were reversed and she was the one saying, 'It'll be fine,' while I was screaming inside.

I got very depressed, and thought I was having a nervous breakdown – which I probably was. I was having real problems with leaving my management and real problems drinking. I had been drinking secretly for the past eighteen months but now it got steadily worse. Put those two together and you have a mess. I was a mess. I had been very down before during the BMG years, and again in 1997 before 'Breathe' was a hit I was pretty depressed, but never so bad that I couldn't face the day without having a drink.

Towards the end I was drinking on Taiwanese time, getting up in the morning and having a sip of vodka. I didn't wake up with a hangover, as I'd gone past that, but my first conscious thought was, Shit, I've got a whole bloody day to get through. I knew there was a bit left in the bottle – there was always a bit left in the bottle – so I'd go and have a sip and I'd feel better. Fantastic, in fact. I'd start getting the kids' breakfast, then that first sip made me feel so good I'd have another one. That made me feel twice as good. I did that and then drove the kids to school. I was putting in jeopardy everything I love, everything I have, everything I hold precious.

I found myself in a very dark place. I couldn't live seeing the world clearly: I couldn't focus on anything without a drink. I thought drink would *help* me deal with my problems, but it made things ten times worse. I was hiding from the truth, living in a fantasy land, not wanting to do anything. I'd go up to my studio, switch all the machines on and sit there for two hours looking at a blank screen. I'd find it more interesting to refile my tapes than create something new. I'd go to sleep in the studio for a bit every afternoon, lying under the desk in case Sheridan came up, when I could wake up and pretend I was fixing something.

It was like somebody had unplugged me: all the drive I used to have had gone. Because my brain wasn't in gear, I wasn't focused, and I didn't have the passion I'd had about my creativity. My self-esteem had been chipped away to the extent that I didn't believe in anything I did any more. Chipped away by the industry but mainly by myself, by the potential failure of everything I'd worked all my life for.

When I was giving one of my regular one-man acoustic shows I found myself doing the same eighteen songs I'd done for a year, because I couldn't be arsed to sit down and relearn some of my older songs to make it more interesting, not just for the audience but for me. The shows were never like wading through treacle – I'd walk on stage and everything went 'ching'. At least I was still a professional.

Driving to the shows got harder and harder. They were what was keeping me alive artistically but none of it made any sense any more, and the pressures outweighed any of the joy. I did some stupid, stupid things, like driving back from London in the dark after a day of meetings, with a bottle of vodka sitting in the passenger seat. That kept me company all the way home. I had lost the plot, trapped in the reality gap between normal thinking and complete insanity.

In January I went to see a variety of doctors – my GP, Chris Morrison's doctor, one in London and a specialist in Bath – but I never told them the truth. To me it wasn't that much different from what I'd been doing a year prior – secretly drinking around the house. They all said I was depressed and gave me mild happy pills which did nothing at all. The local specialist told me that to eliminate any physical causes I had to have a CAT scan. That scared me, because I hate tight closed spaces. In my delusions I actually believed they might find a medical reason for why I was staggering about!

The Thursday I was due to go to Bristol to hear the results – my musician friend Adi had offered to drive me – Sheridan was doing a launch at the house for a health-food product. Unbeknownst to anyone I had a few drinks that morning. Sheri was in the sitting room about to give a presentation to a lot of friends and mums from the school but all she could hear was me next door, sobbing my heart out slumped over the computers. Our friend Charlotte Culkin (Caroline Crowther's sister) heard this and came in. She led out a walking heap – the hood on my parka pulled up pretending I couldn't be seen – through this gaggle of dreadfully embarrassed women.

Charlotte insisted on coming with me and she clocked me halfway to Bristol. She knew, because her family has been through enough similar problems. Ad was driving while Charlotte held my hand saying, 'When did it start? How long has this been going on?' When we arrived at the Priory in Bristol she told me to wait while she went to tell the doctor. He already knew. He told me, 'I have the results of your scan. You have shrunk your brain; there is water round the brain that shouldn't be there, and you have damaged your kidneys. You have to go into detox right now.'

It was such a relief to sit there and admit it all. I went back home and told Sheridan. She was relieved because she thought I had some kind of dreadful brain problem but this was something we could resolve. I told the kids I was going into hospital. The specialist wanted me to go into the Priory that afternoon but it was only a four-week programme and I'd heard stories that the place is more like a hotel than a detox clinic. I knew I needed something longer, maybe tougher, to help me fight it. Fortunately Charlotte's mother was one of the trustees of Clouds in Wiltshire and so by the Monday afternoon I was in Clouds beginning a six-week stay.

When I went in they gave me a Breathalyser and checked my blood pressure. Then they gave me four massive injections in my backside with these great long needles. I needed to be pumped full of high vitamins to get me up to scratch. I was very thin when I went in because by the end I couldn't eat as it made me feel sick. I thought I looked great. They put me on Librium three times a day to bring me down from the alcohol, because it is dangerous just stopping overnight.

The medical staff unpacked my bag to make sure I hadn't sneaked anything in. (Some people do – later on in my stay I found an empty half-bottle hidden under a tree trunk.) They went through my toilet bag and took away my aftershave, a funky little atomiser I was given for Christmas. I asked, 'What are you doing?'

'You might drink it.'

'Jesus, it's Issey Miyake; it costs fifty pounds a bottle. I'd have to take out a mortgage to get drunk on that. How bad would I have to be to drink aftershave?' That was before I heard stories about how other patients would drink Listerine. It was a petrifying learning curve. I had counselling every day and chats, constantly sharing stories with other people – I had never seen so many tattoos in my life, but they were all great characters who made me feel very welcome. Most of the kids in there had had something dreadful happen to them and they had a lot more issues to sort out than I did. My life story was pretty rubbish compared to some of theirs. 'I made lots of money; I spent it; I had a ball. I've managed to do the job I've wanted my entire life without having to drive a van like my dad.'

I learned that there was no traumatic moment in my life, and I wasn't abused as a kid. I had no real excuse except it was fun, the laugh and enjoyment of getting smashed with my mates.

At Clouds I was introduced to a standard twelve-step sobriety programme in which I was required to take stock of my life physically, mentally and spiritually. It sounds easy stated like that but it isn't. It's the hardest thing I've ever had to do because I will be doing it for the rest of my life.

I wasn't ready to leave, as it was too cosy. I ate loads. I spent six weeks completely and utterly devoid of alcohol and there was something really wonderful about doing the breath test as I walked out of Clouds and to see it hit 'zero zero zero'. Something clicked in the back of my head that maybe I was immune to all this, maybe I should just try it again to see what it was like. The first thing I did when I came out was to test myself. I bought a bottle of vodka.

Even as I drank that first bottle I knew I was a complete dick, but I thought I could get away with it again, that I could hide it. Not this time. Sheridan noticed the difference in me. When you stop drinking your skin changes colour and your complexion gets smoother. It went on for a week up until we had this big financial meeting with my tour manager Berenice and her partner Dave who runs the website. They had travelled down from North Wales to go through my cash flow with Philippa my bookkeeper.

I knew what was coming and I couldn't face it so I had a couple of drinks. Halfway through the meeting Sheridan spotted I wasn't quite with it. She went out to my car and found a quarter-empty bottle of vodka still in its plastic bag, so she walked in and plonked it in the middle of the table. I went, 'Oh shit,' and the meeting was disbanded.

Those poor people had driven five hours down from Llandudno and I'd blown it just like I'd blown Sheri's Aloe Vera pitch for her. I went and packed my bags, but she let me stay that night after the vodka was poured away.

I knew there was no sense behind any of my behaviour. Why would I come out and do it again after spending six weeks away from home and everybody I love? But I did. The next day I only bought a small bottle – but why a small bottle? I don't know.

I was talking to Rusty Egan, who has had his own problems and was incredibly supportive, on the house mobile phone, so I wandered out to the car. I sat down, picked the bottle up and had a swig. Sheridan was sitting behind me. That was it. She had had enough of my lying; she'd had to pretend everything was normal for the past six weeks and here I was betraying her again. I was sent packing – quite rightly – though unfortunately everything happened in front of the kids. I checked into a hotel in Bath, sat in the bar and had a couple of drinks. The next day I went to Ad's house and that was enough to jolt me back into reality. When I realised how close I was to losing my family forever it focused me.

When I went back to Clouds for my weekly meeting and explained how I had slipped, the counsellors weren't surprised. One said, 'I could see it in your face you didn't really get it when you were in here; you got some of it but not enough.'

The stumbling point I had was Step Three, where you have to hand your life across to a higher power or a god. Coming from Glasgow and hating organised religion as I do, that doesn't sit well with me. They explained a million times that it can be a god of your choosing, the ocean, a waiter called Godfrey, whatever. I kept saying, 'You are making me play a game here, but you are not telling me the rules.' I don't know whether I was analysing them analysing me or simply fighting it. My way of getting that stuff out has always been to write it in songs.

The only person who can make me stop drinking is me. I can't promise never to drink again. I take it one step at a time, and I can't promise that it will all be great from now on. I find it hard to contemplate the thought of never having a drink between now and the day I die. It's down to will and being strong, and whether I have that or not I don't know. All I have is one day at a time. I didn't drink yesterday and I won't drink today and I'll try not to drink tomorrow.

My children soon outed me to the world. Flossie went into school and announced, 'Daddy's in hospital, because he's an algoloholic.'

I've done some bad things, damaged my family, but I'm not a paedophile or a rapist. I've done something that a huge amount of people do and now I have to fix the mess. I've been drinking for over twenty years, so six weeks in Clouds isn't going to fix that, but I have the ultimate incentive – a great family who need their dad. I've fallen off the stallion, been trampled by a couple of Shetland ponies, now I've pulled myself back in the saddle again.

With each day I stay sober my focus becomes clearer. The problems that at night were magnified a gazillion times, that prevented me sleeping or eating, no longer seem as bad as I once believed. I am falling asleep and waking up, whereas when I was drinking I passed out and revived. Now when I wake up it is with a clear mind, which makes such a huge, huge difference.

Starting to play again was really hard – and a tremendous relief. I sang a couple of songs at the Albert Hall for a benefit concert for Ronnie Lane's Multiple Sclerosis charity. On 24 April 2003 I gave my first solo concert in six months at North Hykenham, just outside Lincoln. It's a special gig for me: that was where I was given the card about the Ethiopian girl, a good place for second chances. I was absolutely petrified, and my fingers were soft, and my brain was too.

The pacing I did up and down in my dressing room was hideous, and I probably wore a hole in the carpet. For the past 25 years I'd have been relaxed, feet up on the table, having a drink – or two – sucking in Dutch courage and false bravado. It took me half the show to get back into the flow, after walking on sober to play a set full of new songs and cover versions. I wanted to shake it up a bit; I needed to shake it up a bit for myself and for my regular crowd. So I did 'Waiting Days', which I had only ever done on a brief American tour. I wrote it in Los Angeles in the early days of AIDS when people were judged and convicted of a love crime. I sang 'Never More' from Queen's second album and somehow managed to remember all the words. I gulped down two bottles of water and realised it was all going to be fine.

The overwhelming response I got from the audience, and from comments on the Net and written in my guest book, was that my voice was 'outstanding'. I heard myself sing out in a couple of places, and the odd quaver, but I was so relieved to make it through. The nerves have gone – until the next one, and the next one after that.

That show was just the start. Suddenly there was a lot happening, stuff stirring inside me that hadn't stirred in nearly two years. I got my studio back up and running – because it had been a while a lot of the software and drivers had expired. Now that my brain was no longer floating suspended in liquid I started jotting stuff down: a list of songs for the covers album I've been threatening for the past twenty years, titles and ideas for songs. I always listen to Radio 4 in the car and heard this documentary with the perfect line 'from the cradle to the grave'. That summed up for me what it is like being born into a bigoted background, of hating someone and not knowing why. There is a song waiting to happen.

I am thrilled and enthused to be writing new songs because I was bored to tears with my old ones. It doesn't worry me that I have no current record deal; if the only vehicle is midgeure.com so be it. In the past, if nobody was going to hear the songs there was no emotional need for me to write. Now I have a reason to start.

The songs don't come out of the night fully formed, but their seeds do. Now that the alcoholic stupor has gone I can feel them calling me again. That's what I have always done. I'm a songwriter who lost his way but, my higher power willing, I have found it again.

CHAPTER 28
THE SONGWRITER

If you last long enough in this industry, if you get really, really old and you are still out there, still doing it, the world starts to believe you are a songwriter. I'm a songwriter.

In April 1992 I appeared at the Oxford University Union Debating Society. After that performance I realised where my future lay. After four years in the commercial wilderness floundering in record company limbo I had no focus about where my career was going. There was much talk about reinvention – hello, I am not a packet of tea – but very little in the way of concrete suggestions. One of the first things I learned was I couldn't do shows on the Ultravox scale. I might sell records the same way, but I couldn't do five-hour sound checks and have huge stage sets. I had to adapt because basically I was starting all over again.

Chris O'Donnell came up with a solution. He was managing Van Morrison and working out of CMO as a tenant. We had all these discussions about stripping my live shows right down, how I could make a statement that showed how I had removed all the pomp. 'It is like a debate,' he said. The idea of a debate stuck in Chris's head to the point that he rang up the Oxford Union, spoke to the president and made him an offer. 'Midge will come along and talk about how you create songs, and you can ask questions.' He fixed the date. Then he told me about it.

I was petrified. I had left school at fifteen, so it was a scary prospect to even enter those hallowed halls. These were highly educated kids at one of the top universities in the world, future heads of state, future doctors, future lawyers, the brains of Britain. I was going to sit there and try and entertain them. If I could have pulled out I would have. On the night I sat down in front of this sea of intellect thinking, If I can face this, armed with just my guitar, I can do anything. The stained-glass windows were backlit, evocative of centuries of history. Nervously I played a song, and there was a polite ripple of applause.

'Does anyone have any questions?' I asked hesitantly.

Nobody said anything. It was like being back at school except I was the teacher. The procedure was very formal: in order to ask questions you had to go through the chair and nobody wanted to start. Up piped O'Donnell from the back with 'What's your major influence?' I lobbed that one back, played another song and answered another couple of questions. I felt like a corpse, but then I was dying a slow, agonising death.

Then some kid asked, 'If you had to write something for Take That, what would it be?'

'An instrumental.'

The whole room roared with laughter, and the ice was broken. That was when I realised what I had become. I was not a rock star, not a pop star. I was a songwriter. I still am. I create music, hopefully interesting music, and I can perform it on my own. Oxford was a full stop: it marked the end of one stage of my career. I realised that I had to change my whole approach to live shows. None of that Ultravox pomposity worked any more. I decided to go out and do a tour where talking to the audience was as important as playing songs. In April 1993 I started my first Out Alone tour, which was literally me, my guitar and a tour manager/sound engineer (Steve Cox) playing Civic Halls and the like. In the next year I played almost sixty shows in various towns, many of which didn't get many acts visiting any more. The money was fantastic because I had no overheads. In twenty years gigging it was the first time I'd ever made any money on the road; up until then it had always cost me a small fortune.

I knew that most venues have to have some form of PA system. In my naïvety I thought it would be good enough. Every night, because the monitors were usually beaten up, not working or just rubbish, the sound check would take hours. I'd end up hoarse before I even started the show. After twelve shows in fifteen days it was starting to take a toll on my voice. We arrived at the Albert Halls in Bolton. I walked in and there was a proper PA, a big stack on either side of the stage, and big wedge monitors, stuff I recognised, thank God. Because the venue didn't have a PA the promoter had hired it in from Berenice Hardman and her partner Dave Claxton. She did front-of-house sound and he did monitors. After two weeks of complete dross, hearing myself sing with a goldfish bowl on my head, that gig was a joy. Two weeks later we played in Llandudno where Berenice and Dave lived. They came along, enjoyed the show and we got on really well.

The second time I went Out Alone in January '94 I decided I had to do it slightly differently and I knew I had to have a PA. I was talking to Cerise Reed who ran the Ultravox fanzine, *Extreme Voice*, and she suggested I hire Berenice to do the sound. That grew into her driving my car when I was tired and a year later she became my tour manager. She still is.

Playing alone I had stripped everything down to its barest minimalist form, getting rid of the stage sets, the lights and everything that I had hidden behind. Just me, my guitar and my songs, as basic as it can get. It's so much easier to connect with an audience that way, I can talk about anything I want, crack jokes. In the past ten years I've done regular tours with a band but I love doing the solo gigs. People seem to like the intimacy, and they want to know how I write songs.

I write in a very strange way, different from anybody else I know. I don't sit down with my guitar, or behind the piano, write a complete song, and then go to the studio with a producer and record it. It takes much, much longer than that. The process always starts with a seed of an idea that can come from anywhere, a story, a memory, a TV image. 'The Leaving' was based on my brother having to move away from Glasgow to find work, but it was also about what might have happened to me had I stayed in my engineering apprenticeship, only to find years later that there were no more jobs. I think it's one of the best songs I've ever written.

In the studio I start laying out a musical bed for this seed to live in. The computer is my surrogate band. I put down the drum patterns, the bass parts, layer it one element at a time, and create the atmosphere to drop the seed in. It evolves and evolves and evolves, until eventually I sit down and write the final melody and the words. I've got to have the musical atmosphere, melodies and the musical arrangement first. Then I write lyrics – which I leave to the last minute because I dread doing it – that will scan and rhyme and sound right. The sound of the words are just as important as their meaning. 'Reap The Wild Wind' is a song about absolutely nothing. It started off as an instrumental and the lyric was only about the rhythm of the words. 'You take my hand and give me your friendship / I'll take my time and sell you my slow reply / Give me an inch and I'll make the best of it, Take all you want / Leave all the rest to die / Reap the wild wind'. It doesn't mean anything . . . but it sounded great.

Generally the music comes easily, the harmonies, the counterharmonies, the countermelodies seem to float in. When it comes to doing my lyrics I spend ages analysing them. At the end of the night I might think, That sounds great, so I'll sing over the backing track and write the lyrics down, but next morning I walk in, hear it and go, 'God, that's dreadful.' I die a thousand times, scrap it and start over again.

I'm not a prolific writer but I am picky. I write ten albums' worth of material and edit it down to one, which takes a long time. I'm not Elvis Costello. I've got this image that Elvis, like Prince, is so prolific he can rattle out two albums a year. I've got to get it right, so it takes me a long time to chisel away and hack a song into shape. Some songs take for ever. After I did the Mandela concert I started writing a song about how dare they do this to him and how I could 'see hope in the morning light'. It took so long to write that the South African government had set him free before I finished it! I was a little miffed to say the least – I'd spent ages on it so I had to turn it into a generic song.

I don't write with other people very often. Every album there's always a couple of tracks that Danny Mitchell's been involved in. It's usually because I'm floundering towards the end, and I've run myself dry. I've done the production, the arrangements, played most of the instruments, written most of the lyrics. So it's nice to shove it onto somebody else.

The best songs I've written are often commercial failures, perhaps because they're more interesting, too long or they don't fit the format of the moment. With 'All Fall Down' I had the brilliant idea of getting Ultravox, the kings of all things plugged in, together with the Chieftains, the kings of all things unplugged, and doing this Celtic protest song. Radio One played it and pronounced, 'It's either going to be the Christmas Number One, or it will do nothing.' It did nothing.

A song about governments around the world claiming to fix our lives by beating up other governments, when in fact it will only get better when we all fall down, isn't really Christmas fodder. At the base it's about the religious bigotry I was born into. I lived through the whole Catholic–Protestant, Rangers–Celtic thing. That's why I never played football. I wanted to play music because music is neutral. It's still going on. I see it in Belfast and in Israel today, people using religion to beat each other up. I have fought against that all my life. My kids haven't been christened, as I don't want them to have any religion at all. They can choose their own when they are old enough.

The song I write is not the one that you hear. It may sound the same but it means something different to you. To me the Beatles' 'Hello Goodbye' will always be a Christmas song. It was *the* song of the Christmas when I was fourteen, walking around school with my big college scarf wrapped round my neck, and hair slightly over my ears, because that's as long as I was allowed to wear it. Whenever I hear 'Hello Goodbye' I picture Scotland, very snowy and cold, and I can remember the people I went out with, see the face of the girl that I fancied.

Listeners place their own interpretation on my songs: they've adapted it to what they need. We associate certain songs with key moments in our lives – had children to it, buried a parent to it – so they have their own personal resonance. Sometimes, inadvertently, songs can become a form of therapy, a catharsis or an aid to forgetting, which are not things I think of when I write. I am getting something off my chest, and making music for people to enjoy. Release it and it's an old song, and it's time to get on with the next one. It's only since the advent of the Internet that I've realised how songs that I have all but forgotten have become the soundtrack to individual lives. I got one email from a kid who was brought up in the Lebanon. The only way he could get away from the bombs and fighting was to put on his Walkman and listen to Ultravox (the music was probably more miserable than the war). Now he's a doctor, living in Paris and he wrote to tell me how much my music helped him to get through that time.

You don't go to school to learn how to write songs: you learn by experience. When I started I certainly couldn't but I learned from my sad mistakes. In Salvation I wrote 'The Bowie Trilogy' in the style of Ziggy but it wasn't three parts of anything except awful. 'Young Girls', on the Rich Kids album, was really cheesy: 'Young girls everywhere I go / They touch my leg at the picture show / How come I can't say no to those young girls.' Glen let me put it on the album, probably to appease me. Within six months I'd gone from writing that to 'Marching Men'.

'Fade To Grey' was another pivotal song. I painted this whole scenario, steeped in European-cinema imagery, about this little guy losing it. 'One man on a lonely platform, one case sitting by his side, two eyes staring cold and silent, shows fear he turns to hide.' I used to flick through filmbooks, looking for old movie titles – *Thin Wall* and *Reap the Wild Wind* are both old films. The titles sparked off images in my head, then I'd sit down to write a story.

I make a distinct division between what is a successful song and what is a commercially successful song. Due to circumstances 'Breathe' somehow managed to be both. They are two different animals. A commercially successful song is something which is put in the machine. It goes through all the processes, all the cogs and wheels, until it gets to radio. It comes out the speakers, and people hear it, like it and buy it. A successful song is one that works on a musical level, as an entity;

it means something: it's got the highs and lows, the emotion that I want in there. But when I put it into the system one of the cogs is missing, so it gets stuck or falls through a hole in the bottom. It doesn't mean that the song's any less worthy, it just means that it hasn't had the luck or opportunity to become a commercially successful one. I could release a fantastic album of all the ones that got away – *Midge Ure's Great Escapes*.

I write about the downside, not just the upside. Most songwriters write about subject number one: love, the good bits, the bad bits, the intimate bits, the 'I love you, you love me' stuff which has been done a million times. To me the other emotions – hate, lust, envy, greed, jealousy – are just as important. We didn't really write about love in Ultravox. It was all about sad subjects, dark and miserable stuff. What do you do if there's four minutes left of your life? You go home, to be with the people you love, play a piece of music, turn it up as loud as you can and just hold on to each other, dancing with tears in your eyes.

I've always liked writers who find interesting paths to their subject matter. Both Kate Bush and Fran Healey of Travis use strong melodies and concentrate on the song rather the dressing the song is wrapped in. They don't rely on production to cover a song's flaws. Other songwriters like Peter Gabriel and John Martyn, who has been criminally underrated his whole career, are prepared to go out on a limb and take chances which don't always succeed commercially.

Sometimes a song can have a bizarre birth. 'Love's Great Adventure' was the bastard son of a jeans commercial. Levi's had spent a small fortune on this TV commercial, until five days before the big international launch one of the advertising bods went, 'I'm not sure about the music. Let's change it.'

Somebody else said, 'What you need on there is "Vienna".'

As it happened one of them knew Peter Wagg, who worked in the art department at Chrysalis. He phoned me.

The agency gave me some speculating money to come up with an idea. I went home that night and watched the commercial. It started in a quarry; rocks blowing up, rubble getting crunched down and then loaded into a truck; the truck hacks its way across America. Then it cut to molten iron, sparks everywhere in this big foundry, close-up on a piece of denim. The stamp goes down and leaves a rivet. The whole commercial was a build-up, so you didn't know what was being advertised until the very end.

I wrote this piece of music which they loved. They came back and asked me to do the follow-up – 'Threads'. They had sent off one of the Scott brothers – either Ridley or Tony – to Mexico for three months to shoot the commercial. This guy is out fishing; he catches a marlin, plays it, then just as he's about to reel it in he cuts the line. You follow the line through the water and you can see that the thread is what they make Levi's with. This time I had three months to get the music right. The original brief was to make it rhythmic, not melodic, so I used lots of mechanical sounds. They came back with, 'It's got no melody.' I wrote a melody, very 633 Squadron, which went brilliantly over the pictures of the fish jumping out of the water. Then I started getting phone calls . . . it's just the way those admen speak: 'It doesn't sound right, it needs to sound a little bit more like the feel of Formica.' What? 'It needs more bass.' What? More bass drum, more bass guitar, more bass on the overall sonic mix?

In the end I got tired of the crap and told them to forget it and give me my bit of music back. I took it away, wrote some lyrics and had a Top Ten hit.

My major life experiences come out in my songs. If I was an American I'd be lying on a couch being counselled, with some guy talking me through my childhood, examining all the stuff that has ever gone wrong in my life. *Pure* was miserable and misogynist. 'Cold, Cold Heart' is all about me, it's a nicely packaged Christmas gift but when you open it up there is a miserable, nasty, self-pitying song inside. Others weren't much better. 'Tumbling Down', 'Pure Love', 'Sweet 'n' Sensitive Thing' – that last one depends how you say the title: try 'sweet insensitive thing' instead – or 'Lied'. I was feeling sorry for myself. Who was to blame? Me. I was part of the problem so I put it down on paper, sang it away on tape. It was a good way of exorcising the ghosts, to help get it out of my system. I don't play those songs any more – except for 'I See Hope In The Morning Light'. I don't need to; my life has moved on.

My love songs usually have a twist in them. One of my most straightforward is 'Guns And Arrows', and it's got two weapons in the title. 'When you're tired of all your sorrows / Just fire your guns and arrows and nail me through my heart.' It's a hopeful song about a breakup and how there is someone waiting for you when you have recovered. I wrote it when Sheridan was pregnant with Kitty.

Some people think 'You Move Me' is a love song. It could be interpreted that way, but it's actually about how popular culture – art, music, books, cinema, whatever – should make you feel something. You should be affected when you hear a piece of music, but it doesn't seem to happen that much any more. When I heard *Ziggy*

Stardust for the first time I had this revelation that there was real music out there. 'You move me in a wild and wicked way' – what a great thing to say, my molecules have been thrown about. There is a reference in 'You Move Me' to Bowie's 'Hang On To Yourself'. I took what I thought was his line 'like a diamond in Vaseline' and put it in the chorus. (I got the line completely wrong, but that's memory for you.)

'Fields Of Fire' is about a volatile relationship. There are moments where it's all lovely and fabulous, and others when you end up screaming at each other. I'm saying, 'You've gone crazy. I don't understand what you're doing; I don't see what you're getting at, because I'm a man, you're a woman. Now let the rains fall on your fields of fire, just to calm you down, to make it nice and smooth again, so we can start over, just forget it and get on with life.' That interests me because it's real, it's what happens in life. My songs come from life: I write about my kids, how I worry about the future, what kind of a world they are going to be living in.

I walked about with the line 'beneath a Spielberg sky' for a year before I found the right story. It implied something huge. The impetus came when I was sitting on the sofa with the kids, watching the news. The report was from Kosovo, and we could see missiles hitting targets. The kids asked me what it was. I explained, 'It's a missile, and it's got a little camera on it, and we see the building explode.'

'Is it real?' they asked. 'Are there people in there?'

Yes, I said, there probably are. I was watching this high-tech war unfolding in my sitting room and then I thought, When the end comes that is how it will be. We will be watching it on a plasma screen with 5.1 surround-sound stereo. We are so far removed from reality that if we don't see it, if we don't taste it, then we're not there. The end of the world will be like watching a Hollywood blockbuster. I wrote the song three years before 9/11. When I watched the Twin Towers collapse it just didn't look real. I couldn't comprehend what was actually happening. It's chilling to watch a song come to life.

That's me, prophet . . . and songwriter.

Bob Geldof and I were given an Ivor Novello award in 1985 for Band Aid. That was fairly inevitable. For a songwriter it is the ultimate accolade, but for us it was something else. We'd written a charity record that had enjoyed huge acclaim. However, I believe that Ivor Novellos should be about what you have achieved as a songwriter. When George Michael was awarded his he burst into tears.

I was in the supermarket last Christmas and somebody was whistling the tune to 'Do They Know It's Christmas?'. I liked that. That meant more to me than the Novello. At the time I felt I didn't deserve it. It wasn't the best song I'd ever written, nor the best tune, but it's lasted. Perhaps it's better than I think. Or maybe one day they'll wake up and give me another Novello.

CHAPTER 29
A 21ST-CENTURY STAR

Behind its brilliant façade the 21st-century record industry is an empty, crumbling shell. The next U2 are playing in a pub, and the next Kate Bush is sitting at home writing brilliant songs because nobody is chasing them. The major talents in the British record industry were signed twenty years ago. U2 are the biggest band in the world and have been for the past decade; there isn't anyone close to touching them. The music business is in a real mess and it blames everyone but itself.

I will never sign another major record deal. That's not a whinge but a simple fact. That may sound defeatest, but it's not – I'm being a realist. I don't fit any more. I am neither young, being the wrong side of fifty, nor an old established rock star. The record business is still very ageist. We have OAP superstars like the Stones, Paul McCartney, Clapton – there hasn't been a new guitar hero since the 60s – who sell a lot of tickets because people want to see history on stage, but their record sales aren't that hot any more.

I'm a problem. I've had more than my fair share of hits, of fifteen minutes in the spotlight, so I think in a certain way, and I don't agree with what is going on in today's music industry. An actor, if he is clever about it, can grow old gracefully. In the music industry you are always Peter Pan, and if you never look in the mirror you can still feel seventeen. That will never go away. But I am not going to pretend to be 25. Not again. To the younger generation I am an old man, who has had his day. I can hear them thinking, Go! It is understandable but it doesn't sit comfortably. Fortunately I don't have to be young to make music.

There isn't much of a future for recording acts of my stature. I am part of a legacy that the British record industry wants to ignore. It has constantly thrown out the baby with the bath water, chucked out what we've got, whether it's good, bad or indifferent, just because it's old, and embraced the new. Unfortunately what is new has brought nothing to the rock and roll party. The business has become a high-tech factory pumping out sausages in white suits and spiky hair.

A lot of modern pop stars are karaoke singers who have been dragged along by a 'reality' TV show – though how real are *Pop Idol* and *Fame Academy*? After scouring through 10,000 kids and being promoted on Saturday night primetime TV for ten weeks, is David Sneddon the best they can come up with? A guy who can write one song that scraped into the Top Ten and quit the moment his year was up?

There is talk of a Live Aid twentieth anniversary concert in 2005. But who would we get to play? U2, David Bowie, Elton John – the same artists who did it last time. Or do we ask the dance acts and the boy bands along and re-christen it Mime Aid. Backstage there'd be a bunch of boy bands fighting over whose CD was coming on next. It might be hard to tell whose backing track it was.

I won't be signed to a major label again because I'm perceived as somebody who has had his years of writing hits. I've had twenty years of making music that is, hopefully, musically successful, but that is seen in a totally different light. Most of the public probably thinks I am a multibillionaire, sitting back and resting on my laurels, playing on my huge big lawn with my seated lawnmower. I wish that was true, but the reality is I am what I have always been: a working musician. The morning after my fiftieth birthday party I drove 300 miles to Hartlepool, did the gig, stayed in a B&B and drove 300 miles back.

I will sign another publishing deal, because I feel I have a lot to offer as a writer. Over the past 25 years I have accrued a lot of information and know-how. I can be constructive, teach young guys how to write songs, show them where they are going wrong. I can produce records across the complete span from Radiohead to Robbie Williams. It would be ridiculous for me to walk away and put nothing back.

Britain has consistently turned out some of the best, if not *the* best, rock music of the last fifty years. But what has the world, particularly America, accepted from us in the last ten years? Dido, Coldplay, Radiohead and the Darkness. And their success is probably as much down to luck as investment of time and creative input from a record company.

In the 90s the industry shot itself in the foot, and started buying one-off dance records. Some guy knocked up a white label in his bedroom and, once there was a buzz in the clubs, the record company bought it. There was no commitment to developing an artist for the future. It was all about short-term profit at the expense of long-term gains. Football teams find players at twelve; they come up through the junior team, and by the time they're seventeen there is a hot new player, who has been developed, nurtured and taught by forty years of experience. The music industry has stopped doing that, and there's no loyalty, no belief in the long term. I may sound like a broken record – I do remember vinyl – but when I started out record companies believed in taking raw talent, developing it over three, maybe four, albums, building a fan base by gigging, and out of that might come a world-class act with the longevity to match.

What happens now is that all the same A&R men go to see the same hot young band and they get into a bidding war. The band ends up with a half-million-pound advance, but once the stakes get so high the machine takes over. They are packed off to a £2,000-a-day studio, give five points to the hot producer of the moment and make an album that smoothes out all the very elements that make them special. The record comes out; they do some crap tour and only sell 20,000 albums, whereupon the record company look at the balance sheet, realise they can't afford to pick up the next £750,000 option and drop them.

Over the last ten years record companies have done that consistently. Mariah Carey had to be bought out of her $70 million contract with Virgin for over $40 million. What were the financial people thinking? What were the A&R people thinking? That girl wouldn't be able to recoup those advances in an entire lifetime. Music's all about changing fads: the door opens for a while, and it's your turn, then it closes. Carey's success was remarkable: she sold 100 million albums, but those were freak numbers; they happen to very few artists once in a blue moon. And they always stop.

First the industry blew its foot off with deals like that, and then it ignored the Internet. Young kids take music straight off the Net, and they can't see anything wrong in that. A huge monster has been created that has whacked the industry over the head, so it's spent years bleating about piracy instead of finding a solution.

I don't know how the future of pop music is going to unfold. I'd hate to be starting out now because so many gates have come down. I drove my Transit van to Inverness in mid-winter, played two 45-minute sets, and drove straight back with icicles on the inside of the van. That outlet doesn't exist any more. I worry about how new music is going to perpetuate itself. Perhaps there will be no new music, and everything will be available to download, but it will all be old.

I don't have to play the record-company game any more, because the record-company game is up. As a 'classic' artist I still have a hard-core fan base, so I can carry on making music. Maybe it's because I'm a paranoid Scot but I always knew the day would come when I was surplus to requirements, when a bean counter would study the numbers, see I didn't add up and pull the plug. So I have always had my own studio.

My first studio cost £150,000 and took a genius to wire up. My current studio is a computer, some software and keyboard. It cost me forty grand – which includes the building and the equipment to make my own videos, so I don't have to ask for £50,000 to make a promo. My recording studio is a high-powered Mac. I use Logic Audio, a music-making sequencing software program. I simply sing through a microphone into a little interface box and it goes straight onto my hard drive. The computer cost under £3,000, the software £600, a top-of-the-line microphone is a grand and I can carry my whole studio in a backpack.

If I make the whole album myself, the only cost is my time and effort. When I ask other musicians to play I usually operate a barter system. He plays on mine, and I play on his. I don't mix the record myself, as I use a proper engineer who takes the hard disc to his home studio. He's got the ear and knows the frequencies to make sure that it's sonically good. Once that's finished we pop into Real World – when they have some cheap downtime – play it through the big speakers, make sure that the bottom end is OK, and make sure it's not too heavy, woofy or wobbly. Tweak it a bit and it's all done. There are companies who cut the album, EQ-ing it to make sure it's technically right, not too messy, that there's not too much bottom end, and it's not too bright at the top. I can make a whole album for under five grand and I'd defy anyone to tell me whether it was recorded in my garden hut, or took ten years at the Record Plant, in New York at $2,000 a day.

Berenice Hardman is one of those people who can fix stuff. When my car broke down, if she couldn't actually mend it she knew exactly what was wrong with it, and she's brilliant at fixing my computer. Years ago when we were driving to a gig she told me, 'You know your web domain name is still available?'

'What's a web domain name?'

'You know, midgeure dotcom, the worldwide web . . . the Internet.'

'Why would I want that?'

'Believe me,' said Berenice, 'you will.' She went on and on about it for over a year until even I realised how important owning something like that might be. Eventually I bought the domain name to stop anybody else having it and then didn't do anything much with it for a couple of years. After the whole BMG debacle imploded Berenice suggested we open a web shop. She had never made a website in her life but she figured out how it worked and built it from scratch. Type 'Midge Ure' into any search engine and www.midgeure.com is the first URL that comes up. It's bloody good, really fast, easy to use and she sits on it like you wouldn't believe, updating it constantly – she's like a ferret who won't let go.

As far as I am concerned now the Internet is a saviour, because I can bypass the middle man. It allows me, or rather Berenice, to run my own self-sufficient micro-industry, a cottage industry for the 21st century. Even for someone like me with no left brain worth discussing, the maths are compelling. If a new band has a royalty rate of 14% and the CD costs £15 their share is a fraction over £2 – after they have paid back the recording costs. Take away manufacturing costs and the rest goes on marketing, putting them on planes to go to promote the record in Japan ... not forgetting the record-company profit.

Admittedly I do have to pay for pressing, artwork, the other musicians who have appeared on the CD, and I have to pay whoever is packaging it and sending it out, but it still makes more economic sense. I won't sell as many copies as I do on a major, but there are bonuses. I can release limited-edition live recordings from past tours and other rarities that my die-hard fans love. I can decide how to spend any money I make: pay a plugger to take the record up to Radio 2, take out adverts in magazines, promote it the way I see fit. It's my choice. I have to run a web shop, and I have to sell stuff at gigs, but it's an ongoing livelihood.

The downside is that I may never appear on *Top of the Pops* again. I've been on *Top of the Pops* in so many different guises it makes me dizzy trying to remember. I may never have a Top Forty hit again, and I can forget ever being played on Radio 1 again. Five years ago Radio 2 was a viable option, but now it, too, has become more controlled with panels and playlists. Radio is becoming more powerful, more selective and more conservative. The next time I get played on Radio 2 will probably be the day I die. 'Good old Midge Ure's popped his clogs today ... here's one of his tunes.' 'If I Was' might be appropriate.

Fortunately there is no substitute for live performance. The only person who can go out and do my stuff properly is me. Mind you, when I was rehearsing the *Move Me* band before the European tour in 2000, we did a warm-up gig in Birmingham. As we were sound-checking some guy came and bought four tickets. 'Fantastic,' he said. 'It's a Midge Ure sound-alike band.'

'No, no, it's Midge Ure. The real one.'

The guy gave the tickets back. Figure that out? He would pay good money to see someone who sounded like me, but not to see me. I can only put it down to the fact that tribute bands do all the hits, wall-to-wall hits, nonstop. When you come to see me you will get the quirky instrumental and me announcing, 'This is one of my favourite songs: I wrote it about depression.'

Live work is being swallowed up by the tribute bands such as No Way Sis and T-Rextasy, who do an hour and a half of songs that everybody knows. It's a nostalgia trip that fills bars. Live venues are stuffing their week's-worth of entertainment with covers bands. That's pretty tough on new bands trying to cut their teeth.

It's not all about going Out Alone or doing shows with Troy Donockley. Sometimes I get a real bonus. In October '98 I was invited to sing at the opening of the Potsdamer Platz in Berlin, which used to be no-man's land in the days of the Wall. Eberhard Schoener was commissioned to produce a show for the opening and asked me to sing 'Breathe' and 'Vienna' with the Berlin Philharmonic Orchestra. It was like being asked to sing in Trafalgar Square in front of half a million people. That stuff is still exciting.

I was musical director for Showtime at the Stadium, which was held at Cardiff's Millennium Stadium in 2001. The idea was a series of songs from musicals performed by pop acts like Blue, S Club, A1, Steps and Atomic Kitten, as well as stars from West End musicals like Ruthie Henshall and Petula Clark, and popular classical singers like Charlotte Church and Russell Watson. Blue wanted to do 'Something's Coming' from *West Side Story*. They played me a dreadful 70s sub-Stevie Wonder thing, so I did a new arrangement for them. I spent ages doing it, counted all the bloody bars, then they turned it down. I was miffed they disliked the version I did, but they were polite in their refusal. Thanks but no thanks came back from their management.

On the Thursday before the concert A1 dumped the arrangement I had worked on for weeks and said they wanted to do the Blues Brothers' 'Everybody Needs Somebody'. I couldn't find any brass players around Bath at that short notice so I used sampled brass and multilayered it to sound like a proper band. I gave them the arrangement with a guide vocal at 9 p.m. on Friday night. By Saturday afternoon they had worked out an entire dance routine, all four of them doing the pose with the black hats and shades, falling on their knees at the same time. I was gobsmacked, and for me they stole the show.

That was an eye-opener, because I'd been slagging them off the week before. These guys really knew their stuff and they can play, too. Some of the other pop acts just mimed, which I thought was a cop-out. Atomic Kitten can sing – two of them went to stage school – so why did they settle on doing their dance routine; it short-changes the fans. I shouldn't be overcritical, though, as I blew my own performance badly. I did a duet with Heather Nova and totally fucked up the words on 'Phantom of the Opera'. It's a duet all the way through so, when I forgot everything and sang the next line in Dutch, Heather just froze and stood there with her mouth open.

There are some things I don't want to do. I won't go down the DJ-remix path – not since I was talked into having a remix done of 'Beneath A Spielberg Sky'. Everyone was on my back, saying I had to do it because that was the way to get a hit. I read an interview with a young band who likened a remix to going out for a walk with a dog, and coming back with a cat. It's a perfect analogy for such an alien thing. All they do is take the vocal and then change all the chords. Even though the song was getting played on Radio 2, I couldn't stand hearing it. That wasn't my song. It was as if I'd come full circle and I was in Slik again singing someone else's song.

I'll never let it happen again. I have accepted that if I don't jump on the dance bandwagon it's going to hurt me financially. Ironically, in Europe they all think I'm the godfather of dance because I came up with Visage and co-wrote 'Fade To Grey'. I'd be seen as a two-faced tosser if a DJ started doing official dance versions of Ultravox and Visage numbers. Not that it matters much, because songs are public property once you release them. There are dance versions of 'Breathe' in Miami, where it is a popular tune on the gay scene. An Italian guy did a cover of 'Hymn', and I've heard thrash-metal versions and really bad dance versions of 'If I Was', but as that's not me doing it I don't care.

Recently I did a track for Jam & Spoon's album, *Tripomatic Fairytales* 3003. They're a pair of Frankfurt remixers and DJs, but this was a proper collaboration, so I'm not being a hypocrite. They sent me the backing track, and I added a top line, the lyrics and sang. 'Something To Remind Me' was based in 80s electronic and textural sounds, but it's not a dance record. I'd like to work with Jam again and I'd always want him to mix it because he's really, really good at it. He's got better ears and equipment than me.

I have talked for the last twenty years about doing a covers album – since 'No Regrets' – and as I'm not bound by record-company restraints any more it may be time to record it. With covers, if I don't like the way a song turns out I can throw it away and no one will ever know. I'd like to do some Small Faces and old blues numbers as well as 'Everyone's Gone To The Moon'. I know it's a slushy, rubbish song but I love it.

I'm a jobbing, working musician. That's what I do. Sometimes that takes me into the realms of fame and recognition. Other times I get in my car and play in seedy clubs halfway up the motorway. A working musician is all I have ever wanted to be. I can't be bitter and twisted, and stamp my little foot and moan about not playing football stadiums. It's not going to happen. I have helped build bandwagons rather than jump on them, but that is what my life has dictated.

I try to be sincere and honest in what I do. I try to strive and make as interesting music as I can, to write songs that will last. I don't like shoving myself to the fore unless it is something I have earned. If I write a song that has done really well I relish it. I love the adulation when it is deserved, but I am prepared for it all to go away again, which it always does.

Peaks and troughs, troughs and peaks. That is the way it has worked through my entire life. Sometimes I have been bloody unlucky and found myself in scenarios not of my doing, tied to a sinking ship, having to escape and swim to the surface. But much of it is my own doing, because I am bloody-minded. I won't do things I don't want to do. I have learned that if I stick to my guns I have to accept the consequences, but I also believe that there are other hit records waiting inside me.

I have to keep working, to keep putting my irons into the fire. If that means producing and writing for other artists, writing film music, directing videos, I have to try it all. I don't live in a mansion in Tuscany. I don't want to retire tomorrow. I couldn't retire tomorrow, not with four kids.

CHAPTER 30
THIS IS MY LIFE

I should have guessed something was up when the BBC sent a car for me. These days I'm no longer considered to be a pop star so I'm allowed to drive myself.

In March 2001 I was doing interviews promoting *Move Me*. One was with Johnny Walker at Radio 2, who'd told me to 'bring along your guitar, do an acoustic version of "Vienna" . . . or anything else you fancy playing'. So there I was talking to Johnny, who I hadn't seen for a long time, and he's asking about the new record, all the regular stuff, Ultravox, Visage, life with Thin Lizzy, right back to my days as a reluctant teen idol. There were TV cameras hovering around but Johnny warned me there was a documentary being made on Radio 2 and to ignore them.

In every interview I ever give I am asked about 'Do They Know It's Christmas?' and Live Aid so it was no surprise when Johnny started asking about it. I sat in the studio, my guitar on my lap, reminiscing away. In my peripheral vision I saw someone move, but I didn't pay it much attention. Suddenly there was Geldof looming above me. My bottle went a little bit wobbly, and I couldn't understand what was going on. All Bob said was, 'Are you able to play it or what?' Well he certainly can't, so I went into automatic, twang on the guitar and I played the opening chords.

The door opened again and in came a camera crew. 'I've waited fifteen years to get you for this, you bugger,' said Bob. 'It's payback time.' Then Michael Aspel emerged from behind him clutching the big red book. I'd been kippered, completely stitched up. I'd done the same to Bob just after Live Aid and now he had his revenge. I wanted to run out of the room. What if they'd wheeled out some hideous teacher I hated from my primary school? It wouldn't be a party, more of a wake with me sitting there like a lemon watching what was going on, listening to everybody saying all these nice things about me just as if I was lying in a coffin in the corner.

Too late. I was trapped. With a beaming smile Michael Aspel announced, 'I needed a bit of Live Aid on this one so Bob has come ahead of me so that I could say: Tonight, Midge Ure, This Is Your Life.'

It was a great honour to be picked for the show, but part of me was muttering, 'Hang on, I'm not dead. I'm not even fifty. My career's not over. It's just different.' Now it's done – and especially as they're not making it any more – I'm delighted to have been a part of TV history.

At least the guests weren't a succession of household names playing the Old Pals act. There was a good collection of mates like Chris Morrison, big Glenn, Mark King, Paul Young, Mark Brzezicki, Rusty, Scott Gorham from Thin Lizzy and Howard Jones. Howard and I had worked together on Prince's Trust concerts before I toured with him in the States. I remember when we played 'Delta Lady' for Joe Cocker, Joe was really taken aback that this synthesizer kid with the silly haircut could actually play serious boogie-woogie piano and delta blues. It was great to see Kenny Hyslop again. Kenny is one of those guys who hasn't been sober for thirty years . . . and that night showed he wasn't intending to be sober for the next thirty.

Chris Cross had changed since he became a counsellor. He'd become shy and a bit diffident in public and really disliked being on the telly. Somehow they'd found Tiger Tim Stevens, a Radio Clyde DJ, who for reasons of his own had championed Slik, and because they needed a DJ from the 80s they had grabbed poor old Bruno Brookes and dragged him along; he was as confused as I was. It was an oddity to have Paddy Moloney walk through the door – not being a pop star from the 80s. He's a great character and rather than hobnob with the other guests he spent ages backstage teaching Kitty how to play the penny whistle.

Yello Kabede, the head of the Ethiopian Support Committee, turned up as did Caroline Crowther – who's married to Dave Taskevedis, Peter Gabriel's tour manager – another reminder of how much I still miss Phil Lynott. There were video messages from George Martin, Martin and Gary Kemp and Michael Buerk.

Chris Tarrant did his thing from the *Who Wants To Be A Millionaire?* chair, and asked the embarassing question: In February 1981, which artist beat Ultravox's 'Vienna' to the Number One spot in the UK charts?

A: Keith Harris and Orville the Duck – 'Orville's Song'
B: Joe Dolce Music Theatre – 'Shaddap You Face'
C: Sheb Wooley – 'The Purple People Eater'
D: The Wurzels – 'The Combine Harvester'

Thanks, Chris – I really needed to be reminded about Joe Dolce one more time. At least he sent me a million-pound cheque, which I've got framed up in the bathroom. It may be a fake but I think it will be the last million-pound cheque I ever get.

The researchers had delved right back into my past and found my first band, the Stumble. When I first heard Alec Baird's voice I was really confused and when they all came through the door there was this hotchpotch of old men – Alec, Alan Wright, Kenny Ireland and Gordan Appacellie – who I could hardly recognise. But they probably thought the same thing when they saw me.

It was really funny to see them. Alec produced this hand-painted crash helmet of mine that I'd customised with the blue crackle paint they used on steelworkers' toolboxes. I'd left it at his house one day 35 years ago – I still don't know how I got home. The best thing he brought was a demo I'd done in my first studio – the shed in Mum and Dad's garden – with my Sony reel-to-reel tape recorder. It had a thing called 'sound on sound' where you couldn't multitrack but you could record a guitar track and then switch it across. If I balanced it properly I could do it four or five times and have something that sounded vaguely real. He played the tail-end of this demo I'd done, though it was so crackly the tune could have been anything. At the fade-out all I could hear in the background was the jingles from the ice-cream van outside in the street.

After the show I had a couple of drinks with Alec. After the Stumble he'd joined Contraband, a folk-rock band, and we all thought he'd really made it because they actually made an album, then he went on to join some hippy-trippy Gong-type band. I asked him what it was like playing with them. 'I had to count to twenty-nine and a half then hit the cymbal,' he said. Then he joined the Jags and enjoyed his fifteen minutes of fame.

Both Linda and Bobby were there, and it was really nice to see them. We have a funny family setup. In Glasgow we were always very close, living on top of each other in the same small house. I didn't leave home until I was 22 and Bobby was still there. It was like an Italian family. My mum and dad were never rid of us kids, but as soon as we fled the nest we all went in different directions.

My life and Bobby's had moved apart slowly. He had girlfriends when I was playing in bands; when I was becoming successful he was getting married, and then I moved to London and I was out there touring the world.

We're not one of those families that get together every weekend for a knees-up. We all live in different parts of the country. If you're not all living in the same town it is difficult to have that close relationship. We don't ring each other every week but that is the way our family has unfolded. Bobby's in Poole, Linda's in Milton Keynes and I'm in Bath. When we do get together everything is great, there is an unspoken thing, a friendship there, but we don't have to show it.

Linda's been married a few times. Her children Michelle and Mark are all grown up now. She ran a plumbing company with her last husband and worked in a nightclub. Ure is an unusual name and with her Scottish accent she's been asked if we're related. Linda was never musically inclined so there was never any jealousy there from her. She always tells me that the boss of the club was a big fan and she's happy to ask me sign photos or get passes for shows. I may not speak to her every week but I'm still her big brother.

I know Bobby was incredibly pleased about my success. He was very proud because he knew how long I'd been working at it, so to see me on *Top of the Pops* was a real buzz the first time. I'm sure eventually that buzz turned to something else – it's very boring being someone else's brother. It must be irksome to say the least, though I think my sister has quite enjoyed it. I can't imagine what it must be like to always be in the shadow of your younger brother, and it must have been hard having somebody rubbing your face in it all the time. Funnily enough, the first time I went on Lorraine Kelly's TV show twelve years ago she told me, 'I've interviewed your brother. He used to work at Rolls-Royce up in East Kilbride and did karate, didn't he? I was the local hack and I wrote this article on him.' That was the first time in my life our roles were reversed.

Bobby also plays music; he picked up guitar after me and used to play in pubs at weekends – he still does – but he always dabbled in it while I was driven by it. When he comes to visit I give him any equipment I don't need any more, so we usually have a scour round to see what bits and pieces of gear I'm not using. He's a bit broader than me, but that is down to thirty years of karate.

None of us Ure kids are ones for picking up the phone and having long chats every couple of weeks. It's more like once a year. We never had any fallings-out, that's just the way we are. We're all dreadful. Bobby did text me on my fiftieth birthday, which was amazing as we never send cards. When my mum told him I'd had to go into Clouds all he said was, 'Maybe now Jim will stop telling everybody what to do all the time.'

My mother and father had been in cahoots with Sheridan for months and months. She'd been sneaking into my personal organiser trying to extract telephone numbers from it without raising my suspicions. She certainly succeeded, because I never suspected a thing. Best of all was that I didn't get any grief from the people in my past who had been left out or ignored. I couldn't, because it was nothing to do with me.

I'm really glad my mum and dad were at the recording. To their generation that show was bigger, more important than Band Aid – they never quite understood what that was all about. They saw *This Is Your Life* on telly every week for 35 years. It was a massive, massive thing for my dad. He died just over a year later. That was difficult to deal with, and it still is. I moved him and Mum close to me in Bath so that I could be here for them. It hurt so much going into the hospital every day and seeing this strong man – dads are always strong – deteriorate as we talked. I knew it was happening and he knew I knew it was happening. We'd sit together in the hospital and he'd say, 'I'm not coming out, Jim,' and all I could reply was, 'I know, Dad.'

My dad had smoked forty a day since he was fourteen and at 82 it caught up with him. He had angina and bad lungs and they put smoking down as the cause of death. When I was a kid he smoked Embassy and we'd collect the coupons. A big night in for the family was counting the coupons and seeing what we could get from the catalogue. My mum had also smoked heavily until Molly was doing a school project about smoking. She asked her grandmother about when she started smoking and she was so mortified she stopped there and then. She'd nag Dad about not being able to give up but he never did.

I have a lot of my dad in me. The placid side, the neutral side, the side that says, 'Let's not argue, let's not fight.' Back away, walk away, let things resolve, that was very much him. My mother's side is in-your-face, much more argumentative. It was tough watching him leave. We were never big, cuddly, huggy characters. He was a good man, but for all we talked somehow neither of us could ever say the things that needed to be said. He knew it, but neither of us could ever say it. I loved him. He loved me. He was proud of me.

Analysing my life has been a wee bit hard. Sometimes it seems like I am just sitting on my laurels, that I haven't achieved anything apart from the halcyon days, but that is not how it is. Things diversify, and priorities change. Which was bigger: 'Vienna' or Band Aid? As a musical moment 'Vienna' was pivotal in my life. Band Aid changed the world more than a little bit, and changed everything for me socially. So did getting married, so did getting divorced, so did having my four beautiful girls . . . and so did getting married again.

We waited a long time, over ten years. Sheri said to me one day, 'It would be nice to get married.'

I nodded. 'Yeah, it'd be great.'

That was it. It's only a bit of paper, a ring, a party, how more committed can you be than having three children together? We started discussing it in the summer of 2002. We went all round the houses, and talked about South Africa (why, I'll never know, probably an excuse for a holiday). It remained on the back burner – there was always something else that needed doing. We finally came to the conclusion that the best place we could go was Mull. We had been on a fantastic camping holiday there once, five days of glorious sunshine, and we loved it dearly.

I was trawling through the Net looking for a rental cottage and I found a castle. As you do. We had been on the Calgary Bay, sitting on the beach, and we looked back and saw this castle nestled in the trees. Calgary Castle is a small castle, and it only sleeps eighteen people. We told our mates we were not organising anything, just where and when the wedding was. If they wanted to be there we'd love to see them. They all turned up.

We were married outside on the lawn on 15 July 2003, a blistering hot day in front of forty family and friends. Sheri had announced months before the wedding that she had found the dress, with the emphasis on *the*. Her friend told her, 'Buy it now because, if you leave it, it won't be there when you need it,' so she did. It was kept firmly under wraps. I was banned from going anywhere near the wardrobe on pain of death, or something much worse. All her friends saw it; a gaggle of girls would stomp up and down the stairs at regular intervals and I could hear the squeals of delight. Everyone in Bath had seen it but me; in fact, there are probably carvings on the Roman baths of Sheridan's dress.

I had to do some snooping because I had found a fantastic jeweller's in Bradford upon Avon. They made our rings, a beautiful platinum engagement ring studded with seven little diamonds all the way round and two very plain platinum wedding bands. While we were in the shop sizing fingers I noticed these beautiful necklaces that looked like Victorian lace, made out of wire and little precious stones. I nicked Sheri's phone book and called her friends to find out what this dress was like, did it have a high or a low neck – one of the necklaces was a choker, the other a low-cut one. The shop eventually let me take both just in case.

She was quite right to hide her dress. I didn't see it until the day she walked out of the castle onto the lawn. She looked absolutely stunning. The dress was white with an asymmetric hem, almost but not quite lacy, V-necked and sleeveless. She had her hair up in a tiara, and wore these fantastic shoes with very high heels and a jewelled strap round each ankle.

All my girls were bridesmaids, and Kitty, Ruby and Flossie were dressed in matching fairy dresses of white chiffon, little flower head-bands they picked themselves and little white slippers. Molly was in something much more grown-up, a deep wine-stain off-the-shoulder dress. She looked much too old and much too beautiful to be my daughter.

The little ones seemed rather more interested in what was under my kilt. I'm a Campbell so I rented the tartan in Swindon and took it to Mull – talk about coals to Newcastle. I had tartan boxer shorts underneath. My daughters would have been so desperate to look at Dad's willy, that kilt would have been up and down like the links of the Forth. Initially Kitty was a bit miffed when she found out we were getting married, because in her view we were perfectly all right the way we were. In her long experience most people who eventually got married all got divorced. That was her outlook on our rosy future together. On the day she was wonderful, running around everywhere in her dress, on the beach, into the water. At seven in the evening we stood on the beach with a glass of champagne, looking over white sand and aquamarine water. Nobody was there. It was a beautiful setting. Even the two journalists from the *Daily Record* missed us. It was private, personal and unpretentious.

On the last night we went to eat at the Calgary Hotel, where they serve excellent food. The owner said to me, 'It must have been a fantastic wedding because all we could hear was people laughing.' That is the best thing anybody could say.

I am the father of four daughters. This is definite payback for my misbegotten youth. At some point I must have wished for four girls and it has been bequeathed to me in a way I didn't expect. What a responsibility to have . . . four lots of boyfriends – Jesus. I love it. They drive me crazy, and they have no logic at all, any of them. Women can multitask; men can't: we are different animals, which I do find very frustrating. But the bottom line is they wander up at the most ridiculous times, sit on my lap and kiss me on the neck. I don't ask them to, but they come up and do it. My girls are just fabulous.

It was hard for Molly when Kitty was born. She was seven, and there was no competition. The night Kitty came home, she sat up all night refusing to go to sleep. I had to sit on the freezing stairs with a blanket round me because she wanted to get into our bed where the baby was. Since then they've been catty, fighting sisters just like they should be, healthy animals who jump on and then cuddle each other. The younger three love having Molly visit Bath – for the first hour, until she shows she's better at the Playstation than they are.

Life is different for Molly. When I was a kid I didn't know anybody who was divorced, but there aren't many nuclear families any more. Of course I want the *It's A Wonderful Life* scenario, but the reality is it's hard work, and there is always a phone call, a situation. Molly was brought up with Brian May's daughter, Emily, who's been through the same thing, living with Mum, seeing Dad at weekends. I've spoken to Brian umpteen times about driving up and down motorways. That is what you do unless you are a useless parent, when you don't bother. The easiest option is always to walk away. Not for me.

Molly has a different outlook on it to me. As long as she can remember her mum lives here and her dad lives there, she doesn't need to know anything else. She has a different life from the other three but I have always been there for her and I always will be. I'm just not living under the same roof as Annabel.

I don't know what it is about girls, but they seem to be more honest, more upfront, pains in the arse but just more open, more confident. When I was growing up in Scotland we weren't allowed to talk about sex or personalities or who you were and what you wanted to do. I was expected to do what my parents wanted me to do.

Now it's a whole different ball game. My kids are going to sing: they are all-singing, all-dancing beauties. I'd like to think they will have something to fall back on but then I realise that's not me, that's my dad talking. The words that come out of my mouth are the same my parents threw at me when I was a teenager when I was so driven, so ambitious I couldn't ever see myself falling back on any trade. The best thing I can do for my children is supply them with a good education. I'm giving them the best they can possibly get right now and that's important to me. I don't care if there are no royalties left when I go.

My girls all sing beautifully, and they have perfect pitch. Kitty and Ruby play piano, and Flossie has just started learning. Molly is really good: she has taught herself piano and guitar and wants to be in musical theatre. If she wants to enough she will do it . . . but I can't help her. That's the strange thing about my name, it can be a negative or it can be a legacy. I don't want to see them not making it because of my background. There are very few of us Ures, so I wouldn't blame her if she changed her name.

I don't have flunkies or an entourage around me. I never have had and I've never wanted it. I don't hang out with Paul McCartney or go for dinner at Elton's every week. That may happen in certain circles, but not in mine. I still have the same friends that I've always had in the music industry, and there are only a few of them. Glenn Gregory is one of my best pals, but we don't see each other from year to year. I don't go out of my way to ingratiate myself with luminaries and to hang out with them. I don't mix in those circles – unless it's on a musical level.

Twenty years ago music, image and style were all interwoven, and they were important to me. As I've got older my hair has receded and I've put on a few pounds, so image has been overtaken by life. I don't wake up in the late morning and flick through my Armani suits before deciding which one to wear for lunch. I get up, force the kids to brush their hair and clean their teeth, feed them and get them off to school. Priorities have changed. I'm bottom of the heap now – most of the time the dog's higher up the food chain – and I love it. Now I have managed to come to terms with who and where I am, and I don't need a bottle to protect me from the truth.

I'm fifty years old and I have finally come to understand that I am just an ordinary guy who has to deal with all the same stuff every other ordinary guy has to. The real truth is that my life has always been pretty normal, punctuated by extraordinary moments. One day I might do a concert in Berlin to 20,000 people, the next I come home and go to Sainsbury's. That is it. It's no great shakes. Real life is what I do. It has just taken me fifty years to realise that I am not Bono, not Sting. I am Midge, the guy round the corner, the dad who does the shopping. There have been moments in my life when I have been elevated to a different stature. That was the easy part. Dealing with my family every day, bread-and-butter, day-to-day living, now that is hard.

As part of my ongoing aftercare at Clouds the counsellors regularly push me, ask me to describe why I always think I can get away with it, and why I have such a hard time dealing with life on a daily basis. I often feel like Chauncey Gardener in *Being There*. He lived in a beautiful garden in the middle of downtown Washington, oblivious to the world, but when his employer died he was thrust out. For years I have been wrapped up in cotton wool, not had to deal with the everyday aspects of living, just gone off and done my fantasy thing.

Now like Chauncey Gardener I have opened the gate and walked out into the world, and found it is rough and tough out here. For the first few months it was really difficult and I was trying to deal with it and hide from it at the same time. That created a mess; I ended up in a whirlpool and got sucked under.

Chauncey found his way a lot easier in the world than I have done so far. But he is my inspiration. At some point I'll have the ears of kings and presidents. Even if it is the President of Latvia again.

That's a start.

DISCOGRAPHY

SINGLES

Slik	Mar. 1975	The Boogiest Band in Town
Slik	Jan. 1976	Forever And Ever
Slik	May 1976	Requiem
Slik	July 1976	The Kid's A Punk
PVC2	Nov. 1977	Put You In The Picture EP
Rich Kids	Jan. 1978	Rich Kids
Rich Kids	May 1978	Marching Men
Rich Kids	Aug. 1978	Ghosts of Princes in Towers
Ultravox	June 1980	Sleepwalk
Ultravox	Sep. 1980	Passing Strangers
Visage	Dec. 1980	Fade to Grey
Ultravox	Jan. 1981	Vienna
Visage	Mar. 1981	Mind Of A Toy
Ultravox	May 1981	All Stood Still
Ultravox	Aug. 1981	The Thin Wall
Ultravox	Oct. 1981	The Voice
Visage	Mar. 1982	Damned Don't Cry
Midge Ure	June 1982	No Regrets
Visage	June 1982	Night Train
Ultravox	Sep. 1982	Reap The Wild Wind
Visage	Nov. 1982	Pleasure Boys
Ultravox	Nov. 1982	Hymn
Ultravox	Mar. 1983	Visions In Blue
Ultravox	May 1983	We Came To Dance
Midge Ure	July 1983	After A Fashion
Ultravox	Feb. 1984	One Small Day
Ultravox	May 1984	Dancing With Tears In My Eyes
Ultravox	July 1984	Lament
Ultravox	Oct. 1984	Love's Great Adventure
Band Aid	Dec. 1984	Do They Know it's Christmas?
Midge Ure	Dec. 1985	If I Was
Midge Ure	Nov. 1985	That Certain Smile
Midge Ure	Feb. 1986	Wastelands

Midge Ure	June 1986	Call Of The Wild
Ultravox	Sep. 1986	Same Old Story
Ultravox	Nov. 1986	All Fall Down
Midge Ure	Aug. 1988	Answers to Nothing
Midge Ure	Nov. 1989	Dear God
Midge Ure	Aug. 1991	Cold, Cold Heart
Midge Ure	Oct. 1991	I See Hope
Ultravox	Mar. 1993	Vienna (re-release)
Midge Ure	May 1996	Breathe (re-released 97/98)
Midge Ure	Nov. 1996	Guns and Arrows (re-released 97/98)

ALBUMS

Slik	May 1976	Slik
Slik	Mar. 1999	The Best of Slik
Rich Kids	Aug. 1978	Ghosts of Princes in Towers
Rich Kids	Oct. 1998	Burning Sounds (compilation of rarities)
Ultravox	July 1980	Vienna
Ultravox	Sep. 1981	Rage In Eden
Visage	Nov. 1980	Visage
Visage	Mar. 1982	Anvil
Ultravox	Oct. 1982	Quartet
Ultravox	May 1984	Lament
Ultravox	Oct. 1984	The Collection
Ultravox	Oct. 1986	U Vox
Midge Ure & Ultravox	Feb. 1993	If I Was – The Best of Midge Ure and Ultravox
Midge Ure & Ultravox	Oct. 2001	The Very Best of Midge Ure & Ultravox

SOLO ALBUMS

Midge Ure	Oct. 1986	The Gift
Midge Ure	Aug. 1988	Answers To Nothing
Midge Ure	Sep. 1991	Pure
Midge Ure	Feb. 1993	If I Was – The Best of Midge Ure and Ultravox
Midge Ure	May 1996	Breathe (re-released 97/98)
Midge Ure	Oct. 1999	Midge Ure – Live in Concert
Midge Ure	May 2001	Move Me

Midge Ure	Aug. 2001	Glorious Noise (Breathe Live)
Midge Ure	Oct. 2001	The Very Best of Midge Ure & Ultravox
Midge Ure	Nov. 2001	Little Orphans

RECORDS PRODUCED
Atrix – Treasure in the Wasteland
Ronny – If You Want Me to Stay
Cold Fish – Love Me Today
Phil Lynott – Yellow Pearl, Together
Peter Godwin – Torch Songs for the Heroine
Modern Man – Concrete Scheme (LP)
Fatal Charm – Crossing
Steve Harley – I Can't Even Touch You
Strasse – A Stairway to You
The Messengers – I Turn In (To You)
Rodeo – When You Smile at Me I'm in Heaven
Visage – Visage, Anvil (albums)
Ultravox – Vienna, Rage in Eden, Lament (album) Love's Great
    Adventure (single)
Band Aid – Do They Know it's Christmas?
Midge Ure – The Gift (album), Answers to Nothing (album), Pure
    (album), Move Me (album)
Michel Van Dyke – Reincarnated (LP)
Ryoichi Yuki – Dear God (LP)
Countermine – LP & Singles

VIDEOS DIRECTED
Ultravox – Reap The Wild Wind, Hymn, Visions In Blue, We Came To
    Dance, Monument, Dancing With Tears In My Eyes, Lament,
    Love's Great Adventure
Phil Lynott – Yellow Pearl
Visage – Damned Don't Cry, Visage
Fun Boy Three – Telephone Always Rings
Banarama – Really Saying Something, Shy Boy
Monsoon – Shakti
Midge Ure / Mick Karn – After A Fashion

Midge Ure – No Regrets, If I Was, Answers to Nothing, Cold Cold
    Heart, I See Hope (in the Morning Light)
Martha Ladley – Light Years From Now
Truth – Step in the Right Direction
Andrew Strong – Same Old Me
Midge Ure – Move Me
Midge Ure – Beneath A Spielberg Sky
Russell Watson & Faye Tozer – Someone Like You

INDEX